Race and Radicalism in the Union Army

Race and Radicalism in the Union Army

Mark A. Lause

Urbana and Chicago
University of Illinois Press

Library of Congress Cataloging-in-Publication Data
Lause, Mark A.
Race and radicalism in the Union Army / Mark A. Lause.
p.   cm.
Includes bibliographical references and index.
ISBN 978-0-252-03446-6 (cloth : acid-free paper)
    1. United States. Army of the Frontier. 2. Indian Territory—History, Military—
19th century. 3. United States—History—Civil War, 1861–1865—Social aspects.
4. United States—History—Civil War, 1861–1865—Participation, African American.
5. United States—History—Civil War, 1861–1865—Participation, Indian. 6. Radicalism—
United States—History—19th century. 7. Brown, John, 1800–1859—Influence.
I. Title.
E505.95.L386   2009
973.7'1—dc22   2009015041

Contents

Illustrations follow page 66

Acknowledgments

This book owes much to many. Early in this project, it benefited significantly from the goading of my medievalist office mate, L. J. Andrew Villalon, who has always had, among his many other sterling qualities, a good nose for a great story. Our colleague Janine Hartman has always made herself available as a sounding board on drafts and approaches to problems. At crucial points, Paul Buhle and Louis Proyect helped keep my focus on this project. Bryce Suderow, an independent scholar in Civil War history, generously shared what he had found in his painstaking work on the *National Tribune*, where he found R. M. Peck's recollections. Kenneth W. Burchell shared his insights into Masonic history. Bruce Laurie offered extremely helpful input after reading an earlier draft of the manuscript. The extent to which we have a book worthy of the subject is owed largely to the diligent and patient editorial advice of Laurie Matheson, Angela Burton, and Bruce Bethell of the University of Illinois Press.

My interests in the Transatlantic dimensions of these problems and the necessity of taking a genuinely multicultural approach go back to graduate school and my work under Professors Leo Schelbert and Marion S. Miller at the University of Illinois at Chicago, and Elizabeth Balanoff of Roosevelt University. I would like to dedicate this volume to them.

Race and Radicalism in the Union Army

Introduction

On July 17, 1863, a little army of Indian, black, and white soldiers advanced against a much larger force. They moved south across the prairies, alongside the Texas Road, toward Elk Creek, just north of the Honey Springs Depot in the Creek Nation of the Indian Territory. In the heat of the day, the soldiers "had stripped themselves of everything in the way of clothing and equipment that could be dispensed with," leaving piles in the rear of the line. Artillerists "stripped to their undershirts and pant," but the African Americans "had even taken off their shirts, and their black skins glistened in the sun."[1] On no other battlefield of the American Civil War did the sun illuminate such a willful display of diversity.

John Brown's soul seemed to be marching on more directly with this part of the Army of the Frontier than with any other Union force. Their commander, General James Gilpatrick Blunt, had ridden with Brown, as had Colonel William Addison Phillips, one of his two brigade commanders. In the black regiment on the field, so had Lieutenant Colonel John Bowles and Captain Richard Josiah Hinton, who would have recognized the terrain, which he had scouted years before on behalf of Brown's abolitionist guerrillas. Perhaps others had, too. White abolitionists, particularly in the Kansas units, had been fighting for nearly a decade before they moved across the field alongside black and Indian soldiers, and surely some of the former had not so carefully documented associations of their own.

In those earlier years, Federal authorities had hunted those white radicals as renegades. Reaching the battle line near Elk Creek, Blunt, Phillips, Hinton, and Bowles shared a taste of that experience with others, including Jake Perryman, a runaway former slave, and Su-nuk-mik-ko, the Seminole chief who had spent a generation fighting the United States in Florida. That July all these North Americans of different races and backgrounds wore the same uniform and took their places under the Stars and Stripes, daring all for what was, in varying degrees, a shared vision of the future. The war in which they engaged would, in part, determine whether such hopes had any realistic prospects.

Straddling the road to their south waited a Confederate army, commanded and officered by white veterans of Southern sectionalism. Having dominated the United States for a generation, Southern slaveholders now sought to dissolve it in order to secure, among other things, African slavery, an absolute authority over the future of the Indians, and the option of conscripting whites unwilling to volunteer to preserve these things. That morning these veteran Indian fighters and slaveholders counted almost 6,000 men, about twice the size of the Union forces.

These armies clashed in the most significant Civil War battle fought in the Indian Territory, in the area that would become the present state of Oklahoma. Whereas veterans of other similarly important battles often celebrated their memories of them, however, the participants in this one neglected it almost completely. Elsewhere, veterans who had experienced the terrors of such places would return to commemorate their contribution to history and to mark the crucial locations on the battlefield for future generations. Participants in this battle felt little compulsion to do so.

This book explains why and how this happened.

Most fundamentally, I seek to define more closely the general scholarly assessment that the Civil War of 1861–65 entailed a "Second American Revolution," albeit one with severe limitations. Shifting coalitions, converging interests, and irrepressible clashes shaped the possibilities of the war. The interaction of races at the western edge of the Civil War demonstrates just how rapidly that war became revolution—revolution that turned on issues of class.

Diverse groups built American civilization. The most powerful among the Euro-Americans looked beyond the limited realities of their lives to imagine mythical Cities of Gold, with boundless wealth shimmering to the west just beyond their grasp. They came to espouse a freedom and justice that minimized restraint on the individual's buying, selling, investing, or divesting anything anywhere. Although some African or Native Americans have equally embraced acquisitive, exclusive, and hierarchic values, new nation's clearly racialist social structure directly minimized their freedom to exercise them.

Conditions on (and beyond) the edges of white settlement permitted greater fluidity in ideas, values, and institutions. There, three distinct racial groups (as the whites defined them) regularly interacted in a new setting. Familiarity with the activities of these groups, either in Kansas or the Indian Territory, undermines any static view of race in nineteenth-century America.

As the sectional crisis erupted into armed conflict, the dominant standards and institutions increasingly lost their hold over the people. The very survival of the American Union required the people themselves to mount the stage of history, write their own dialogue, and direct their own actions. Whenever this happens, nothing is determined or easily predictable, even in civilizations defined by their inequalities.

Although later recast as marginalized "cranks," adherents of a broad spectrum of social reforms proliferated in the decades leading to the war. Literally as well as figuratively, Kansas seemed to open wider possibilities for a free society and drew many reformers to the West. The insurgent Republican Party—and, later, a wartime Unionism—included numerous gun-toting radicals of all sorts. As circumstances made social reconstruction the order of the day, their innovative radicalism would have an important, though rarely dominant, influence.

In fact, the proponents of a radical version of the emerging free-labor ideology shared much with Republican political leaders and wartime Unionist leaders, as well as with the nation's founders. All feared that strong government and centralizing economic institutions would become inherently less accountable to the people and that those eager to exploit the exercise of power in their self-interest would gravitate toward such institutions. To them slaveholding typified this process, and secession represented a fundamental challenge to whatever the republic had achieved since declaring its principles in 1776. However much the struggle required revolutionary transformations in both the South and the North, it also severely limited those transformations.

Certainly, these socialists, abolitionists, land reformers, trade unionists, woman suffragists, and spiritualists opposed slavery, but they also advocated a "free labor" that went beyond its abolition. Most desired a vastly more decentralized and democratized civilization, one dominated by free labor liberated from the dictates of capital as well as slaveholding. Over time they would help secure—at least on paper—the acceptance of racial equality. The subsequent course of their war suggested an even broader view of equality that would include the continent's native peoples. Such impulses would recast radical Unionism in light of that "maroon" legacy. Augustus Wattles—aptly, a denizen of Utopia, Ohio—became an adviser on Indian affairs for Abraham Lincoln's administration; this is remarkable given that his circle had long entertained such ideas as an autonomous Indian state that would simultaneously ensure full U.S. citizenship for all adult residents, including representation in the national government.

Wartime Unionism in the region, then, fostered a mutual interdependence among whites, blacks, and Indians in the face of the enemy. It tended to suspend racial prejudice, at least under the duress of combat. "Citizenship in a free country amply rewards the war-worn soldier," wrote James M. Williams of the First Kansas Colored. To prove that this experience could survive off the battlefield, Phillips cited the examples of other nations that had "no such thing as color caste."[2] Some Unionists, at least, articulated a triracial dream of the nation's future that increasingly loomed larger as the only practical means of securing the Union's survival.

These radical views existed within a Unionist coalition with many contradictory elements. While abolition may have been an essential prerequisite for equality, its advocates did not necessarily seek racial equality, any more than did political leaders using the rhetoric of free labor want the same things as the radicals. It took the war, however, to define the nature and depth of those differences and to work out their resolution. The well-trained West Pointers and regular army officers pressed for reassignment to the East, leaving war in the West disproportionately in the hands of "nobodies" who had never expected to be soldiers. In the upper Trans-Mississippi, the heirs of John Brown shared the management of the war with those of Napoleon.

While Civil War historians describe an evolution of the conflict into a "total war," it had actually never really been anything else in the vast Trans-Mississippi, where the haziest of lines demarcated soldiers, militia, and civilians. In the absence of established civil authorities, war entailed a conflict among the peoples with respect to whom various parties, governments, and armies scrambled to retain their balance. However intense, the rivalry between South Carolina and Massachusetts did not involve armed struggle until it reached Kansas, and the nature of the Civil War as a total war first became evident in the Indian Territory. In the end, the contending armies churned back and forth between the Missouri and the Arkansas rivers, over roads twisting for hundreds of miles, leaving in their wakes the burned shells of farmhouses and abandoned villages. Massive refugee camps grew along the perimeter of this largely depopulated region or clustered about scattered and blighted garrisons. Nowhere did the essentially handicraft mode of warfare create a more modern scale of destruction.

Given the intensity of the war and the eagerness with which officials sent white troops raised west of the Mississippi to the East, the Trans-Mississippi war first tapped the interests of "colored volunteers." Over a year before the Fifty-fourth Massachusetts made its famous assault on Battery Wagner, black soldiers fought at Locust Grove in the Cherokee Nation. Months before their début in the East, a black regiment fought in Missouri and began to inspire the enlistment of African Americans in neighboring states.[3] By the war's close, over 15,000 blacks had joined the Union army in an area where the entire Federal volunteer force fluctuated between 30,000 and 50,000.

Realities on the western border confronted not only slavery but the presence of Indians. While largely overlooked, at least five thousand Indians joined the Union army, serving in various units from neighboring states as well as the Indian Home Guards. They sought a union that would respect and tolerate, if not sustain, traditional Native American values, as opposed to the Confederacy, which would destroy them. The U.S. Army briefly reversed its history to foster and protect genuine civilian self-government and to cooperate with such governing bodies as the Cherokee National Council, which sent to Washington, among other officers, Captains James McDaniel and James S. Vann, who were buried at Arlington National Cemetery.[4] In no other part of the Civil War did Federal aspirations turn so heavily on the work of so diverse a population of nonwhites as in the upper Trans-Mississippi.

Then, too, many whites in Missouri and western Arkansas—and many further south, in places such as northern Texas—viewed secession with anything from passive indifference to outright hostility, despite the insistent and noisy views of the elite. Claimed by secessionists as a Confederate state, Missouri furnished overwhelmingly greater numbers to the Federal armies and its own Unionist militia. Official sources credited Arkansas with 8,289 white Union soldiers and unnumbered others in its unofficial "home guards." Thousands more served from Texas. Many Southern whites served in the volunteer regiments raised by other states or in the expanded units of the regular army. In contrast, during the course of the war, the Confederacy raised most of its soldiers in this region by rigorously applying conscription, which it had, in effect, sought to impose from the onset in the Indian Territory.

For the South, the "War between the States" was more accurately a war *within* the states. Given how secessionists promulgated their project, those unwilling simply to follow their course had few options. Early in the conflict white Missourians overthrew their secessionist government. Residents of the Indian Territory faced similar problems, albeit with far fewer prospects of success. By the close of the conflict, residents of Missouri, Arkansas, Louisiana, Texas, and three of the five major nations of the Indian Territory had two governments, one allied to each side. Clearly, nothing like that happened in Kansas or Illinois or Iowa.

Maintaining slavery required an ever more centralized, intrusive civic power. Increasingly, the political authorities systematically censored the press, repressed opponents, and imposed a wartime conscription earlier and more thorough than anything later adopted in the nonslaveholding states. Throughout, those planters explicitly denounced the "Agrarianism" of the free-labor radicals as an egalitarian attempt to evade the imperatives of the marketplace. Their arguments for slavery embraced the demands of that market and the innate rights of property ownership.

Paradoxically, the later, dewy-eyed architects of "the Lost Cause" mythologies rewrote the realities. Reading postwar results into antebellum interests and aspirations, they asserted that the North represented the centralizing force in American history. Conversely, they embalmed their planter self-interest into a nostalgic "Agrarianism" unencumbered by egalitarianism, just as their notion of "liberty" omitted any application to people of color. The postwar powers in the North generally accepted these revisions, which placed them at the cutting edge of Darwinian success, recasting slavery as merely a particularistic obstacle to the flowering of market capitalism. The agreement eased the way for a national reunification that left racism's human impact unaddressed.

The notion of race identity as the primary loyalty of white Americans finds a strange echo in the more recent discussions of "whiteness." Among others, the Marxist sociologist Theodore Allen's two-volume *History of the White Race* draws on sources other than North American to offer insights into the social and cultural construction of "whiteness," and David R. Roediger's *Wages of Whiteness* applies these insights to the United States. Although imitators have generally not done as well, this sociological model has provided a professionally acceptable mechanism for white historians to address the fascinating and essential issues of race, just as masculinity studies have become an acceptable, if indirect, way for male academicians to explore issues of gender.

Whatever the intentions of its proponents, the focus on "whiteness" often embraces some innately elitist and conservative assumptions. The top of Euro-American white society, from its colonial inception, sought to ground white supremacy in law rather than rely on custom. Left to the latter, race relations were anything but simple and straightforward. The further one got from ruling circles—either socially or physically—the weaker the gravity of interest that made racial practices and ideas coherent. The result was an increasingly diverse spectrum of behaviors, running the gamut from attempts to ape the ruling values of the dominant elite to easy movement across race barriers or to communities' lack of action to institutionalize such barriers. Somewhere in this vast unaddressed American reality are the particularly complex interactions of Indians and Africans, which the "whiteness" model not only fails to illuminate but actually renders invisible. This model is perfectly capable of misinforming as well as not informing and, in some respects, misplaces the major responsibility for racism.[5]

Imposing such rigidly generalized models on what was actually a more complex spectrum of race relations poorly equips us to explain how John Brown emerged as a self-consciously American figure. Or why others chose to ride with him. Or how several thousand white, black, and Indian Unionists formed a common line of battle on the western edge of the Civil War. Or even how a radical rethinking of race in the United States could ever become possible.

Such approaches also define individuals such as Phillips, Hinton, Blunt, or even John Brown as ultimately marginal. In this study, I seek to demonstrate how they were, in fact, integral to the unfolding of the conflict that led to the Civil War. I also attempt to explain how the dynamics of the Union war effort made such views and those who hold them integral to its success. Finally, I try to explain why their memorable vision failed to have the impact that many of us would have wished.

ONE

The Shadow of John Brown

John Brown and other abolitionists, black and white, discussed many questions beyond slavery. William Addison Phillips remembered that, among those who knew him, Brown openly criticized the nation's "forms of social and political life." He "condemned the sale of land as chattel" and "thought society ought to be organized on a less selfish basis; for, while material interests gained something by the deification of pure selfishness, men and women lost much by it." According to one of his sons, Brown's "favorite theme was that of the *Community plan of cooperative industry*, in which all should labor for the common good; 'having all things in common' as did the disciples of Jesus in his day." At one point, Brown and his men imagined what they called the "State of Topeka," a utopia in which neither race nor gender barred citizenship and equal rights; its logo was the image of a black man with a cannon and sword over the slogan "Justice to all Mankind."[1] In extraordinary circumstances, such a vision helped to detonate and shape a crisis national in scope, global in its implications, and expansive in its possibilities.

Phillips and others who would later face the Confederates at Honey Springs in 1863 had brought west with them a view of "free labor" as more than the absence of chattel slavery. Their activities in Kansas grew not only from their moral opposition to slavery but from their fear of its effects on the American republic, which inspired John Brown and others to take direct action against slavery and the proslavery authorities. Conversely, contemporary elites sought the social, economic, and political development of the territory, as quickly and profitably as possible, replicating the standards of white civilization. Simply excluding slavery from the territory, then, could not have resolved the tensions underlying "Bleeding Kansas."

⌐⌐

As the battleground in a national struggle over resources, Kansas paradoxically had little to offer early settlers. On the edge of what had long been regarded as "the Great American Desert," development there faced formidable obstacles of geography and climate. The introduction of capitalism, particularly coincident with a national economic depression, meant that most of the settlers would remain economically marginalized for some time. The specific attempt to introduce slavery into the territory made Kansas the flashpoint for what was becoming a national crisis.

After six years of white settlement, Kansas averaged a bit more than one person per parched, windswept square mile, reaching a population only about a quarter that of Arkansas and a tenth that of Missouri. Most residents huddled in isolated little cabins or crude dugouts along with their dogs, pigs, and chickens. The proportion of females had only begun to approach that in the states, and only around a tenth of the overall population exceeded the age of forty-five. Almost all the towns on the map amounted to no more than a few buildings over a wide spot on an ungraded trail. Only Leavenworth, Atchison, and Lawrence topped a few thousand residents, and even well-known towns such as Fort Scott or Moneka numbered its residents in the hundreds. The seasonal passage of the legislature through Topeka overtaxed the capacity for housing in not only the capital but also the surrounding towns. Few were as well off as Augustus Wattles, who hosted John Brown and his men in a little structure at Moneka that could barely seat a dozen adults. Overall, about a quarter of the whites who went to Kansas abandoned the territory, and "hard times" left another quarter of them bogged in a barter economy.[2] In practical terms, most who went west to better their lot had certainly not done so.

Fundamental problems defied rapid development. The territory had so little timber that construction usually required importing lumber at great cost. Commerce choked on poor transportation and a circulation medium clogged by the paper promissory notes of the "wildcat" banks, the value of which deflated with the Panic of 1857. The gold rush to Pike's Peak in 1858

drew thousands farther west. Plagued with bitter winters and broiling sum-
mers, Kansans faced particularly brutal conditions with a drought, lasting
from the fall of 1859 into the fall of 1860. July drove temperatures as high
as 132 degrees, and September 1860 brought a plague of grasshoppers.[3]
More than politics seemed to conjure biblical imagery.

The most ambitious and influential gentlemen brought west the aspirations, ideas, and values of the antebellum states. Entrepreneurs positioned
a few logs as an "enclosure" and then used claims of improvements in lieu
of currency, thus establishing "towns" that made money through real estate
speculations even though they existed only on paper. Increased land prices
in turn helped to exclude the landless from access to the soil, creating a class
of wage earners. Speculators made inroads into tribal lands and agitated
for the negation of Indian claims. The new patriarchs of Kansas explicitly
restricted citizenship to "white" male residents.[4]

Even among white men, though, the cherished American image of an
egalitarian West required very selective memories. Settlement replicated
familiar social structures and hierarchies, and the human material for this
replication tended to come from neither the utterly impoverished nor the
largely successful, such as Horace Greeley, who freely advised young men
to go west but had little incentive to move there themselves. The process
created opportunities at the top for some of humbler origins, generating
anecdotes of upward mobility mistakenly embraced as representative, while
the relative standing of most would remain unchanged or even worsen.

Specific political conditions shaped another set of obstacles to any egalitarian future for the territory. The 1854 Kansas-Nebraska Act opened the region
to the possibility that those Americans who could afford it might establish
their legal right to own other people. Struggling to maintain its dominance
in national affairs, the Democratic Party grappled with new "Southern rights"
arguments asserting the universal legality of slavery, which moved other
Democratic leaders to propose a "squatter sovereignty," leaving the matter
to the settlers in the territories. Thereafter, though, the stability of the party
required demonstrating to the Southern faction that this new doctrine could
bring Kansas into the Union as a state that sanctioned human slavery.

Those who emerged at the top in this process of replicating "civilization"
justified the outcome and the process. A contemporary novelist depicted the
explanation of one such apologist: "the weak are made to serve the strong
in the same manner that the little fish serve the big ones, the bugs the birds,
the bird, the hawks, and they in turn serve us."[5] Certainly, some slaveholders

believed that the natural world—human nature—mandated hierarchy and slavery, which justified the imposition of a nonrepresentative proslavery territorial government by force of arms.

Sectional tensions framed the development of Kansas. In November 1854 a population with only 1,114 legitimately resident voters cast 2,871 ballots, and in March 1855 officials tallied 6,320 votes in a territory with only 2,892 possible voters.[6] Based on such returns, the federal authorities ascribed legitimacy to what the "free-staters"—settlers from the nonslave-holding states—called "the bogus legislature" at Shawnee Mission, which hoped to bring the territory to statehood with slavery. Essentially, the Democratic administrations had to secure the unity of the party and the nation by demonstrating to southern elites that "squatter sovereignty" could establish slavery in Kansas.

Hostile paramilitary groups took the field in Kansas, sanctioned by an alleged proslavery majority actively supported by the federal government. They named themselves the "Social Band," the "Friends' Society," or the "Sons of the South," but their victims believed they acted at the command of a centralized leadership in the three-degree "blue lodges" associated with the Southern Jurisdiction of Scottish Rite freemasonry. Then, too, many would-be *filibusteros* patrolled the territory, their organization variously attributed to the Order of the Lone Star or the Knights of the Golden Circle. All offered a romanticized and abstract ideal of Southern rights and comradeship with prominent Southern leaders. Such veteran Indian fighters and freebooters set the tone for the participation of those whose legacies of political terrorism and violence would haunt the West for years, individuals such as the Missouri slave traders and businessmen Jo Shelby and Thomas R. Livingston or the Ohio schoolteacher turned horse thief William C. Quantrill.[7]

Political violence in Kansas grew naturally from interest in expansionism, which unified Southern Democrats in a way it never quite did for Northern elites. Charles Robinson—leader of the free-staters in Kansas—noted that earlier, in California, he faced Ben McCulloch, the Texas Ranger and future Confederate general. Florida's "Colonel" Harry Titus counted as another "chief pillar and ornament" of the early territorial government; his career included filibustering adventures against Cuba and Nicaragua.[8] A society free of slavery may develop rigid social hierarchies sustained by bodies of armed men and a corrupting political system, but the presence of "the peculiar institution" and the need to defend it by any means virtually mandates these features.

No less than the proslavery forces, the free-staters—who favored the organization of a state without slavery—looked to people with prior political leadership, such as Charles Robinson. During the California gold rush, settlers angry over "land monopoly" formed armed bands of squatters that confronted the authorities in the streets of Sacramento before launching the Settlers' League, which became active for many years in local and state politics. A Massachusetts-born sympathizer wounded during the Sacramento squatters' uprising, Robinson thought the fighting in California had foreshadowed that in Kansas in several respects. The titular head of the "Topeka movement," he later became the first free-state governor of Kansas.[9]

Even more important, James H. Lane, a Democratic politician from Indiana, seized the opportunity Kansas presented to remake himself. Although he had long repeated white supremacist arguments about African Americans and had favored the Kansas-Nebraska Act, the "Grim Chieftain" made a frighteningly smooth transition into a free-state spokesman. As did other radicals, Phillips found Robinson increasingly too conservative, though still "a man you can honor for his ability without feeling ashamed of his character." In contrast, Phillips liked what Lane said but alternately "admired him, and again shrank from him with the conviction that the public interest could never be safely entrusted with him."[10]

The logic of seeking and holding public office would leave participants more concerned with "development" than with mapping out social changes. As in any settlement, the civil and military authorities exercised power through institutions that had grown from the specific needs of a ruling class or dominant elite. Under most circumstances, these factors permit shifts to resolve contradictions endemic to the dynamics of a changing society. The mid-nineteenth-century American republic, however, experienced two related problems. First, clashes among these authorities reflected an unprecedented crisis in the coherence of the ruling elites and their institutions; second, an ideology of American republicanism had introduced a usually minor factor in such considerations: the aspirations of ordinary people unwilling to accept the status quo.

⌒⌒

While western settlement replicated time-honored structures and values, it also imported dissenting traditions and frequently drew disproportionately from those discontented with the old order back east. Phillips thought settlement drew "a class of *thinkers* to the territory, who are, of all others, the worst to *manage.*" Perhaps nowhere did they constitute so prominent and influential a proportion of settlers as in Kansas. The Vegetarian Settlement Company, socialist German Turners, and others attempted to establish colonies in the territory, and freethinkers organized a library to combat the influence of religious denominations. Opponents equated temperance with abolitionism, because a vocal hostility to alcohol seemed so characteristic of settlers from the free states.[11]

Political abolitionism played an understandably critical role in Kansas, largely because it had, over the previous decade, embraced a broadening set of other concerns and fostered a much wider antislavery political movement. The Liberty Party had started in 1839 with a single-issue condemnation of southern slavery and began building a wider constituency with a "broad platform" that officially or informally expanded to include a spectrum of antebellum reform ideas, including a quasi-socialist notion of land reform. Particularly after 1846, critics of slavery, regardless of strategic differences, tended to share a sense that the institution not only constituted a gross injustice to the slaves but undermined republican values and the dignity of free labor. Political antislavery attained more successes, and in the wake of the Mexican War, the new Free-Soil party entered national politics in the 1848 elections.[12]

The popular agitation for radical land reform by northern "lacklanders" introduced a cause that brought vast numbers of whites into conflict with "Slave Power," which stood in the way of their personal and collective hopes for success. Rooted in the working-class politics that had episodically erupted in New York for years, the National Reform Association (NRA) had begun its work around "the land question" in 1844 and within two years began regularly collaborating with sections of the abolitionist movement, particularly the one headed by Gerrit Smith, John Brown's benefactor. By 1852 the NRA had inspired as many as a quarter of a million Americans to sign petitions for a series of radical "Agrarian" measures, including the establishment of a legal limitation on individual land ownership. Among the most radical of the abolitionists, Smith envisioned a broad but explicitly abolitionist coalition embracing the Germans, particularly "such of them as breathed the revolutionary spirit of 1848," and the Agrarianists, since "every real land reformer is an abolitionist."[13]

As early as 1850 midwestern land reformers imagined Kansas to be a reasonable testing ground for free-soil politics. Relentlessly pushed by the demands of western development, as well as those of eastern social reformers, Congress reluctantly passed the Homestead Bill, inspiring the NRA to undertake the largest nationally coordinated petition drive in American history to date (1850–52). The Kansas-Nebraska Act, wrote William Addison Phillips, ignored "the right of the settlers to the soil," marking the triumph of "Manifest Destiny" over Anglo-Americans as surely as it did over the Indians or Mexicans.[14]

Phillips had not yet turned thirty when congressional passage of the Kansas-Nebraska Act enabled the organization of the territory. Born in 1824 at Paisley, in Scotland's Renfrewshire, he had learned and devout Presbyterian parents, who placed him in an academically oriented grammar school where he "uniformly stood at the head of his class," especially in mathematics and Latin. Phillips's formal studies came to an end, however, when the family immigrated to Randolph County, Illinois, during 1838 or 1839. He followed his eclectic interests in his new country, in 1852 writing regularly for Benjamin Franklin John Hanna's *Chester Herald*. While studying law, he became Hanna's partner and started writing for Horace Greeley's *New York Tribune*. Both these newspapers ardently advocated National Reform politics, and Chester had a circle of the pro-NRA Brotherhood of the Union, in which Hanna and likely Phillips held membership.[15]

Described as "a Free State knight errant" and the "bell wether of Horace Greeley's flock," Phillips went west as a correspondent for the *New York Tribune*. He soon found himself periodically "hunted like a wild beast." In response he cultivated his physical strength and stamina, becoming a formidable fighter. He also quickly found a dedicated group of volunteers that sought to master troop evolutions "from the old-fashioned sergeant major polka to the Crimea drill." Through it all, he remained an uncommonly bookish man, regarded by those who knew him as "an original thinker, especially on all subjects of religion, morals, general politics, economics, and civilization." Although Phillips never discussed religion, he did not share Brown's piety and characterized himself as "not a full believer in the orthodox dogmas of the church." Still, Phillips fully shared Brown's conviction that moral duty required resistance to slavery.[16]

Other settlers came, quite literally, from Utopia—Utopia, Ohio, that is. Just upriver from Cincinnati, the town had enjoyed a series of incarnations as a spiritualist and socialist community, largely under the leadership of John Otis Wattles. Fifteen years Phillips's senior and the son of a Connecticut musical instrument maker, Wattles was a National Reformer, abolitionist, and "no-government man." After spending his life involved in one communitarian experiment after another, he now began planning a railroad. His somewhat older brother, Augustus Wattles, had been involved in the 1834 schism in Lane Seminary but chose not to join the general withdrawal to Oberlin College. Staying in Cincinnati, he built a black school system, which he replicated at Columbus, Chillicothe, Circleville, Zanesville, Dayton, and many other Ohio towns. After a flood swept away the town of Utopia, the Wattleses slowly planned its rebuilding, but Kansas put an abrupt end to their plans. Augustus put his family and belongings in three wagons and set out for the territory, arriving in May 1854. By 1856 the brothers had heavily invested what they had taken west in building a new community at Moneka.[17] In the process, they established a natural base for paramilitary operations along the border.

Kansas also drew a number of talented immigrants, such as Richard Josiah Hinton, an English workingman turned journalist. He had been born November 25, 1830, to the family of the chief stonecutter working on the archaeology exhibit at the British Museum. After serving an apprenticeship as a mason himself, Hinton had learned printing and shorthand at a mechanics' institute. His father had been president of an illegal labor organization, and young Hinton became an ardent radical by 1848, when he learned his "'facings' and how to handle and load a musket in the ranks of a seditious company of 'physical force' Chartists" (a supporter of "the People's Charter," demanding universal manhood suffrage in England). With the defeat and repression of that movement, he came to New York in 1851, where he studied topographical engineering and worked as a reporter. As a visitor to Boston in 1854, he helped try to rescue a runaway slave from the local authorities. Still retaining an accent that dropped the *h* from his speech, he made arrangements with various newspapers to support his freelance reporting and, in 1856, went to Kansas.[18]

Adopting the term from ancient Roman advocates of reform, such free-labor radicals saw themselves as "Agrarian" critics of the status quo. They viewed slavery as a threat to the republic, the Democratic and Whig parties as co-sustainers of the institution, and the "lacklanders'" demands for equality as the key means of righting the republican experiment. Veterans of the NRA proposed using the "republican" name for a new party, deeming it appropriate to opposition against a slave-based imperial course of American development. In their own civilization's pursuit of Manifest Destiny, they discerned the danger of the kind of imperial ambitions that consumed the

Roman republic. For a generation, Democratic administrations had been removing native peoples they had encountered. Rather unusually, Phillips wrote that "the Indian aspects of the Kansas question" underscored an official "breach of faith" by the U.S. government and observed that the subject had been "too much overlooked" and "comparatively lost sight of" owing to the struggle over slavery.[19]

Phillips later recounted how the Roman city-state had begun as a market town dominated by the more powerful Etruscans, who had fostered slavery and employed mercenaries in their army. After it gained independence, Rome established "a higher conception of government" based on "the equal rights of all its citizens." As it started acquiring power, however, it also began to attract ruthless individuals drawn to power. Justified by the hostility of neighboring tribal people, Rome secured its borders, albeit in a way that disproportionately benefited the leading families over ordinary citizens. The former, having access to cheap and enslaved labor, created vast estates, the *latifundia* that dominated the economy and impoverished ordinary citizens. In addition to the titled patricians, untitled men of wealth in the equestrian orders functioned as businessmen, bankers, and government contractors, forming the patricians' natural allies in monopolizing land, labor, and capital. The nature of these new hierarchies militarized politics and politicized the military in the interests of the leading families. Dependent on the elite for bread, distracted by circuses, and viewing the army as one of its few means of social mobility, citizens sold votes and accepted the meaningless party rivalries of *optimates* and *populares*. This left the old Roman republic to choose "between one great tyrant and a thousand small tyrants."[20]

Given this reading of history, Phillips and the other radicals saw the expansionist faith in Manifest Destiny as a crisis in the American republic. The annexation of Texas, the seizure of California, the invasion of Mexico, and the conquest of the Southwest, all of which extended the United States from the Atlantic to the Pacific, introduced what Phillips called "a feature foreign to our republican institutions." Both inside and outside the federal government, southern leaders openly spoke of a new Caribbean empire for slaveholding and encouraged a succession of private expeditions of filibusters, or freebooters, who reinvaded Mexico a half-dozen times, raised troops to attack Cuba at least three times, planned the annexation of the Yucatan, seized Nicaragua, and placed armed Americans in the field from British Guyana to Ecuador. It required no "paranoid style" to see official complicity in such activities, for U.S. officials meeting in Europe justified any future American seizure of Cuba in the Ostend Manifesto, which the *Tribune* called "the greatest piece of villainy since the days of the first Cain."[21]

The new Republican Party emerged directly in response to this perceived threat to "republican liberty." News of the Kansas-Nebraska Act inspired an important series of protest meetings at the former Wisconsin Phalanx at Ceresco, a socialist community inspired by the ideas of Charles Fourier. Along with their neighbors in the renamed town of Ripon, they assembled under the gavel of Alvan Earl Bovay, the former national secretary of the NRA, to form a new party under the banner of republicanism. By the fall of 1856, with the newly minted Republican Party fielding John C. Fremont as its presidential candidate, Bovay accompanied several hundred of his neighbors into Iowa, on their way to Kansas. Leading Bovay and his cohort was Edward Daniels, a Boston-born geologist and an Oberlin graduate who had taught school at the Fourierist community and served briefly as Wisconsin's first state geologist before taking on his duties with the Kansas Aid Society. U.S. dragoons stopped and disarmed Daniels's contingent of settlers.[22]

Opposition inspired not only the Republicans but also the Radical Abolitionist Party. John Brown attended its founding convention at Syracuse, June 26–29, 1855. Concerned about the Whig origins of the Republicans in New York, white and black abolitionists—including African American leaders such as Frederick Douglass and Dr. James McCune Smith—founded a party to agitate explicitly for immediate emancipation, equal rights, and a distinctively antislavery interpretation of the U.S. Constitution. At their founding convention, Gerrit Smith read letters from Brown's sons to the convention, which declined to endorse violent measures but informally provided John Brown with firearms and seven broadswords to take west. By the time he reached the territory, in October 1855, legions of settlers from nonslaveholding states were sporting a red string in a buttonhole of their coats as a "red badge of resistance." The newcomer Brown impressed Phillips as "a volcano beneath a covery of snow."[23]

When John Brown addressed questions beyond slavery, he spoke the language of other free-labor radicals. Phillips thought Brown had "read much and *thought* more," largely embodying those radicals' antebellum utopian and millenarian aspirations. Brown's faith in the dignity of the individual grew from both the Bible and the secularist Declaration of Independence. He had personally witnessed the aftermath of the 1848–49 uprisings in Europe and spoke of both the Haitian revolution and the repeated attempts at slave rebellion in the United States—just as he readily discussed how Spartacus might have won the Servile wars had he either marched on Rome or led his men into the mountains to fight as guerrillas. He saw chattel slavery as both one of "an infinite number of wrongs" and the "sum of all villainies" that pervaded American life. "If the American people did not take courage, and end it speedily," he warned Phillips, "human freedom and republican liberty would soon be empty names in these United States."[24] It was a language that Phillips, Hinton, and the Wattleses well understood.

The uncompromising radical insistence on equal rights had direct implications in Kansas that reached beyond antislavery. In the spring of 1859, "some twenty-five earnest men and women of the John Brown type" launched the Kansas Woman's Rights Association, with Susan E. Wattles—Augustus's wife—as secretary. John O. Wattles presided until his death later that year. Supported by James Hanway and James H. Blood, the future husband of Victoria Woodhull, the association persuaded the free-staters to schedule a special session on suffrage at their upcoming Constitutional Convention. The future Federal commander at Honey Springs, James G. Blunt, agreed that he would not oppose the motion should women "ask to be put upon an equality with men." Although Charles Robinson, Samuel C. Pomeroy, and other territorial politicians endorsed woman suffrage, they pleaded for a constitution more easily acceptable to the U.S. Congress. One of the suffragists quipped that there had been "too many old lawyers in the convention."[25]

Spearheading the suffragist effort was John Ritchie, a midwestern abolitionist who also opposed limiting citizenship to whites. A tough-minded and ambitious man, he had been pushing forty when he brought his family to Topeka. There, in 1856, he built "the Ritchie Block," the town's first block consisting entirely of brick structures. His involvement in the armed struggle and the underground railroad made him periodically a wanted man. After the Constitutional Convention, Ritchie won a shoot-out with a U.S. marshal and won acquittal in a short trial.[26]

Even amid the desolation and the gunslingers, a meager little labor movement appeared. Printers in the territory produced over two dozen newspapers, including three dailies. Employees at Leavenworth, Lecompton, and Lawrence established affiliates of the new National Typographical Union (NTU). These NTU members, likely never more than forty or fifty, waged an uphill fight to keep owners from reducing wages by frequently using "'strapped' typos" just arrived from the East. Then, too, erratic employment sometimes forced union members to odd jobs, such as driving cattle to Pike's Peak or

Salt Lake City. Workers for the territory's highly politicized press, such as Charles Lenhardt or John Swinton, found it almost impossible not to take sides, and after the sack of Lawrence, Lenhardt "and thirteen others, a majority of whom were printers, took the 'brush' against the Border Ruffians."[27]

Notwithstanding these other questions, radicals could not help but focus on the issue of slavery. Brown and his men spoke scornfully of those free-state businessmen and conservatives who opposed the extension of slavery in hopes of making the Kansas Territory a "Free White State," whereas these abolitionists viewed slavery as the "sum of all villainies," because it denied the very humanity of working people.[28] Since the proslavery forces insisted on resorting to arms, the radicals had to postpone any resolution of their divergent visions of free labor in a free state. The violence also meant that John Brown, who had complained for years about the way a few powerful capitalists had dominated the wool business at Springfield, Massachusetts, would gain fame for defending a town financed by—and named for—one of those capitalists, Amos A. Lawrence.

Although John Swinton described John Brown as "a man like unto whom Kansas at that time of strife and stress had not a few men," few free-staters had taken it on themselves to rewrite the rules imposed on them. Northern backers agreed to send arms to settlers on the condition that they not be used in clashes with the territorial and federal authorities who protected the "ruffians." When proslavery men sought to keep local free-staters from going to help defend Lawrence by threatening their families with violence, Brown took decisive action. On May 24 he seized and presided over the execution of five proslavery settlers in what became known as "the Pottawatomie Massacre." Blunt thought the act sufficiently intimidating to provide a needed opening for the free-staters. "I justified it then, so did Robinson and everybody else," added Hinton. "I have had no reason to change my mind upon that subject since." Phillips called it "one of those stern and remorseless acts in civil war," placing the ultimate responsibility on "the corrupt government and perverted official authority" that failed to protect free-staters.[29] The militia seized prisoners after the Pottawatomie Massacre, after which Brown's company captured and held proslavery men hostage, releasing them only to avoid a clash with U.S. dragoons based at Leavenworth.

The Pottawatomie killings haunted John Brown. It seems likely that Lane, Robinson, and others encouraged his original preemptive executions at Pottawatomie, but they were not the parties who did the deed. Brown himself—and those closest to him—remained emotionally conflicted, if intellectually convinced. While consistently admitting to having led the band that killed the five victims, he repeatedly made a point of adding that he had not personally raised his hand against any of the prisoners. Yet, as Brown said to his friends, the Hanways, "If it was murder, I am not guiltless." One acquaintance described him as having gone somewhat mad that summer, though most who knew him, such as Luke F. Parsons, insisted that his judgment remained unclouded.[30]

The alternative to this kind of conflict would require neutralizing the military, which had been siding with the proslavery authorities. In a document worthy of the European revolutionaries they admired, Brown's men addressed the "Duty of the Soldier" for circulation to the officers and soldiers of the U.S. Army in Kansas. "In the ancient Republics every man capable of bearing arms was, up to a certain period of his life, bound in duty to the public to fill his place in the ranks of the soldiery to secure his country against invasion or insult." But "in assuming his armor," they added, "the man did not engage to confine his mind in a strait-jacket." The terms in which this argument is couched demonstrate these armed abolitionists' relationships to wider ideologies of revolutionary republicanism. The soldier would either behave like the citizen of a republic or mindlessly carry out orders, as do subjects of an imperial monarchy. The Kansas experience posed the question, "Will the soldiery of a Republic consent to become *living machines*, and thus sustain Wrong against Right?"[31]

The U.S. cavalry celebrated the Fourth of July in 1856 by dispersing the free-stater government in Lawrence, inspiring the generally Democratic crowds to defiantly cheer for John C. Fremont, the Republican presidential candidate. The honest but generally nonconfrontational Robinson went back east to plead for arms, and Lane fled the territory a wanted man. That summer, as Hinton arrived, the free-staters seized "Fort Titus" with firearms and a howitzer, using the melted lead type of a demolished antislavery press to deliver "double-leaded editorials." When the two sides clashed over a wagon train of supplies, U.S. troops arrested the free-staters, allowing the proslavery forces once more to turn to Lawrence.[32]

A few weeks later Hinton, who had met John Brown on his way to Kansas, encountered him on the streets of Lawrence. At the time an imminent raid by the proslavery bands had forced an emergency town meeting that had bogged down over what to do in response. The terrified residents had sent word to the U.S. cavalry, which was too far away to help even if it tried, and were debating whether to petition Washington. Hinton rushed Brown into the meeting, where he exercised some forbearance before he "mounted a dry-goods box" and quietly explained what his auditors needed to do: keep silent until the riders came in range and then aim low.[33] Almost immediately those at the meeting emptied into the street to see to the town's defenses.

John Bowles, a Kentucky slaveholder turned abolitionist, placed himself under Brown's command that day. Bowles led the small group up Mount Oread, overlooking the town. At dusk the would-be raiders rode into what they expected to be a defenseless community only to get a lively firefight. Shortly thereafter his brother died from the poor food and conditions of confinement by the "bogus" authorities.[34] Bowles joined Hinton as a lifelong defender of John Brown and his legacy.

In stark contrast to those in Lawrence, the town fathers of Fort Scott saw the border war over slavery as a noisy, dangerous, and irrelevant distraction. Nestled safely in the protection of the army, the local courts took action to disarm the antislavery residents, inspiring two new antislavery warriors. A former schoolteacher and a minister in Kentucky and Missouri, James Montgomery raised a band that supposedly profited from the punitive raids on proslavery settlers, but his defense of the free-staters made him a natural ally of the Wattles brothers and Brown. Although Montgomery's junior by twenty years, the New York–born midwesterner Charles Jennison had ridden with Brown before moving to Mound City and joining Montgomery's "jayhawking" forays. They sponsored and protected their own "squatters court" as a rival to the official system of law enforcement at Fort Scott and helped free-staters escape that system's clutches.[35]

This kind of resistance around Fort Scott invariably involved Brown's old followers. Dr. James Gilpatrick Blunt—nephew to Dr. Rufus Gilpatrick, one of the judges in the "squatters court"—had grown up on a farm in Maine and spent time at sea and in a military academy before going to Ohio and becoming an ardent Republican. In 1857 he had settled not far from the Wattleses and "hired a 4–mule team and wagon" to bring reinforcements when proslavery forces threatened Montgomery and Jennison's base at "Fort Bayne," on the Little Osage. August Bondi, a Jewish veteran of the 1848 Vienna revolution and "the only survivor of this expedition," later remembered that "during the engagement Wm. A. Phillips the *N.Y. Tribune* correspondent came on in a gallop," leaped into the defenders' "breastworks and was received with 3 cheers for the *N.Y. Tribune*."[36]

At one point, during a jailbreak at Fort Scott, Jennison horrified the community by taking a shot at the richest man in town, Alexander McDonald. A Pennsylvanian merchant then in his midtwenties, McDonald had followed his brother to Kansas, where he opened a dry goods business and built the town's first sawmill in town, first bank, and first large house, "the palace of Fort Scott." A member of the Masons and the proexpansionist Sons of Malta, McDonald also served on the town council, filled the post of city treasurer, and worked with anyone worth knowing in town, including the prosecuting attorney, Charles W. Blair. For decades to come, residents pointed out Jennison's bullet holes in McDonald's door.[37]

From one perspective, the fate of Kansas had always been contingent on the interests of the capitalists and investors, particularly those in the western settlements. They wanted development, which required settlement and a government that would protect the settlers in their homes. What William Henry Seward called "the Slave Power" threatened all that; these elements had prevailed in their own states by repressing any views opposed to them, but the attempt to introduce this system in Kansas interfered directly with the free development of the territory.[38]

Victory for slavery required restricting settlement, usually using armed bands from outside the territory, and neither the end nor the means suited business interests in development. The violence and insecurity proved especially offputting to new settlers. Dramatizing this, on May 19, 1858, one such band from outside the area dragged eleven men and boys from their homes and summarily executed them in a ravine near the Marais de Cygnes. While apologists pointed to the Pottawatomie killings, that action had been a response to an overt armed threat, whereas Marais de Cygnes had been a reprisal killing of people whose only crime had been their state of origin, making it apparently gratuitous. Although the Fort Scott authorities made no effort to identify the killers, let alone bring them to justice, they certainly came to see the folly of permitting them to enter the territory and function with impunity.

Still, the militant free-staters' decision to take up arms in their own defense made possible a constitutional and legal victory. They defied the local officials, the "bogus" legislature and its militia, and even the federal authorities, including the U.S. Army. While the proslavery forces ratified the Lecompton Constitution in January 1858, the free-staters met, wrote, and ratified their own constitution that spring, under the vigilant protection of Lane's "Ballot Box Guards." The armed minions of the Grim Chieftain also escorted so many free-staters into the territory that it settled its future with regard to slavery. The sheer weight of numbers overcame federal intransigence and forced acknowledgment of the legitimacy of their free-state elections.

Despite the victory, John Brown urged caution and skepticism about electoral successes and the new Republican Party. "A professional politician you never could trust," he complained to Phillips, "for even if he had convictions, he was always ready to sacrifice his principles for his advantage." Even as the new party took form, Brown warned that "many of the leaders would jeopardize the principles of the party in order to get power." Even those of his men who were actively involved with the party, such as James Redpath, complained that on the big questions, "the Republican Party has sold us out."[39]

⌒

John Brown never accepted the idea of human freedom as a conditional state to be compromised or negotiated into existence, but he drew clear conclusions about the way the free-staters had triumphed in Kansas. By the end of the border troubles, for example, even the most respectable free-staters—such as South Carolina–born Martin Franklin Conway—sheltered runaway slaves. Formerly an active leader of the Baltimore printers and a charter member of the National Typographical Union, Conway had become the territory's congressional delegate and a contact man for the New England abolitionists. He asked Bowles, a fellow southerner, to report on activities with the underground railroad. Bowles reported that as many as two dozen runaways weekly passed through Lawrence, choosing this town precisely because Missouri slaveholders damned it as an abolitionist center.[40] For Brown, the citizens' willingness to defy unjust laws opened unbounded possibilities for freedom.

Brown saw that this approach raised possibilities beyond Kansas. Bowles's later novel dramatized plans for "a highway" for runaway slaves going "right through the State of Missouri," with "organized bands to protect it all along the way," thus shielding "an irresistible torrent toward freedom." The Radical Abolitionist Party's newspaper reported "private information, from a high source," that victory in Kansas would lead to abolitionist raids to liberate slaves in Missouri, though, it added, "the movement will not stop in Missouri. The war, if it begins, will run through the slave States. It will be a war of revolution, and make other work for the administration, besides subduing Kansas. It will probably embroil the whole nation."[41] Learned at great cost in the West, John Brown's lesson would now be applied nationally.

TWO

A Free West in a Slave Nation

Some four years before the 1863 battle, the Creeks near Honey Springs probably took little notice of Dick Hinton as he rode along the Texas Road. As did other followers of John Brown, he believed that a slave rebellion might detonate a general uprising of nonslaveholding southerners and specifically that "the best place of attack would be in the South-Western States." So he passed through the area with a topographical eye for militarily strategic positions from which to fight such a war. The San Antonio socialist Dr. Karl Adolphus Douai had suggested to Frederick Law Olmsted—that Fourierist designer of parks and cemeteries—that the Germans there might want to form an independent nonslaveholding territory in northern Texas or beyond. Between there and Kansas, the Indian Territory—present Oklahoma—provided a strategic link. Moreover, Hinton thought the tradition of maroons among the Creeks made them "the best of men" as allies in this projected multiracial revolution.[1] When later captured at Harpers Ferry, Brown carried a copy of Hinton's report proposing an initiative that would take place in not Virginia but the far West.

The westward extension of the sectional conflict between the North and the South brought new forces to bear. Nowhere else did the threatened federal union face the distinct problem of dealing with large populations of American Indians, who generally had a distinct disinterest regarding the distribution of slavery laws. Abolitionists, free-labor radicals, and the ascendant Republicans had a range of views about Indians and race, which posed the possibility of something other than the rigidly defined standards of white supremacy that reflected the needs of the southern slave owners, who had run the country for decades. Most directly, the West contributed to John Brown's plan for resolving the sectional conflict over slavery in a way that would thereafter make race a question difficult to ignore.

⌐⌐

The 1860 U.S. Census counted roughly 300,000 Native Americans. These included, with a great margin of error, 55,000 in present New Mexico and Arizona, 40,000 in the Dakotas, 31,000 in Washington, and 20,000 in Utah. The largest concentration—and that closest to a large white population—occurred in the Indian Territory, which was home to 65,680 Indians (along with over 8,000 blacks), many of whom had close tribal connections to the 13,000 Indians in the Kansas-Nebraska territories.[2]

A generation before the expansion of southern labor relations threatened Kansas, slavery contributed much to the removal of tens of thousands of Indians from the southeastern states to the Indian Territory. The Cherokee, Choctaw, Chickasaw, Creek, and Seminole nations—the so-called Five Civilized Tribes—had generations of contact with the whites and had adopted Christianity, literacy, or slavery to whatever extent they thought appropriate. White travelers noted unexpected "elements of culture and refinement" among them.[3]

Within the territory each nation had its designated homeland. Tucked in the corner between Arkansas and Texas lived 18,000 Choctaws with nearly 2,400 slaves, and up the Red River to the west were some 5,000 Chickasaws with nearly 1,000 slaves. Along the border with central Kansas were 13,600 Creeks with over 1,500 blacks, while 2,300 Seminoles with a black population estimated between 500 and 1,000 occupied the central part of the territory, in the forks of the Canadian River. Wedged along the eastern border, between the northern and southern nations, resided some 21,000 Cherokees with over 2,500 slaves, though the nation also owned vast tracts of land in Kansas. The Neosho District, in the northeastern corner of the territory adjacent to Missouri, contained as many as 5,000 Osages, Quapaws, Neoshos, and Shawnees, along with various "New York" groups—Cayuga, Seneca, Mohawk, Oneida, Onondaga; these groups were mostly Iroquois in origin and often closely associated with tribal members relocated to Kansas.[4] In the Leased District were over 2,500 Indians of mixed background, including Wichitas to the north; Tonkawas and Euchees to the south; and Arapahos, Kiowas, Comanches, Apaches, and Cheyennes to the west.

Although American Indians, with their characteristic pragmatism, sought to use the arrangement for their own purposes, the United States had super-imposed on each native group an artificial identity as a "nation" defined by an executive "principal chief" and a legislative "general council." While this hardly reflected the decentralized and organic nature of authority among Indians, the U.S. government needed such structures to legitimize the great concessions it demanded of each "nation." If the chiefs resisted the removal and treaty terms, the U.S. authorities simply found members of the tribes willing to accept those terms and made them chiefs. Each Indian group, how-ever, struggled to respond to removal in its own fashion. When Georgia tried to remove them, the Cherokees filed a lawsuit, which the U.S. Supreme Court decided in their favor. Nevertheless, President Andrew Jackson brushed aside the ruling to implement the goals of Georgia and other southern states.

The Seminoles resorted arms. Su-nuk-mik-ko (also known as Halpat-ter Micco, Holata Micco, or Halpuda Milkho, meaning "governing chief") emerged as a leader of the Arpiucki band. He, Halpatter Tustenugee, and Coacoochee—known also as "Billy Bowlegs," "Alligator," and "Wild Cat"—drew the United States into a succession of expensive and bloody quagmires known as the Seminole Wars. Many surrendered in 1842, but Su-nuk-mik-ko withdrew deeper into the swamps, reportedly rebuffing a $10,000 bribe to surrender. The Third Seminole War—waged against his band and pressed by U.S. Secretary of War Jefferson Davis—lasted into 1858, when Elias Rec-tor, of the Office of Indian Affairs (OIA), persuaded Su-nuk-mik-ko to leave Florida. *Harper's Weekly* described the chief at the time as "a rather good-looking Indian of about fifty years" with "a fine forehead [and] a keen, black eye," as well as two wives, a son, five daughters, and, on paper, fifty slaves.[5]

The OIA, which supervised these mass extortions, had long been the most lucrative area of federal employment. By 1861 its commissioner had thirteen superintendencies and nearly three dozen additional agencies charged with doling out the large federal annuities to tribes struggling to eke out an exis-tence on the poorer and unfamiliar lands to which they had been removed. Of-ficials deducted from those payments reimbursements to any white claimants for debts, damages, or depredations. Collusion with claimants and contractors became standard.[6] The politics of the appointees reflected the dominance of the southern faction of the Democratic Party in national government.

The federal government also sought to control all business done between whites and Indians by restricting trade to a designated licensed business. Originally justified as a means to bar the unscrupulous from the trade, the entrepreneurial opportunities of a chartered monopoly drew "gamblers, whiskey-traffickers, fugitives from civilized justice and desperate men of every known vice," as well as more superficially respectable types who adopted the norms appropriate to their newly chosen profession. Usually awarded their licenses based on OIA or congressional recommendation, the traders set their own prices, kept their own books, and submitted their yearly claims against the annuities; OIA officials usually accepted those claims on face value and paid them before the Indians saw their government money.[7] Other businesses might also get special contracts to perform specific functions under OIA supervision.

Just as whites moving west brought conflicting ideas about slavery, lingering issues over removal divided the Indians. Although the timing, pace, and geographic details of their forced migrations varied, these nations' common subjugated status inspired both assimilationist and traditionalist aspirations among their people. The assimilationists included leaders such as Robert M. Jones, of the Choctaw; Stand Watie, of the Cherokee; Daniel and Chilly McIntosh, of the Creeks; and John Jumper, of the Seminoles. As did their white peers, they tended to measure progress by their own factional and personal successes, and the increasing cultural inroads of the white South magnified their influences.

In contrast, Indians who remained hostile to the treaties of removal also tended to mistrust the standards of their white neighbors. Creek traditionalists followed Principal Chief Oktarharsars Harjot and Opothleyahola (also called Gouge), an elderly full-blood who clung to the old ways despite his relative wealth and slave ownership. Their cothinkers among the Seminoles turned to Su-nuk-mik-ko, Halpatter Tustenugee, Coacoochee, and John Chupco. Even in the shadow of white Texans, the Choctaw Peter Perkins Pitchlynn decried the uncritical acceptance of the values of the whites.[8]

Traditionalists themselves inaccurately spoke of the difference in terms of Indian blood, full-bloods as opposed to "mixed bloods" and "half-breeds." Among the Delaware in Kansas, Panipakuxwe—"He who walks where leaves fall," or "Fall Leaf," as he was known outside the tribe—worked as a guide, interpreter, and adviser to the U.S. Army but complained that "half breeds" imposed "white man's law" by becoming "government chiefs." He hoped "to live as before," cherished the old long-house religion, wanted "lands in common," and urged loyalty to chiefs "who will take care of the poor people—of the women and children and of the interests of the whole tribe." Among the Cherokee, however, the full-blooded Stand Watie articulated assimilationist aspirations, while traditionalists looked to Principal Chief John Ross, a slaveholder with only an eighth Indian blood, who resided in Rose Cottage, a southern-style mansion at Park Hill.[9]

The very notion of "traditional" Indian ways required a creative recasting of Native American identity. Indeed, the joint occupancy of the Indian Territory by diverse Indian peoples created the preconditions for finding mutual traditions. Seasonally, young braves of these nations shed the clothes of the whites, painted themselves, and went west to hunt buffalo. There, the "half-savage" tribesmen who continued to resist government provided "civilized" Indians with a hint of life before the advent of the whites. What emerged, though, was an amalgamation of practices, rituals, and stories centered on the lodge, dance, ball playing, and a prophetic shamanism that had already begun to experiment with psychoactive substances such as peyote, which came north from Mexico.[10] Of course, the wealthier, respectable assimilationists derided all such practices, just as their white peers had scoffed at spiritualism and occasional spiritualist uses of hashish and opium.

Cherokee traditionalists formed the Keetowah. Drawing on Cherokee origin myths and an important village back in North Carolina, the name also evoked a spiritual vision of "the beloved community." After growing to about three thousand among the Cherokee, the secret society seems to have spread among the Creek, the Osage, and presumably other neighboring peoples. Meeting in caves and forests, they often used ball-playing to cover the organization's business, and opponents began referring to them as "pin Indians." Authorities have identified the term's source as not only the crossed pins worn by the movement's adherents but also Washington Irving's *Rip Van Winkle*, in which the magical little people created great thunder by going into isolated, secret places and bowling. That such an arcane literary reference even entered into the discussion is perhaps a measure of the extent to which the critics of the "pin Indians" had assimilated white civilization. Then, too, the Keetowah formed at the Peavine Baptist Church and always retained a close association with the territory's Christian missionaries, who spoke of all men as brothers and used old Indian words to talk of "life, liberty and the pursuit of happiness."[11] In the end, the most traditional feature of Keetowah may well have been its embrace of the historical pragmatism of the Indian peoples.

Most of the roughly 13,000 Indians resident in the Kansas and Nebraska territories occupied designated homelands, as did those to the south, in the Indian Territory. From north to south along the territory's border with Missouri, vast tracts still belonged to the Iowa, Sac and Fox, Kickapoo, Delaware, Wyandotte, Shawnee, Peoria, Miami, New York, Cherokee, and Quapaw. Toward the interior of the territory, there were reserves for the Sac and Fox of Mississippi, Ottawa, Pottawatomie, and just west of the Cherokee Neutral Tract, the Osage.

Indians there well knew that the proslavery territorial government of Kansas did nothing to prevent white land-grabbing. As John Brown pointed out to Augustus Wattles, the government early targeted its violence on the only OIA agent in Kansas of northern birth. Under the auspices of the proslavery government, so many whites squatted on the Delaware lands and stole "corn, hogs and other articles" from the Shawnee that even the Shawnees' OIA agent protested. The authorities themselves, however, secretly negotiated treaties and imposed them on the Otoe and Missouri, Kickapoo, Kaskaskia, Weas, Delaware, Shawnee, and other tribes, wresting from them large tracts of ceded land. Partly because of this, many Shawnee, Delaware, Pottawatomie, and other Kansas groups had already left their designated homelands to live as "absentees" in the Indian Territory. Short of changing the government, there seemed little hope of relief.[12]

Nonetheless, many of the most militant abolitionists simply failed to recognize any similarity between their concerns and those of Indians. The *National Era* lamented how the social and political institutions of the Indian Territory fell "under Pro-Slavery influence." A celebrated 1860 Iowa trial pit James Vincent, a transplanted Oberlin ally of John Brown, against the Indian owners of four runaways.[13] Abolitionists back east often saw Indians as simply slaveholders of a different race.

More important, those free-state settlers in Kansas preoccupied with development shared a range of assumptions and values with the southern elite. Men such as Perry Fuller proved perfectly capable of treating the Indians as nothing but a source of profit. Although he later claimed to have opposed slavery, Fuller did business with proslavery interests and worked to influence the appointments and contracts in and around the Southern Democrat–controlled OIA. A founder of both Centropolis and, later, Mineola, he quietly seized thousands of acres of land from the Sac and Fox, who complained bitterly about him, as did the Chippewa. Another free-stater, the New York lawyer Robert S. Stevens, became "a veritable Indian ring

by himself." When the Sac and Fox contracted his services to raise buildings, he constructed a much larger sawmill than they needed and used it
himself. He constructed a number of shacks, submitting a bill for $109,000,
and managed to wrangle $179,000 of Indian money from the OIA, causing
Jim Lane to remark, "The contract as originally made is a gross fraud. The
buildings themselves are a fraud. Stevens is a fraud." None of this kept Lane
and others from partnering with Fuller in the effort to locate the new state
capital at Mineola or with Stevens on other projects.[14]

Aspiring antislavery political leaders appealed to the interests of the
business leaders among the free-staters, some of whom openly speculated
in the future value of Indian lands, such as the Cherokee Neutral Strip or
the "floating" rights of the Wyandotte. Indeed, William Henry Seward, the
front-runner for the Republican presidential nomination, made a major address not only urging the removal of the Indians from Kansas to the Indian
Territory but asserting that the demands of a transcontinental railroad and
farming meant that the "Indian territory . . . south of Kansas must be vacated
by the Indians." That some white free-staters embraced the "unjust and in-
humane" removal of tribes to "closely-guarded reserves" disgusted William
A. Phillips, who nevertheless despaired at finding any "honorable escape
from the dilemma in which the Kansas Bill place[d] these matters."[15] Still,
if Indian relations would not vary in the hands of the Southern Democrats
who had shaped and managed them, the success of the free-staters might at
least allow for the possibility of change.

The simplistic top-down institutional standards of race relations that prevailed in the settled areas could rarely be replicated immediately on the
frontier. In the most general sense, Indians, blacks (often runaways), and
whites had anticipated a genuine New World by intermingling and giving
birth to biracial and triracial "maroons" beyond the control of the coloniz-
ers in the Americas. (Indeed, the colonial authorities had made the initial
American contribution to the western legal tradition by instituting a new
capital crime, that of running off to live with the Indians.) The first proposal for American independence had been that of Johann Gottlieb Priber,
who suggested that the eighteenth-century Cherokee should embrace their
destiny as an ingredient in a genuine "melting pot."[16]

Unlike whites, native peoples never conjured an idea of race linked to
forced labor. They had long taken captives in war, partly and temporarily

putting the prisoners to work, but they did so without the explicit racialism, the hereditary obligations, or the exploitive mechanism found on southern plantations. Removal had rooted the legal existence of slavery among them, just as it had imposed on them the political status of a nation with laws necessarily compatible with those of their white neighbors. As the United States prepared the Indians for removal, authorities confiscated unowned blacks among them, holding them for resale, but agreed to send those owned by Indians to the West, along with their other property. As a result, many blacks living among the Indians seemed to have asked the local chiefs to claim them as slaves and thus prevent their resale to the planters.

The result established a widespread slavery on paper that actually reflected an incredibly broad spectrum of day-to-day practical relationships. Generally, slavery tended to resemble that among the whites most among the Choctaws and least among the Seminoles and Creeks. The Creek Opothleyahola owned many slaves on paper but lived the life of an impoverished "blanket Indian" while his nominal slaves lived as free people among the Creeks or in their own in communities, such as North Fork Town. Su-nuk-mik-ko frankly attributed much of his shrewd diplomacy to the part African Seminole Ben Bruno (or Ben Bruner), who understood the white world better than did the Indians. *Harper's Weekly* thought this illustrated unnatural race relations among the Indians, where the "the negro slaves are, in fact, the masters of their red owners," adding that Seminole slang described a particularly smart person as having "nigger wit."[17]

Whether enslaved or not, blacks generally enjoyed higher status and greater freedom among the Indians. Certainly white slaveholders in Texas, Arkansas, and Missouri did not want to buy slaves from any of the Indian nations, where African Americans sometimes intermarried, gained their freedom, and assimilated into tribal life. The slaves themselves were well aware of their better treatment among the Creeks and Seminoles, one recalling that they could "go and see one another sometimes and often they were sent on errands several miles with a wagon or on a horse." One former slave grew up not knowing she was actually owned by the head of the household. Another among the Creeks recalled, "We didn't have to be under any overseer like the Cherokee Negroes and lots of times, we didn't have to work if they wasn't no work to do that day." These blacks knew that "the Chickasaw people didn't treat their slaves like the Creeks did. They was more strict, like the people in Texas and other places." Even among the Choctaw, a female slave married to a man belonging to neighbor recalled that they lived together on a cabin between the farms of their owners, adding, "I don't 'spect we could of done that way iffen we hadn't of had Indian masters."[18]

African Indian peoples also established their own communities. Upon removal, some blacks from the Creek and Seminole nations clustered about Fort Gibson in an effort to avoid forced labor. Many among the Creeks settled at North Fork Town, while the African Seminole chief Cohia, or Gopher John (also John Cavallo, or John Horse), who had had been Hal-patter Tustenugee's interpreter, founded a village of black people on Deep Fork in that nation. In addition to the one at Deep Fork, black settlements formed on Wewoka Creek and Little River. Gopher John also worked with Coacoochee and John Chupco to project a major colonization project along the Texas-Mexico border.[19]

Then, too, some Indians had cultivated explicitly antislavery traditions. The Seminole practice of helping runaways had provided the United States a key motive for driving them west. Prior to their removal, the Ottawas had their own leg of the "underground railroad," and the Shawnees told their children "horrible stories about slavery" as they helped runaways. One Indian in Kansas said simply, "God make white man, God make red man, God make black man, but God never make slave."[20]

Conversely, some blacks and whites in the antislavery movement culti-vated a genuine sympathy from considering the conditions of the Indians. Black abolitionists appealed directly to Indian antislavery traditions, as did Martin Delany through his novel *Blake; or, the Huts of America*, whose pro-tagonist forged a psychological alliance with the native people. Dr. James McCune Smith adopted the pen name of "Communipaw," a multiracial colonial settlement on the Jersey side of the Hudson River. The Radical Abo-litionist Party asserted the right of Indians to defend themselves and their lands and discussed that resistance as a model for African Americans.[21]

Along with the Radical Abolitionists, some adherents of Phillips's Na-tional Reform movement linked the treatment of Indians to slavery. One NRA leader described the United States as existing on lands "obtained through fraud; and force that part of it which was not acquired by blood." Their satiric "Modern Dictionary" defined the terms *democracy*, *liberty*, and *the republic* through the example of "Northern troops" making "Glorious War" on a few Indians for the purpose of catching a handful of free and equal, "liberty loving, runaway democrats." They quoted Black Hawk and published an autobiographical sketch of him and a remarkable interview with a white tailor among the Seminole. They quoted the latter as saying,

"There's a great deal of talk about liberty, equality, and such great things among white people, but the divil a bit of liberty or equality did I ever find till I came amongst the Indians.... There's no one to drive you, nor can you drive any body but yourself, and that's what I call liberty and equality."[22]

Other, less sanctioned views of race developed alongside the ideological claim of supremacy through whiteness. In a land reform version of the Declaration of Independence, free-labor radicals asserted "that Labor on the Soil, in the workshop or factory, is, and of right, ought to be free, without reference to sex, color or condition." Their avowed goal was to "restore their rights to the blacks, the Indians, and the landless whites of this continent" and to bring about "the liberation of universal man." Humanity being "irrespective of sex, character or colour," their argument assumed "the rights of women or of colored people" and urged "the right of voting and ruling" without regard to "race, sex, color, intelligence, residence, majorities, compacts, laws, wealths, inheritance, [and] divinity." Nonwhites should enjoy what "every other right and privilege allows to the whites." Speaking on behalf of the "working classes," such National Reformers did not exclude those especially oppressed "laboring people, because they were so unfortunate as to be born of Black Mothers, and Black, White, and Indian fathers." Not without reason did some Democratic papers denounce the NRA with the abolitionist Libertymen as the "Amalgamation Party."[23]

Such strident criticism of racial exclusion within the broader Republican coalition did not extend beyond the abolitionists. Former National Reformer and Republican Party founder Alvan Bovay thought that "the future history of this continent" would be "written in the blood of the Spanish, Indian, Negro, and Anglo-Saxon races, and in such a contest the latter have much to fear." He declared that "the Indians have a right somewhere, and it was certainly time now that their oppression should cease." The *New York Tribune*—with which Bovay had been associated—had long protested the "costly, cruel, and unnecessary expatriation" of Indians to the West. Phillips, another of their associates, saw how western settlement eclipsed any discussion as to the future of the Indians.[24]

Most dramatically, though, the emergence of the Republican Party framed the career of the British-born Illinois farmer John Beeson, who became the noisiest advocate for the Indians among the whites. Beeson had gone to Oregon, where the push for settlers and officials bent on Indian removal or extermination provoked the Rogue River War. When he protested "the wrongs perpetrated by both Government and settlers on the Indians in that quarter," the more rabid of his neighbors drove him out. Under the auspices of any association that would sponsor him, he toured the country, once infuriating the Washington press by denouncing the segregation of blacks at his meetings. He refused to be diverted by charges of amalgamation or talk of "whether the Negro or the Indian has received the greater wrong." Beeson consistently focused on "whether the red race and the white race and the black race [had] . . . the inalienable right to their complexion, to their language, to their religion, and to their freedom and to their homes under the administration of a great Government." One supporter added that "the pitiless fate of those ancient republics," such as Rome, awaited an America "struggling for its constitutional life, and all because of injustice to the Indians and the Africans."[25]

Some radicals in Kansas had flouted the color bar for years. Both John Bowles and Augustus Wattles had helped to settle former slaves in free states. During his school-building days in Ohio, Wattles had founded Carthagena as a refuge for former Kentucky slaves. Bowles, a slaveholder turned abolitionist, transported his manumitted retainers to Illinois, where each family got land and "the dignity of proprietorship." As the troubles intensified in Kansas, members of Bowles's colony joined their former master and benefactor to assist in the antislavery work.[26]

Radicals who went west urged the extension of rights to Indians. For years Wattles and other radicals complained that the extension of full rights to Indians, wherever and however they lived, "ought to have been adopted long ago." Wattles later used the idea of military service not only for securing civic equality for Indians but "for confederating the various Indian tribes, in Kansas and Nebraska, into one, and giving them a Territory and a Territorial Government with political privileges." Men such as Wattles and Phillips understood clearly that "the imperfections of our civilization made it unacceptable to Native Americans," asking, "What have we offered them in return for their native freedom? Luxuries for a few, and misery for the mass! The grasping after land, and the insatiable avarice caused by the traffic in it, have been the bitter source of the continual hostility between the whites and the Indians." Indeed, Indians shared with African Americans this complete dispossession of rights: "We have given the Indians land in return for that of which they have been robbed. The blacks have the same right, in lieu of that from which they have been stolen away."[27]

Further, they acknowledged the rights of Indians (and blacks) to live unfettered by the "prejudice against color." "If 'the people are to govern themselves,'" argued Phillips, "we have no business to govern even the Indians." The old NRA idea of an Indian state loomed as the best assurance of maintaining a distinct identity and political autonomy.[28] With some vague notion of a dual citizenship as a possibility, radicals clearly believed and expected that Indians or blacks might themselves participate in shaping a common future.

The standards of white supremacy prevailed, of course, even though some whites grappled with differing ideas, including genuinely egalitarian impulses and possibilities. Those imposed by the national government, itself shaped by the southern elite, remained unambiguous, and the legal imposition of "black codes" in the nonslaveholding northern states demonstrated that racism ran deeper than just the profitable exploitation of slavery.

The Indians in Kansas certainly seemed to understand that the crisis and its concommitant rethinking of race held implications for them. They had sought an alliance with the free-staters against the extension of slavery. The Delaware provided armed antislavery bands with guides and protection through their reserve lands. In late 1855, when the proslavery forces had converged on Lawrence, both the Delaware and Shawnee "volunteered the services of the warriors of their respective tribes to aid in repelling the invaders." Unwilling to provoke the U.S. authorities, free-state leaders had declined the offer. Nonetheless, Chief John Tecumseh Jones, of the Ottawa, and Baptiste Peoria remained among John Brown's most consistent allies.[29] Clearly, this problem went beyond Kansas to the heart of western expansion.

The immediate issue of race in Kansas centered on slavery. John Brown believed both that an open and armed defiance of the law had thwarted it in Kansas and that the same thing might end it throughout the nation. Early on he discussed writing a book with Wattles to publicize what had been done in the West but settled on a more direct plan to strike a single, decisive blow that would "change the seat of war" to other "points of egress" from slavery. Almost twenty years before, Brown had surveyed the Virginia hills around Harpers Ferry, land owned by Oberlin College. Once armed, local blacks and their allies could make a mad dash into those mountains, where they might establish an armed maroon force, whose very existence and survival would inspire an ever-increasing number of runaway slaves. It would entirely undercut the profitability of southern slavery and destabilize the system.[30]

At this point Brown acquired his military adviser, Colonel Hugh Forbes. A veteran of Britain's Coldstream Guards, Forbes entered the silk business in Italy, where he became involved in the revolutionary movement and trained volunteers to fight for Giuseppe Garibaldi, an experience leading to his insurrectionary two-volume *Manual for the Patriotic Volunteer.* By 1850 Forbes had turned up in the United States and became involved in broader efforts to unite various associations of European émigrés with the American radicals. The most consistent participant among the officers of the Universal Democratic Republicans and the later Convention of Liberal Societies, he sought to make Kansas and slavery issues of importance to "the working classes." An ardent abolitionist himself, Forbes leapt at the offer of a six-month contract, at one hundred dollars a month, to train Brown's volunteers with a more usably edited version of his *Manual.*[31]

Forbes's hopes disintegrated in September 1857 when he reached Iowa to find a handful where he expected a small army. When Brown laid out his plans to raid the federal arsenal at Harpers Ferry, Forbes cited the lack of men, the absence of any direct communications with the slaves in Virginia, and the not inconsiderable fact that raiding a U.S. arsenal involved a direct confrontation with the federal military, which they had carefully avoided in Kansas. Instead, he suggested a series of bands along the border to raid into slave states, remove slaves, and undermine the value of slave property. Forbes argued that this strategy, which would roll back the borders in which the institution would remain viable, reflected good sense, and others not so directly involved with John Brown were actually formulating it independently. Lysander Spooner—a radical abolitionist later viewed as a founder of American anarchism—independently came to Forbes's conclusions, proposing to his New England friends the organization of armed squads to stage regular short raids into slave states. Similarly, a black student at Oberlin, William Ellaby Lincoln, reminded Brown that the Seminole Wars had cost the United States dearly and urged him to consider taking one or two thousand volunteers into the swamps of Florida as "an armed diversion a la Garibaldi."[32]

Meanwhile, the eastern backers who had pledged to fund Brown's operations left Forbes without the salary his family in Paris expected. Concerned about the apparent insincerity of the wealthy "humanitarians," Forbes went east to sort them out. Early in 1858 they responded by shelving all Brown's plans, pleading ignorance, and denouncing Forbes as a madman, a mercenary, or a soldier of fortune on the off-chance that he had said anything to someone not already in the circle. Most slanderously and groundlessly, some even called him a "Judas," implying that he had provided the authorities with information. Although scholars lazily mummified these undocumented and groundless charges, neither Brown nor any of those closest to him used such terms to condemn Forbes for his course.[33]

One of Brown's most consistent defenders, Hinton wrote that he could not believe Forbes "to have been deliberately or intentionally treacherous." Probably owing to his close ties to radical internationalists at New York City, Hinton knew "details of this imbroglio which tend to show that Colonel Forbes must have about this time got into relations with a small coterie of clever colored men in New York City, revolving around a well-known physician of that race," who responded to the injustices of slavery and white supremacist ideas with "a counter race contempt, antagonism, and rage." Hinton referred to the protonationalist militancy of Dr. James McCune Smith. Indeed, some of Forbes's comrades scandalized local Freemasons by hosting Jacques Étienne Marconis de Négre, who sought to establish an American branch of the Order of Memphis, which ascribed the origins of freemasonry and Western civilization to Africa. While in New York Marconis flouted American taboos by acknowledging as brother Masons the so-called Prince Hall lodges of African Americans.[34] This specific black perspective certainly informed Forbes's critique, as did his experience with various revolutionary plans abroad.

In contrast—and notwithstanding their heroism—the Harpers Ferry raiders never fully incorporated black self-emancipation into their plans. True, when Brown called for a May convention at Chatham, Canada, the African American agitator Martin Delany presided, and African Americans constituted more than two-thirds of the delegates, who approved a provisional constitution for an egalitarian republic in armed rebellion against "the Slave Power" and made Brown their commander-in-chief, but they took no measures to get advance word of a raid to the slaves. When Luke Parsons reported that blacks had formed their own Masonic-like secret society around "African Mysteries" or "African-American Mysteries," his white comrades dismissed it as "some such confounded humbug."[35] As it was, the Harpers Ferry plan engaged none of the preexisting networks among African Americans that influenced Forbes.

Hinton himself saw some of the same problems as had Spooner and Forbes. His solution was to stay in the West, and his strong initial impression was that Brown planned to concentrate on the Missouri border, where developments in December 1858 provided a trial run. Missouri's 115,000 slaves and several thousand free Negroes constituted roughly a tenth of the state's population. Short of the grave, the lottery of life rarely delivered a black Missourian from bondage. As with most slaves, the idea that they might themselves influence events must have seemed as intangible as any article of religious faith; to white observers, blacks had not only assimilated Christianity but also infused it with an enthusiasm that could not have been entirely counterfeit. For many blacks, a faith in divine justice blurred into an unexperienced eternity—"thy Kingdom Come"—in which the humble would be raised and the mighty humbled. Thousands acted as though they truly believed that the escalating conflict among the whites might lead to the Jubilee, creating, in the process, a testimonial to the power of faith.

One of these slaves escaped to Brown's friends over the border. Explaining that his family was about to be sold, the runaway pleaded for help. Brown's hastily gathered armed force crossed the state line and carried off the slaves, who were then sheltered briefly in Kansas by James G. Blunt, Augustus Wattles, and other sympathizers. Brown then sat down at Wattles's home, not far from where they were hiding the runaways, to write "Parallels," justifying this raid. When the authorities turned up in the area looking for the runaways, Brown quickly arranged to move them safely into Iowa, thwarting pursuit at what Hinton called "the battle of the Spurs" in January 1859. By March none other than the ex-Chartist Allan Pinkerton helped get this particular group safely into Canada.[36] After all, slave-liberating raids had worked in the West, far from the federal power that ultimately sustained the peculiar institution.

Nevertheless, the plan Brown presented to Wattles and James Montgomery indisputably centered on Virginia. Wattles later told a local man that Brown "had laid before them his maps, places, and data; and after explaining every phase of the contemplated movement, and *predicting failure* invited and urged them in eloquent terms to join and assist him." Both Wattles and Montgomery "argued against the enterprise, but . . . at last Brown arose, and said, 'My friends, this is our last meeting. I go to prepare the way for Freedom. I shall not live to see the work accomplished, but you shall both live to see the nations of the earth bless my name and sing my praises.'" Brown told them, "I leave with you these papers for future uses when, in your judgment, the proper time shall have come." Montgomery put the documents "in a bear skin covered trunk."[37]

The white-haired warrior also approached Phillips, who had just been elected to the U.S. Senate by the free-state legislature, an honor even if no more than a gesture of defiance against the recognized proslavery legislature. More substantively, though, Phillips was organizing the new town of Salina and planning a marriage to "Carrie"—that is, Margaret Carraway Spillman. As a state marshal for the free-staters, he was immersed in organizing a territorial census prior to elections when Brown proposed that he come to Tabor, Iowa. "As means are limited, those who *can must* do this," wrote Phillips to Brown, explaining that he could not go. He assured Brown that at that time the territory had "no necessity for active military preparations now, at this time." He proposed that Brown come to Kansas instead and added, "It will be our duty to see you are protected." Upon arriving, Brown found Phillips immovably opposed to the proposed raid in Virginia.[38]

Old Brown warned Phillips against trusting political action, citing "the fearful wrongs carried on in the name of government and law." When Phillips asked whether the slaves on whom Brown counted might prove too stoically resigned to fight, Brown replied, "You have not studied them right and you have not studied them long enough." In the end, though, Phillips feared a bloody foray that would accomplish little beyond the loss of abolitionists. Rising from the table, Brown expressed regret at his failure to convince Phillips and confidently predicted that he would understand this course when events would shatter his household gods." Offended, Phillips, too, rose to leave, but the old man stopped him, explaining tearfully that he only wanted his friend to understand his thinking. Brown kissed him on the cheek, and Phillips recalled, "I never saw him again."[39]

Phillips's opposition did help dissuade some. The realization that Brown's target would be not proslavery bands in the West but a U.S. arsenal in Virginia discouraged Parsons, who consulted his family at Byron, Illinois, and finally declined to join the Harpers Ferry raid. Another, the pistol-packing printer Charles W. Lenhardt, decided to hang up his guns and enter law school at Cincinnati.[40]

The raid on Harpers Ferry electrified the country. Brown, two of his sons, a handful of whites, and a few blacks moved through a heavy rain on Sunday night, October 16, 1859, to reach the town at dawn. They captured the federal armory and arsenal and rounded up sixty town residents as hostages, although it seems likely that several of the slaves among them had joined the raiders. The local militia pinned the raiders in the engine house until U.S. military forces under Col. Robert E. Lee arrived. The confrontation left most of the raiders dead, as it did two slaves of their hostages, likely killed because they had taken up arms with the abolitionists. The authorities quickly moved the wounded Brown to nearby Charlestown and announced plans to try all the survivors for treason against the Commonwealth of Virginia. When the authorities searched Brown's papers, they found Hinton's report on a western strike through the Indian Territory and quickly made copies to convince the Indians there that "the agrarian rapacity of the North" had designs on their rights and property as well as that of the white slaveholders.[41]

Brown's friends also moved into action. Determined to rescue the prisoners, Hinton retrieved James Hanway from Dutch Henry's Crossing and rode on to meet with Montgomery and Wattles at the Moneka Hotel, above the post office. Only days before, these two, along with Charles Jennison, Henry C. and Benjamin Seaman, and others, had crossed into Missouri and freed Dr. John Doy, who had been convicted of spiriting away slaves through Kansas to freedom. Hinton proposed recruiting up to a hundred "eligibles" to repeat this in Virginia, with a commando attack on the jail at Charlestown and teams stationed at decisive points to cover a retreat through the hills of Maryland into the North. Wattles thought it "only possible with a carefully selected few, and the exercise of the keenest tact and highest courage."[42]

Other such plans for action were also on the table. Spooner proposed kidnapping the governor of Virginia and holding him as a hostage until the state agreed to an exchange. On his own, Lenhardt hurried to Charlestown, where he used Masonic signs and passwords to identify himself as a proslavery loyalist from the West; he "went to work in one of the printing offices and joined a militia company then guarding the prisoners." The abolitionist John W. LeBarnes had sought volunteers for an assault on the jail among Forbes's old comrades, the German socialists at New York, and discussed forming a combined storming party of sixty with Hinton, who had joined Montgomery, Wattles, and Benjamin Seaman at Harrisburg. Henry C. Seaman scouted toward Martinsburg for possible escape routes. The jailer did allow Brown to see his wife, Mary, without supervision, and she served as "a very reliable medium of communication with the rescuing party." Meanwhile, the Massachusetts-born Kansan George H. Hoyt reached Charlestown to serve as Brown's attorney.[43]

In the end, though, Brown refused rescue on the grounds that further bloodshed could achieve nothing more than had the raid. He told the court bluntly: "Had I so interfered in behalf of the rich, the powerful, the intelligent, the so-called great, or in behalf of any of their friends—either father, mother, brother, sister, wife, or children, or any of that class—and suffered and sacrificed what I have in this interference, it would have been all right;

and every man in this court would have deemed it an act worthy of reward rather than punishment." Before going to the gallows on December 2, Brown passed a note that expressed his grim view of the future: "I, John Brown, am now quite certain that the crimes of this guilty land will never be purged away but with blood." In the crowd, Lenhardt waited to assist a rescue attempt that never came.[44]

With Brown's execution, security grew more slack, and Hinton redoubled his efforts to save the remaining raiders. Lenhardt made himself known to one of the prisoners, and they planned an escape, thwarted only when the guard was increased. After it became too late to save that prisoner, Lenhardt still hoped to free the last two. Particularly goading to Hinton was the fact that his report—written over the signature of "William Harrison"—had been ascribed to one of the captives, who faced the hangman under that name. By this time allies included the Boston abolitionist Thomas Wentworth Higginson, and the Kansas Republican Daniel R. Anthony—an associate of the Radical Abolitionist Party and the brother of Susan B. Anthony—contributed to the effort; Hinton went to New York to meet with German volunteers under Frederick Kapp, the historian and president of the city's *Kommunist Klub*. As Montgomery's volunteers continued to scout the area, would-be rescuers periodically loitered in the alley behind the jail, one of them getting a meeting with the prisoners by having himself arrested as "an Irishman on a spree." Ultimately heavy snowfalls and the unwillingness of the prisoners themselves ended the project.[45] The last two raiders died on the gallows on March 16, 1860.

In drawing together a broad spectrum of radical free-labor proponents, the raid's outcome replicated the lessons of Kansas nationally. Ever larger meetings in the North united on the same platform both whites and blacks, abolitionists and radicals known primarily as freethinkers or socialists, such as Ernestine L. Rose. At Cincinnati Peter H. Clark—a black printer, schoolteacher, and former Wattles student—stood alongside the Unitarian minister Moncure D. Conway and convicted Cologne Communist August Willich. At Boston the socialist Turners under Karl Heinzen of *Das Pioneer* and individuals such as Hinton provided armed protection for abolitionists threatened with kidnapping and deportation to the South. Before one meeting Wendell Phillips asked Hinton whether he was "prepared," while "taking from a drawer in his desk a six-inch 'Colt' and slipping it into an inside pocket." Hinton replied by flashing the handle of his navy revolver.[46]

In Boston as on the prairies of Kansas, the time for "passive resistance" was gone; no more would white supremacists enjoy a monopoly on violence.

Indeed, the thwarted rescue attempts evolved into plans for "a second armed invasion of the south under the leadership of John Brown, Jr." This involved a paramilitary organization variously called the John Brown League, the John Brown Liberty League, or the League of Freedom. At least in some places, members took "a binding oath to devote [their] lives to the destruction of American Slavery: to engage in no occupation that could prevent . . . marching at an hour's notice, and to obey an order to march without question." At Salem, Ohio, Joseph Kennedy Hudson's father printed the pro–National Reform abolitionist paper the *Anti-Slavery Bugle;* Hudson said that "a considerable number of young men in that community joined the League and met in the late hours of the night in the loft of a mill in the outskirts of the town." The order had officers, grips, signs, and obligations, like a fraternal order, but it remained, "in fact, a military organization," with state leagues functioning as regiments. "The John Brown League," wrote Hudson, "numbered 25,000 members, scattered through Kansas, Iowa, Northern Ohio, New York and Canada."[47] Although he likely exaggerated the numbers, legions now stood where before had been only a lonely few.

As Harpers Ferry nationalized the ethos of armed Kansas, it helped to unravel the political alliances that had dominated the nation's life for a generation. Northern Democrats shifted wildly to keep their electoral balance, while the southern wing of that party would not compromise its agenda. The residues of the Whigs and nativists urged the electorate to focus its attention elsewhere than slavery. The new Republican Party not only wanted to exclude slavery from the territories but also revived the NRA's old proposal for the Homestead Act in the teeth of southern opposition. As voters of the nonslaveholding states largely abandoned their old Democratic and Whig allegiances, they raised nationally a vital question about the country's future that had already sparked guerrilla warfare on the western border: Should the newly settled areas be turned to small family farms and a social republic or the large-scale landholdings of an aristocracy? After a mere six years, the new Republicans faced a presidential election with both some realistic hope of success and looming danger within such a success.

Despite Brown's Radical Abolitionist warnings, antislavery men back in Kansas played a key role in its Republican organization. Initially they preferred the presidential nomination of Seward, despite—or sometimes because of—his stance for development at any price. Moreover, Seward had been overseas during the planning and execution of the Harpers Ferry raid, which meant he had been neither responsible for the raid nor associated with other antislavery politicians' unseemly attempts to distance themselves from it. Hinton wrote a campaign biography of Seward, and Phillips went to the national convention for the Kansas delegation pledged to Seward. They readily accepted the nomination of Abraham Lincoln, however, particularly when southern gentlemen described supporters of the former rail-splitter as "mudsills and greasy mechanics." Hinton in Kansas, Greeley in New York, and John Locke Scripps of the old Chicago NRA wrote the popular campaign biographies of the former rail-splitter.[48] Following Lincoln's victory, those who had lost the election decided to destroy the country they could no longer control.

⌐⌐

Later admirers of John Brown brooked no criticism of the wisdom of the Harpers Ferry raid, largely because, on the surface, the immediate outcome seemed to vindicate virtually all the criticisms of his plans. Nevertheless, Brown had no intention of continuing to raid individual slaveholders in the distant West and evading a direct moral confrontation with the federal government. Nor, at his age, did plans that would take years to come to fruition have much appeal. Before launching the raid, Brown and several of his men told others that they expected the plan to fail, and their conduct after capture reinforced the sense of a group decision for martyrdom. Psychological and logistical issues obscure rather than clarify what was actually a cold and calculated political decision. The killing of the abolitionist newspaper publisher Elijah Lovejoy had shown Brown that those determined to make slavery safe would take the lives of whites as well as blacks. He and his cohort expected their raid to teach the same lesson to thousands across the North, particularly the Republican Party.

John Brown, the scion of the American Revolution, sometimes puzzled his black comrades with his insistence on fighting for liberation beneath the Stars and Stripes. He believed that the government's concessions to slavery had betrayed the promises of 1776 and the standards of republican government. Conversely, the only meaningful and genuine freedom for slaves had to be the work of the nation as a whole. Rejecting abolitionist purists who sought to separate themselves from a federal union tainted by "the sin of slavery," Brown's Radical Abolitionist Party warned that the "geographical separation of the North from the South will be no *moral* separation on the ground of principles" but rather "a dereliction of duty to the nation and to the enslaved." Brown's attack on a U.S. arsenal near the federal capital aimed to confront the practice with the Radical Abolitionist sense of a national promise: "We are one people, one nation. We have no right to permit the enslavement of any part of the nation. And God will punish us by the loss of our own liberties if we do."[49] Ultimately, the success or failure of Brown's strategy would turn on the responses of his countrymen.

THREE

War in the Far West

The day after Christmas in 1861, a small army closed on thousands of civilian Indian Territory residents at Chustenahlah, or Patriot Hills. By late
afternoon the Texans rolled over the few outgunned and outnumbered warriors who had challenged them. As the Indians scattered, nobody had much
detailed information about how many they left behind. The Confederate
authorities reported capturing about 160 women, children, and runaway
slaves and killing 250 of those who had resisted them. The ratio of killed
to captured underscores accounts that the white soldiers slaughtered many
Creeks and blacks. The rebels tried to return some runaway slaves who had
been "shot and wounded so bad the blood run down the saddle skirts," until
some of them toppled from the mounts, dead.[1] The number of fatalities in the
short fight surely made this forgotten clash between the new Confederacy
and its own civilians proportionately one of the bloodiest of the year.

The secession crisis disintegrated the structure of national power, with
particularly dire consequences for the peoples of the western border. Nowhere else did the conflict have a more immediately disruptive and devastat-
ing impact than it had among the most systematically marginalized Native
Americans. Presaging the future of the war among the whites, among people
of color the conflict never drew clear lines between soldiers and civilians.
The war almost immediately began to destroy slavery, with little regard for

antebellum legal niceties. As a result, this new kind of war created an inescapably multiracial refugee problem that demanded innovative multiracial proposals.

⌒

The election of 1860 shattered the Democratic Party's control over national affairs, which had continued, with few breaks, for a generation. The Republican Abraham Lincoln won by a plurality over the Constitutional Unionists (formerly Whigs) and the Democrats, split between the regulars and the "Southern Rights" faction—the only one of these four that considered secession a viable solution to the sectional tensions. Voters in Kentucky, Missouri, Tennessee, Virginia, and much of the South found other alternatives preferable to even the threat of secession, while mere pluralities carried Delaware, Georgia, Louisiana, and Maryland for the Southern Rights Democrats, who won a total of only about 570,000 slave-state ballots. Given the long history of rhetorical brinkmanship and sectional posturing, many of those voters probably intended to express no more than a bluff or a willingness to entertain secessionist arguments. Reflecting one southern perception, a Virginian living in St. Louis later dismissed secession as "started by a number of politicians who had been defeated in the national election and were sore on that account."[2] Nevertheless, the president-elect avoided anything that might translate prosecessionsts into a majority after his election.

The conservatism of the white southerners provided an initial brake on their political machines, and at first more slave states remained in the Union than seceded from it. State conventions in Missouri and Arkansas flatly rejected secession, although the governors of both states ignored the popular will to order their officials to seize federal property. When a U.S. soldier tore down a secessionist flag in Arkansas and defied an officer's order to replace it, both civilians and other soldiers cheered as the fellow defiantly tore it up on his way to the guardhouse, and the local blacksmith refused to place the man in irons.[3]

Nonetheless, the government that admitted Kansas to statehood in March teetered on the brink of disintegration. On April 12–13, 1861, U.S. authorities refused to abandon Fort Sumter in Charleston harbor, resulting in Confederate bombardment, the fort's surrender, and President Lincoln's call for the states to provide troops for the suppression of the rebellion. This presented the eight slave states still in the Union the alternatives of secession or cooperation in the "coercion" of the seceded Southern states.

Delaware never seriously considered secession, and hesitant Kentucky adopted neutrality, while armed clashes erupted in Maryland and Missouri between Unionists and secessionist local officials. Virginia, North Carolina, Arkansas, and Tennessee seceded, and the Confederacy subsequently claimed Missouri and Kentucky as well.

The white male voters of these thirteen Confederate States generally had little voice in the matter. Only three—Texas, Virginia, and Tennessee—submitted the politicians' decision to the voters, and two of these referenda took place only after the onset of war, martial law, and the de facto suspension of a two-party system. Denied a voice, white Southerners held a broad range of views on the subject, which in most cases seriously limited the sacrifices they would willingly endure for secession.

The narrow base of that initial secessionist impulse recalled John Brown's warning about politicians. Brown had told William A. Phillips that the planters "never intend to relinquish the machinery of this Government into the hands of the opponents of slavery." "The moment they are unable to control they will go out," he predicted, "and as a rival nation alongside, they will get the countenance and aid of the European nations, until American republicanism and freedom are overthrown." Scarcely a year after Brown's hanging, rulers brazenly unfurled over their entire states the lone white star on a blue field, the historical symbol of filibustering.[4] In its new guise as the "Bonnie Blue Flag" of secessionist song, it made its first conquest over Southerners.

Antisecessionist sentiments in the South remained essential to the strategic questions facing the Unionist coalition in the North. Lincoln and his allies pragmatically came to Brown's Radical Abolitionist hope of making allies of whites in the South, but Unionism there remained rooted in areas removed from the plantation districts. In contrast, the professional military—trained in the Napoleonic arts of territorial conquest through the subjugation of strategic points—thought in terms of the most logistically accessible areas, that is, the coasts, rivers, and trade routes developed to serve plantation agriculture.[5] The military strategy, which centered on those parts of the South most favorable to secession, tended to marginalize the Southern Unionism on which the president's political strategy relied.

On the border the federal authorities faced the immediate alternatives of pursuing military subjugation or fostering homegrown revolution against the secessionist power structure. In Maryland they opted for military occupation and martial law, while in western Virginia they encouraged local Unionists to move toward establishing their own government. Kentucky neutrality would be respected until Confederate invasion tipped the balance toward the Union. In the end, Lincoln pursued his pragmatic approach, doing whatever seemed to work in each particular circumstance.

By early summer open warfare had broken out in Missouri, where a mere 540 whites held more than twenty slaves, with only thirty-eight having more than fifty, and the average slaveholder had fewer than five. Still, small-scale slaveholders generally followed the political lead of those more heavily invested in "the peculiar institution," and three-quarters of the state's population came from other slave states or from Southern families moving west by way of Illinois, Indiana, and Ohio. Most of these men regularly voted for the Democratic Party, which claimed a mandate to rule the state. The more active of them expressed their views of their antislavery neighbors by leaving a sign on the burned cabin of John Bowles denouncing him as numbering among the "traitors to the South."[6] Antislavery views, then, were no more welcome in most of Missouri than in South Carolina.

Nevertheless, Missouri had many critics of secession and slavery. Along the rivers of eastern and east-central Missouri, centered on St. Louis, large numbers of Germans gave the Republicans an anomalous and virtually unique foothold in a slaveholding state. Even in the secessionist Southern-born parts of the state, there were tens of thousands such as Wiley Britton, who became one of the most reliable chroniclers of the trans-Mississippi war. A modestly educated farmboy from Newton County, Britton reported that the southern back country as far as Texas included "many strong Union men" and even readers of Greeley's *New York Tribune*, and he blamed secession on politicians and preachers who controlled public opinion.[7]

The secessionist governor Claiborne Fox Jackson had ordered the Missouri State Guard (MSG) to seize the U.S. arsenal at Liberty and establish its Camp Jackson within striking distance of the much larger installation at St. Louis. Fresh from Kansas, Captain Nathaniel Lyon armed a force of largely German volunteers who captured the camp on May 10 and secured the city despite several days of rioting. The former governor and Mexican War hero Sterling Price assumed charge of the MSG and established a short-lived truce with Lyon's superior, though this broke down on June 11. Jackson called out 50,000 men to repel the invaders, but only a fraction of the number responded, and Lyon's little army reduced the area controlled by the state government to the far southwest corner. There, Price's MSG joined forces with a small Confederate army under Ben McCulloch, the Texas Ranger who owed his reputation to fighting Indians, Mexicans, squatters, and free-staters. On August 10 Lyon's 5,500 men attacked the 12,000 rebels along Wilson's Creek near Springfield. In the bitter engagement, the tiny army of Federals inflicted severe damage on the secessionists but lost nearly a quarter of its own force, including Lyon, who was killed while leading them.

The outcome of Wilson's Creek placed a victorious secessionist army on the doorstep of Kansas, which turned increasingly to Jim Lane, whose authority already eclipsed that of Governor Charles Robinson. Lane's friend, Martin F. Conway, the territorial delegate to the Congress, had convinced the Lincoln administration not to fill any federal posts in Kansas until the legislature elected its U.S. senators. Through a series of brilliant and unscrupulous maneuvers, Lane flanked Robinson and won his election alongside Samuel C. Pomeroy, formerly of the New England Kansas Relief Committee. Already a friend of Lincoln's distant relative, Mark W. Delahay of Leavenworth, Lane endeared himself to the new president when he reached Washington. As rebel flags floated within sight of the Capitol and the White House, Lane turned out the "Frontier Guards," a few score of western politicians and functionaries in the capital who took turns protecting the White House. When Indiana gave Lane a colonelcy, he used his Kansas office to secure the appointment of Indianan William P. Dole as the commissioner of Indian affairs, again defeating Robinson, who had wanted Thomas Ewing.[8]

Secessionist victories in Missouri gave Lane an even freer hand in raising Kansas regiments, which opened the door to participation by the most radical abolitionists. As Joseph K. Hudson recalled, the friends and admirers of John Brown from across the country and abroad knew to "go to Kansas and enlist under Gen. Lane or Col. Montgomery, because no fugitive slaves [would] be returned by them." Hudson joined James Montgomery's Third Kansas, officered by former Brown associates such as Dr. James G. Blunt and Barclay Coppoc. John Ritchie took the Fifth Kansas Cavalry regiment; Charles Jennison, the Seventh; and the Ohio land reformer Edward Lynde, the Ninth. John Bowles declined a colonelcy in Kentucky to serve under Ritchie, while George H. Hoyt, Brown's lawyer from his Virginia trial, joined Jennison's force, as did John Brown Jr. Other allies of Lane organized the Sixth Kansas Cavalry.[9]

Lane's people drew their first blood in September. The new Kansas regiments probed into southwestern Missouri from Fort Scott, clashing with the MSG on September 2 along Dry Wood Creek. By then the main body of Price's army had moved north to the Missouri River, where it captured the Union garrison at Lexington. On September 21–22, within hours of the Union surrender at Lexington, Lane's Kansans drove a small rebel column from Osceola, Missouri. Finding supplies and munitions precariously close to the Kansas border, Lane ordered the entire town put to the torch. "I feel ten years older for these five hours of cruel destruction," confessed Bowles, one of those charged with the task.[10]

Although the federal military had yet to adopt an emancipationist policy, the officers of the "Lane Brigade" targeted the institution of slavery for destruction. Bowles's novel described the kind of earnest discussions that took place among Kansas officers, slaves, and their owners. The book's fictional protagonist orders the confiscation and movement of all slaves into Kansas, thus freeing the slaves from any responsibility for openly defying their masters. Should they then wish to return to the sway of slavery after a few days away from it, he reasons, it will be their own freely made choice. (In reality the Kansans almost immediately sent home some five hundred Missouri slaves.) As one general officer replied to a complaining Missouri slaveholder, "Sir, if your slaves are in Jim Lane's camp you might as well try to get them out of hell."[11]

Those radicals who had critically discussed the "duty of soldiers" four years before soon had to demonstrate the strength of their convictions. In his account, Bowles recalled that General Samuel D. Sturgis—the officer who had earlier arrested a U.S. soldier in Arkansas for tearing down a secessionist flag—ordered Lane to arrest his officers and retrieve runaways. Lane warned Bowles, "See that you have none of them in your command when the order is received." Ritchie resigned, but Bowles, along with Captains James M. Williams and Henry C. Seaman, defied the orders. As a result, all three men received several months of a token arrest, with "the liberty of the camp which includes the city," and a court-martial in which they were defended by Colonel Daniel R. Anthony, one of John Brown's would-be rescuers.[12] The incident became one of several that focused attention on the army's role in returning runaway slaves and contributed to reversing that inhuman and self-destructive policy.

Partly in response to such interest in emancipation from his soldiers, Union general John C. Fremont, the Republican presidential candidate of five years before, proclaimed the freedom of Missouri slaves in the fall of 1861. When the Lincoln administration reversed this and removed him from command, old comrades and admirers of John Brown in the East, such as Friedrich Kapp of the New York *Kommunist Klub*, tried to mobilize support for Fremont.[13] In fact, Fremont faced persistent charges of corruption and military failures, and his token and ineffectual gesture demonstrates how a declaration of emancipation could involve complex motives and entail more grandstanding than substance.

⌒

Disunion and war clarified the extent to which the removal treaties made the nations of the Indian Territory hostages to fortune. Even in the teeth of national self-destruction, work on Indian affairs provided officials with temptations that seemed irresistible, as shown in the rumored disappearance of $830,000 from the Indian Trust Fund. Most probably, President James Buchanan's secretary of the interior, a Mississippian then agitating for disunion in North Carolina, had sent a clerk from South Carolina back to Washington to break into the department's safe and return south with the funds.[14] The robbery might have been a major scandal, had it not been overshadowed by secession.

What seemed to be much greater robberies were taking place across the South. To the south and west of the Indian Territory, those insistent on secession bulldozed their opposition. After ruthlessly running roughshod over Governor Sam Houston, Texas secessionists had no scruples about sending armed men to their northern borders with the Choctaw and Chickasaw nations. To the east, Arkansas had declared itself out of the Union; to the northeast, Missouri seemed likely to follow. In the course of taking all federal property, Arkansas secessionists also seized all U.S. supplies on their way into the territory.

The U.S. treaties with the Indian nations of the territory promised military protection in return for which the "civilized" tribes gave up their own means of waging war. Federal troop levels there had dropped steadily from roughly 1,400 soldiers in 1842 to fewer than 300 ten years later. In April 1861 even these few, garrisoned at various outposts, gathered into a united column and marched north into Kansas. Within weeks Lincoln's incoming secretary of the interior, Caleb B. Smith, questioned Secretary of War Simon Cameron on the abandonment of the Indian nations, but the latter replied simply, "The exigencies of the service will not admit of any change in these orders."[15] For whatever reason, the United States unilaterally set aside its treaty obligations to the resident Indian nations.

Some Indians helped bluecoats escape. Fluent in English, French, and eight Indian languages, the old "cosmopolite" Suck-tum-mah-kway (or

"Black Beaver") of the absentee Delaware had long represented his people with the whites, the army, and the now-secessionist OIA agent in the
Leased District, Matthew Leeper. On April 16 he warned the soldiers that
the Texans would invade the territory, which had been claimed by Texas
before it joined the Union. Suck-tum-mah-kway personally escorted the
soldiers back to Fort Leavenworth, leaving leadership of the Delaware in
the hands of the forty-five-year-old Chief Jim Ned, "a remarkable specimen
of humanity" who wore a turban on his shaved head. Impressed observers
estimated his African blood to be from "a slight admixture" to half, noting
that he displayed "all the social vivacity and garrulity of the negro" in his
mannerisms. An indisputably courageous leader, he persuaded many Indians
around the Wichita Agency to abandon the Leased District. While Leeper
confiscated the property of chiefs such as Suck-tum-mah-kway, Jim Ned
headed a Confederate death list.[16]

More generally, residents had long received information about government affairs mostly from the OIA agents, historically appointees of proslavery Southern Democratic administrations. Officials such as Leeper and
Douglas H. Cooper, the hard-drinking Mississippi friend of Jefferson Davis,
simply lied, saying that the United States would no longer provide annuities,
supplies, and protection and advising the Indians that the white government
with which they now had to contend was that of the new Confederacy. The
Confederate States, they explained, would take up all payment of annuities
owed by the United States and would also give the Indians nonvoting territorial representation in the Confederate Congress. The secessionists also
sought to provide Indians the Unionist side of the argument they opposed,
circulating the statements by William H. Seward advocating another removal
and Richard Hinton's plans for bringing armed abolitionists into the territory. A special Confederate emissary, the Massachusetts-born Albert Pike,
seasoned this approach with a flattering white appreciation of Indian life
and culture.[17]

Unionists had no opportunity to make any contradictory arguments.
Even before secession, the proslavery OIA officials had taken action to ensure the removal of troublesome characters such as John B. Jones and his
father, Evan Jones, missionaries to the Cherokees. After Lincoln took office,
the new Republican OIA official Peter Percival Elder reached the Neosho
Agency and refused to leave his post, even when the troops headed north
and he could no longer get his peoples' annuities, supplies, and protection,
but his influence was far too little and way too late to change things in the

territory. (Elder remained until the Indians for whom he was responsible had themselves begun fleeing to Kansas.)[18]

Still, the Indians groped toward a common position that would be not so much Unionist as neutralist. Cyrus Harris of the Chickasaw called a council of the Five Nations in February 1861, which showed real promise. The Creek diplomacy of Micco Hutke galvanized considerable sentiment for concerted neutrality by a "United Nations of the Indian Territory." Seminole, Cherokee, Quapaw, Sac, and Fox representatives attended the April 8 meeting at North Fork Town, which was sponsored by the Creeks, though spring floods kept the Choctaw and Chickasaw delegates absent. The Creeks and Seminoles scheduled a meeting for May 1, but it failed to take place. Even in the Leased District, Creek diplomats and Robert Deer of the Shawnee stumped for a united Indian neutralism. To attend one such gathering, small groups of Shawnee slipped away one family at a time to Council Grove—"a meeting ground of the naked, or Plains Indians."[19] Spokesmen agreed to meet at Boggy Depot on May 25.

Confederate leaders nipped this move toward neutrality in the bud, using time-honored white techniques for imposing their will upon Indians. Back in February Robert M. Jones's faction of the Choctaw General Council had agreed to discuss future relations with the United States, but only as part of a common Indian response. As the general council gathered to elect its delegates to Boggy Depot, an ever-helpful delegation of white Texans crossed over to assist in the voting, threatening the life of neutralist leader Peter P. Pitchlynn and convincing Principal Chief George Hudson that the Choctaw had to act on their own, without reference to the other nations. Just to be sure, though, armed Confederates crossed the Red River into the nation. In June Pitchlynn did attend the Council of the Nations at Antelope Hills, but the government of the occupied Choctaw had already repudiated their treaty with the United States. The much smaller Chickasaw Nation had much the same experience. On July 12 both nations accepted formal treaties with the Confederacy that placed every male of military age at the disposal of the Richmond government. While some Choctaws and Chickasaws fled west or even south, others began moving north.[20]

The Creeks and the Seminoles required a different approach. On July 10 secessionists got a treaty signed by Creek leaders Daniel and Chilly McIntosh, as well as by Motley Kennard, who got a sword and a Confederate commission by abandoning his earlier neutrality, even as Oktarharsars Harjot continued his futile quest for allies. On August 1 Confederate emissaries among the Seminoles bestowed a similar status on John Jumper, claiming a mandate persistently challenged by leaders such as Su-nuk-mik-ko and John Chupco, who flatly refused to acknowledge any such alliance with the secessionists.[21] Among both nations Confederate officials authorized their allied chiefs to raise troops, which would also be used to impose an unprecedented control over their own people.

The government of the more populous Cherokees successfully stalled this process. Conjuring fears of an alliance between the "civilized" nations and the "wild" Indians to their west, Governor H. M. Rector of Arkansas, himself a former OIA agent, made his views explicit. Months before Arkansas left the Union, he wrote Principal Chief John Ross of the Cherokee that the state would secede "in consequence of repeated Northern aggression" and that the adjacent geography of the Indian Territory precluded "the idea of discordant or separate action." Ross replied on George Washington's birthday, saying that the Cherokee Nation would still honor its treaty with the United States.[22] While state conventions in Missouri and Arkansas resisted secession, Rector had no choice but to accept the Cherokee response.

The prospect for maintaining Cherokee neutrality deteriorated when Arkansas seceded and confederated its forces with those of Texas, but Ross continued to dodge demands for action. The Confederates made ever more thinly veiled threats that they would not violate Cherokee domains "without good cause" or "unless circumstances compel." On behalf of his people, Ross declined "to participate in the threatened fratricidal war between the 'United' and the 'Confederate' States" and hoped "persons gallantly tenuous of their own rights [would] respect those of others." Stand Watie, however, the last leader of the old treaty party, had already begun recruiting Cherokee soldiers for the Confederacy and making his bid among the whites to replace Ross as principal chief. Matters came to something of a head at Webber's Falls in July when 150 of the traditionalist "Pins" forcibly prevented the raising of a Confederate flag.[23] Union defeat at Wilson's Creek, however, ended Ross's hope that the United States might retain enough military strength nearby to keep the Confederates occupied.

With rebel regiments on his borders, Ross opted to maintain the leadership and unity of his people. On August 21 some 4,000 Cherokees assembled in the public square of their capital at Tahlequah, a small town that had grown from an old supply depot just west of the Illinois River; the rally confirmed the new official Cherokee alliance with the Confederacy. Ross's acquiescence averted the Confederate imposition of Watie as the nation's new chief. While

Watie had unofficially raised a small force of fifty to sixty men, Ross now appointed his niece's sixty-five-year-old husband, John Drew, to take charge of the official Cherokees regiment, which had 1,200 men by November. Its officers included prominent Keetowah members and sympathizers: Lt. Col. William Potter Ross; Major Thomas Pegg; and Captains John Porum Davis, George Scraper, James McDaniel, and James S. Vann, as well as the thirty-eight-year-old chaplain Rev. Lewis Downing. Although nominally in Confederate service, the First Cherokee Mounted Rifles served as the armed wing of the Ross faction, what one account described as "the Loyal League in the rebel service."[24]

Eager to avoid a fratricidal war among the nations, Ross still strove "to preserve and maintain the Brotherhood of the Indian Nations in a Common Destiny" and urged neutralists to follow his course. Into the fall he lobbied the Quapaw, Shawnee, and Seneca, as well as the Osage whose lands were also in Kansas, declaring it essential "for all the Red brothers to be united among themselves" while also urging Confederate forbearance in dealing with the reluctant. Largely as a result of his efforts, Confederate diplomacy made impressive gains among these smaller tribes, of whom the Euchee, Delaware, Wichita, Caddo, and others eventually consented on paper to the new arrangement. War-te-she of the Quapaw, Little Town Spicer of the Seneca, and Lewis Davis of the mixed Seneca and Shawnee proved to be tough negotiators, holding out into October to ensure exceptional treaty guarantees exempting their warriors from muster into Confederate service. Of these smaller tribes, the Osage agreed to furnish a battalion of volunteers for their new allies.[25] In most cases substance rarely fleshed out the illusions.

⌐⌐

Confederate policies turned neutralism to Unionism among the Indians. The new alliance authorized a unilateral Confederate decision to impose universal military service on them. It also provided assimilationist leaders, such as John Jumper and Chilly and Daniel McIntosh, with a virtually unchecked authority over those of their own people they believed to be backward and primitive. What amounted to conscription raised "volunteers" for the Confederacy but drove many more into exile.[26]

The direct threats of conscription and the white imposition of assimilationist political authority drove many Indians into active opposition. Creek leaders claimed to have a letter from Lincoln—since disappeared from the record—that professed continued friendship for all the Indian nations and asked only for their neutrality in the conflict. In the midst of this chaos, a handful of chiefs cooperated to seek federal assistance. On November 4 a delegation of four Creeks, two Seminoles, and two Chickasaws approached Federal Major George A. Cutler in Kansas, asking for arms, clothing, and aid. Back in the territory, the aged Creek chief Opothleyahola defied the secessionists and sent runners to begin pulling together small groups of Indians across the territory, including some three hundred at Roro-Culka, on the North Canadian River.[27] Everywhere, the desperate, innovative struggle for united neutrality created an unprecedented level of intertribal unity.

Among the Seminoles, Su-nuk-mik-ko announced that he would "go North to the President" and told his countrymen, "We will Suffer whatever he Suffers . . . all who want to Join [Albert] Pike can do so"; he, however, "would go on the Side of the President." They, too, sought the protection of Opothleyahola near North Fork Town in the Creek domains. Many Seminoles and Creeks refused to believe that the Union had abandoned them to their fate or that secessionist Indian brothers would move against an encampment of largely women and children. Warriors heard and repeated rumors that the legions of the new Great White Father might yet descend from Kansas to their rescue.[28] The numbers grew from a few hundred to as many as 10,000, making Opothleyahola's encampment a desperate, almost religious standing protest against the impositions of the white authorities.

Imposing pro-Confederate governments on the Indians inadvertently destroyed the security of slavery in the territory. In an effort to demonstrate that they were capable of the kind of rigidity the Indian nations had so long avoided, the Creek secessionist authorities gave all blacks ten days to "choose a master" or face seizure and sale, which inspired hundreds to flee the territory or declare their choice of Opothleyahola. This moved the enslaved, who had even more to gain. As far south as Honey Springs Depot, at the southern edge of the Creek Nation, "all de slave begin to slip out and run off." Years later one former slave remembered how her Uncle Nick responded when the master decided to rent his slaves to Texans: he simply headed off on his own for Union-held territory.[29]

The same process rolled through the territory. Former slaves remembered how rumors of the Cherokee resistance inspired plans of escape. Jake Perryman met other men at night in the woods and decided to escape; the women would remain behind with the children and await their return. One morning the cabins simply emptied of the men. The "Pins" helped

Perryman's band of runaways reach Missouri, from which they crossed into Kansas. Meanwhile, his brother-in-law took his family to join Opothleyahola's Creeks in order to "make a break for the North."[30]

The Confederate authorities could not ignore the fact that as many as one in seven territorial residents had sought refuge with Opothleyahola or that hundreds of blacks, including runaways, had also joined the encampment. At first officials offered amnesty to all—with the exception of Jim Ned, the black Delaware leader. Opothleyahola refused to respond.[31]

Chief Ross, of the Cherokees, worked tirelessly to avoid open warfare among Indians. Several times between mid-September and mid-October, he advised Opothleyahola to cooperate with the Confederate authorities. Conversely, when those authorities marched nearly half the 1,200 men of Drew's Cherokee regiment to join a general military movement against Opothleyahola, Ross redoubled his efforts to dissuade the Confederates from military action. The former OIA agent—now colonel—Douglas H. Cooper, however, had grouped such Indian units with the Fourth Texas Cavalry, forming a makeshift brigade to crush Indian resistance to the Confederacy.[32]

The chill of autumn moved Opothleyahola before the rebels reached him. Deciding that the encampment would not survive on lands generally stripped of forage, the refugees decided to move on in search of better pasturage, with Cooper and some 1,400 Confederates in pursuit. Even without the women, children, and the aged, Opothleyahola's wanderers might have been able to match the rebels in the number of possible combatants, but their pathetic arsenal ranged from short-range hunting pieces to bows and arrows.

Confederates caught up to the hungry and cold column of civilians at Round Mound on November 19. Given no choice but to surrender or fight, Jim Ned, Halpatter Tustenugee, Su-nuk-mik-ko, and other warriors organized the available braves. At sunset impatient and overconfident Confederates charged in properly Napoleonic fashion. To the chagrin of Cooper and the other Confederate officers, their Creek "volunteers" simply refused to participate in this assault on their own people. The warriors of Opothleyahola remained under heavy cover and picked off enough attackers to demoralize the rebels, forcing their withdrawal as night fell on Cooper's numerical and logistical advantages. In the darkness Opothleyahola's people slipped away from their tormentors.[33]

By then, though, Fremont's small force of Federals—preceded by Panipakuxwe and fifty-four Delaware scouts and joined by the "Lane Brigade," from Kansas—had reestablished a Union presence in southwest Missouri.

This forced Cooper's chastened expedition to countermarch to the east. For some weeks the Confederates occupied themselves in chasing smaller parties of refugees. Never sufficiently numerous to matter in the diplomatic considerations of Richmond, the Quapaw had already fled north, and Watie's efforts to extend Confederate Cherokee control over the territory of the Seneca and Shawnee drove these tribes north, through the abandoned Quapaw lands and toward a refugee center near Leroy, Kansas, where OIA agent Elder relocated them. While the nominally secessionist Osage did field a small war party under Confederate colors, some two thousand of them reportedly opted for their own version of the Keetowah.[34]

The Osage and other Indian groups in Kansas had already tried to join the war for the Union. Through Lane's influence, the Lincoln administration gave Augustus Wattles credentials as something of an OIA troubleshooter. He began helping the Osage to organize a militia against the pro-Confederate renegades and guerrillas. As early as August 22, 1861, Lane told agents of the Sac and Foxes, Shawnees, Delawares, Kickapoos, Pottawatomies, and Kaws that he wanted to form an Indian brigade and sent Wattles to confer with the chiefs and "adopt such measures as will secure the early assembling of the Indians at this point." In September U.S. Indian affairs commissioner Dole brought talk of Indian recruitment to a quick end. Nevertheless, the strength of Wattles's argument grew with the Union military reversals in Missouri and the increasing numbers of Senecas, Shawnees, and other ostensibly Confederate allies fleeing north from the Indian Territory.[35]

The Confederates inadvertently continued to push Indians toward the Unionist cause. Near the close of the year, Cooper's brigade once more turned its attention to Opothleyahola's people. In the second week of December, the strengthened rebel units located the refugee encampment in the interior of a horseshoe bend of Bird Creek, a tributary of the Verdigris River running north of Tulsey-Town. Known as Fonta-hulwache (meaning "little high shoals") in Creek or Chusto-Talasah ("caving banks") in Cherokee, the creek protected the camp on three sides. Ross had once more failed to keep the Confederate high command from including Drew's Cherokee regiment in this fratricidal exercise. On the night of December 7, Drew's unit held the most advanced position, and Capt. James McDaniel took pains to assign his Keetowah to picket duty.[36]

This time the nominally Confederate Cherokees engaged in a curious exchange with Opothleyahola's people. "Who are you?" came a voice from the darkness. "Tahlequah—who are you?" came the ritual response. "I am

Keetoowah's son!" Erstwhile enemies then emerged to shake hands, and de-
fectors to the encampment included such Keetowah as Major Thomas Pegg
and Captains James Vann, George W. Scraper, and Albert Pike (no relation to
the Confederate general). All joined McDaniel in crossing over into Opothleyahola's camp, along with Lieutenants White Catcher, Eli Smith, Samuel
Foster, John Bear Meat, and Nathaniel Fish. While the estimated numbers
for those crossing over to Opothleyahola varied—depending on who did
the counting and when—the sun rose on December 9 to find many as nine-
tenths of Drew's detachment unavailable for Confederate service. Protected
by the banks of Bird Creek, hundreds of Cherokee ex-Confederates stood
alongside Su-nuk-mik-ko, Halpatter Tustenugee, Jim Ned, and the other
warriors.[37] Cold and discouraged, Cooper's brigade again trundled back to
Fort Gibson.

A different, mostly white brigade led by General James M. McIntosh—
no relation to the Creek brothers—thundered down on Opothleyahola's
people on December 26 at Chustenahlah—or Patriot Hills—along Shoal
Creek, another tributary of the Verdigris. It is hard to see this "battle" as
much more than a ruthless assault on largely defenseless Indians led by
whites and rebel mixed bloods proving themselves to be sufficiently white
for Confederate service. Weakened by hunger, exposure, and attrition, the
outnumbered and outgunned warriors did what they could for as long as
they could. Nevertheless, around 5 P.M. their heroic but futile resistance
broke. At some point Halpatter Tustenugee—"Alligator," the hero of the
Seminole Wars—was killed. As a contemporary noted, the proportion of
reported killed to those wounded or captured seemed "too large, unless the
Confederates killed the women and children they captured."[38] Scattered into
small bands, the remaining braves used the gorges and recesses along Shoal
Creek to cover the flight of other civilians.

~~

Through the winter of 1861–62, federal authorities, scrambling to mobilize
the minimal resources needed to wage their war, faced an unprecedented
refugee disaster. Thousands more shivering, hungry, and footsore Indians
left a trail of frozen corpses from the territory into Kansas. Opothleyahola
and Halleck Tustenugee wrote Lincoln on their behalf, as Su-nuk-mik-
ko crisscrossed southern Kansas, giving assistance where he could. (When
Billy Bowlegs arrived at the refugee community near Humboldt, Kansas,

in February 1862, officials already discussed making him an officer.) The former Confederate captain McDaniel publicized the coerced nature of the Cherokee treaty with the secessionists and cited as irrefutable evidence of the coercion the armed resistance with which those encamped around him responded to the secessionists.[39]

Between a third and a half of white Kansans already faced poverty because of the panic, the drought, and the war, which had removed thousands of breadwinners from households now desperately struggling for survival. By early 1862 thousands gathered with Opothleyahola around Roe's Fort (south of present Belmont) on the Verdigris River, though the travails of the season reduced the official spring count to 7,600, with 600 more on adjacent Shawnee lands, another 5,000 elsewhere on the Neosho River, and more Chickasaws and Choctaws on the Verdigris. Flight from slavery began swelling the black population, which grew from 620 in 1860 to 12,527 by the war's close. As well, the state hosted several thousand white Unionists from Arkansas and western Missouri.[40] In the first year of the Civil War, some 90,000 mostly impoverished Kansans found themselves hosting 25,000 to 30,000 refugees, mostly nonwhite and entirely destitute.

Even those federal officials willing and eager to help had no mechanism for—or experience in—addressing a refugee problem on such a scale. Both the army and the OIA claimed authority over what they wanted to control, while neither wanted any responsibility. The OIA refused to pay annuities to peoples not in their designated homelands, never mind that they were not there because of what the agency knew to be the army's decision to withdraw the troops defending them there. Even a relatively unsympathetic Union officer saw the Indians as "ground between the millstone of the War and Indian Department."[41] As officials from Fort Scott to St. Louis and Washington bickered over jurisdiction, refugees froze, starved, died, and pleaded for help to return to their lands.

Confederate military reversals in the West accomplished little immediately. In January and February 1862 Union victories secured Kentucky and inspired the desperate and unsuccessful Confederate bid for an April success at Shiloh, an operation requiring so many troops that the Union won spectacular gains in now poorly defended areas in northern Alabama and along the Mississippi, bringing them, by June, to the bluffs near Vicksburg, Mississippi. Far to the west, during February and March 1862, the ill-fated Texas filibustering into the vastnesses of the New Mexico failed miserably.

Throughout, the architects of the ritual slaughter on the battlefield fretted, with an astonishing lack of self-consciousness, whether the bloodshed might stir the "savage" instincts of "primitive" Indian and Negroes.

Such concerns came to a head at Pea Ridge, in Arkansas. General Samuel R. Curtis successfully led the Federals back into Springfield, Missouri, driving scattered Confederate units along Telegraph Road into the pro-Unionist northwest corner of Arkansas. Shielded by the terrain of Pea Ridge, 12,000 men of a reunited army of Confederate and MSG units under Generals McCulloch and Price hit Curtis's army on March 7–8, a battle that eclipsed Wilson's Creek in the ferocity of the fighting and introduced Indians into the war. The presence of the Confederate general Albert Pike's Indians inspired widely publicized atrocity stories, including the alleged scalping of wounded Union soldiers. In reality, these units comprised the more assimilated mixed-bloods, and atrocities were also attributed to white Texans. Unlike the ferocity and brutality unleashed against Opothleyahola's Indian noncombatants, outrages against white soldiers sparked formal protests.[42] Certainly, though, the Confederate use of Indians dissolved any remaining Union reluctance to do.

Secessionist policies also made certain that the tide of refugees to the north would not ebb. The ink on their treaties with the new Confederacy had hardly dried before the agreements were ignored. Secessionists in the territory pursued their ruthless war on any who balked at accepting their political course, and they did so all the more viciously because they were, in this case, Indians. After Chustenahlah, Watie's men began shooting and scalping known Keetowah, despite Chief Ross's grant of amnesty to any Cherokee who had fought for Opothleyahola. Then, too, the repercussions of Pea Ridge drove Pike to withdraw to an Arkansas cabin where he turned to revising Southern-based Scottish Rite Masonry, leaving Confederate-Indian relations entirely in the hands of old OIA officials and Indian fighters, such as Cooper and McCulloch. By June 1862 Ross protested to these officials that they had provided none of the arms, pay, supplies, and clothing the Confederacy had promised the Indians.[43]

What Ross protested represented regional as well as racial priorities, a focus on eastern affairs that framed policies for both North and South. To defend Richmond, the Confederacy invested heavily in General Robert E. Lee's new Army of Northern Virginia, to the great detriment of all its forces farther west. In an unsuccessful effort to match this, the federal high command acted similarly. Troops raised in Tennessee or Ohio frequently went east to fight, while those enlisting in Arkansas or Kansas could face each other in Tennessee or Mississippi.

Secessionist policies among Indians in the West presaged those later imposed generally across the South. It took only few months of Confederate administration to drive into exile half the Creeks, most of the Seminoles, and virtually all the Neosho Agency. After the new treaties with the Confederacy imposed on Indians a de facto conscription at the whim of the Richmond government, authorities across the South began imposing martial law, requiring residents either to embrace the new government or leave and authorizing the punishment of those who chose the latter course with confiscation of property, imprisonment, or even death. The able-bodied whites who stayed tended to be enrolled in a militia that would then be called into service, with direction conscription following in mid-1862, thus nationalizing the mandatory Confederate military service first imposed on Indians.

On the Federals' side, the grand strategists placed little emphasis on the radical proposal to raise and equip Indians and blacks. Authorities in Kansas, however, had become increasingly desperate to rid themselves of the refugees, who in turn asked only for arms and organization to liberate their homelands themselves. In the winter of 1861–62 General David Hunter met informally with OIA officials and "the head men and chiefs representing the various tribes among the Refugees." All agreed "that two Regiments should be raised of loyal Indians, to act as Home Guards, who, with a military force of white men to accompany them, would move into the Indian Territory, to expel the Rebel Forces and hold the country; and that the Refugee families should then be taken home."[44] In the end, preservation of "the Union as it was" already required actions that, if it survived, would change it radically.

Despite his erratic record and mixed motives, Lane became the most influential proponent of this radical project, partly because he wanted to take a column under his own command south through the Indian Territory and on through Texas to the sea. Although Governor Robinson and his followers mocked Lane's efforts to hold simultaneously a military commission and political office, the senator pursued both a political and military project in what the newspapers called "the Lane Expedition," which probably bore a more than passing resemblance to Hinton's antebellum plans to strike south from Kansas. Lane's superiors ridiculed the entire project, citing not only the greater demand for troops elsewhere but the very real logistical problems of supplying such an operation and their reluctance to give such a vast command to a nongraduate of West Point. Others, however, such as the new OIA agent Elder, testified to the virtual emptiness of the adjacent Neosho District in the northeastern Indian Territory, generally abandoned by the Indians when the Confederacy took charge. Further, Baptiste Peoria undertook a secret mission into the Cherokee Nation, returning with confirmation that Chief Ross actually remained hostile to the Confederacy.[45] Months before formal federal authorization, Lane started recruiting refugee blacks as well as Indians in hopes of moving south into the largely undefended Confederate frontier.

Enlistments proceeded quickly. Of the ten companies in the First Indian Home Guard, eight consisted of Creeks, and two came from the Seminoles, including "black Muscolge." The regiment carried the sacred objects of the Creek and Seminole nations; many of its members had served in Opothleyahola's resistance, and others, such as Su-nuk-mik-ko, had fought the United States to a standstill in Florida. Blunt recalled that, despite his advice on the subject, Ritchie's Second Indian Home Guard had been "composed of Indians of various tribes." Individual Creeks and Seminoles joined, as did groups of Cherokees and a smattering of Choctaws and Chickasaws. Among the former residents of the Neosho Agency, some sixty—eventually eighty—Quapaws enlisted, along with many of their Shawnee and Seneca neighbors. Kansas Indians remembered that "the Missourians had not left them alone," and the Delaware supplied Captain Panipakuxwe's Company D with eighty-six warriors. Other recruits included Osage and Kickapoo warriors, with some Iowas, Weas, Piankeshaws, Peorias, and Miamis.[46]

Open to all residents of the Indian Territory, both regiments recruited soldiers of white or black parentage as well as Indians, making them the first formally to introduce African Americans into the war. A runaway slave from the Creeks, Jake Perryman joined Company C of the First Indian Home Guard. "Most of the colored men who had belonged to Indian masters had enlisted in the Indian regiments," recalled one Kansas cavalryman, "and of course their families encamped with the Indian families." Perryman's outfit included at least sixteen black Creeks and numerous black Seminoles. In the Second Indian Home Guard, the Delawares' Company D included Jim Ned among its commissioned officers.[47] The Indian Home Guards not only brought black soldiers into the war but placed them in racially integrated units and even commissioned them as officers.

Radicals, particularly the former associates of John Brown, plunged into the work. Wattles and OIA agent Elder ardently espoused the arming of the Indians. Dr. James G. Blunt, formerly of the Third Kansas, won an April commission as brigadier general and a May appointment commanding the Department of Kansas. Joseph K. Hudson had a commission in the Tenth Kansas. Newly commissioned, Major William A. Phillips served in the First Indian Home Guard, as did the Nebraska settler Stephen H. Wattles, a distant cousin to Augustus and the late John O. Wattles. Ritchie, formerly the colonel of the Fifth Kansas Cavalry, was to raise and command the Second Indian regiment. Both Ritchie and Phillips had been out of the service since acting as aides-de-camp for the abortive Lane expedition. Other radicals also participated in the operation.[48]

Federal reoccupation of the Indian Territory reflected not only a radical agitation to do justice but also the brief triumph of Lincoln's political strategy over logistical considerations, something made possible by officials with very mixed motives. Lincoln consistently repeatedly his belief that the nations of the Indian Territory had been coerced and that the antebellum treaties remained legitimate, but officials began actively sheltering him from what they were doing in this regard. Commissioner Dole and Superintendent William G. Coffin of the OIA hoped to renegotiate these treaties and had already told Opothleyahola and Oktarharsars Harjot that the Creeks had abrogated their agreements. With studied ambiguity, the U.S. Congress amended the Indian Appropriation Act on July 5, authorizing the president to declare null and void any treaties with Indians allied to the Confederacy. When a Creek delegation reached Washington to discuss what this meant, Lane and other officials strove heroically to keep them from meeting the president. Indeed, OIA officials cynically introduced one of their number to the Indians as "Lincoln," apparently leaving the president ignorant that the delegation was even in Washington.[49] Rather clearly, officials of the OIA and the army had interests in this campaign not only different from those of the radicals but also much more well defined than they wished to share with their pragmatic chief executive.

Nonetheless, war had forced renegotiation of Indian relations. From the outbreak of hostilities, both governments had accepted the premise that the future of the Union would remain exclusively in the hands of whites, as would the future of African slavery, Indian removal, and labor relations. As with every other definition of "whiteness" or "white skin privilege," these matters represented innately top-down imperatives. Specifically, those white men with power and wealth shared a common vested interest from which an official, operative view of race grew. As from colonial days, these imperatives were imposed on a vibrant society of diverse peoples who shared no such vested interest. Indeed, even in the face of these imperatives, the people formulated views and practices on race that constituted a significantly broader and more fluid spectrum. From such a mix of motives—ranging from a principled egalitarianism to opportunistic reaction to the exigencies of war—the struggle to preserve the Union opened a challenge to "whiteness."

John Ritchie. The gun-toting abolitionist had a shootout with a U.S. lawman but became the commander of an Indian regiment. Courtesy of the Kansas Historical Society.

William A. Phillips. The Illinois newspaperman had been a radical land reformer before going west, where he eventually found himself the commander and advocate of the Union Indian Brigade. Courtesy of the Kansas Historical Society.

Richard J. Hinton. The former Chartist and future socialist proposed that John Brown's men strike south from Kansas, laying the foundations for what became the "Lane Expedition" after the outbreak of the war. Courtesy of the Kansas Historical Society.

John Otis Wattles. A resident of Utopia, Ohio, with diverse radical interests, Wattles remained consistently hostile to electoral politics after leaving for Kansas with his brother. Courtesy of the Kansas Historical Society.

Augustus Wattles. A Cincinnati educator, abolitionist, and socialist resident of Utopia, Ohio, he established black schools and refuges across Ohio before coming to Kansas. Courtesy of the Kansas Historical Society.

Alexander McDonald. A business developer at Fort Scott, he remained uninterested in the antebellum border troubles but early secured lucrative contracts with the U.S. Army and Office of Indian Affairs. From *Memoirs and Recollections of C. W. Goodlander of the Early Days of Fort Scott* (Fort Scott, 1900), opposite p. 38.

Billy Bowlegs. The last war chief of the Seminoles in Florida, he fought the United States to a standstill for twenty years before his removal to the West, where he became a Union officer. From *Harpers Weekly Illustrated*, June 12, 1858, p. 376.

Cohia. The African-Seminole chief and other blacks accepted among the so-called "Five Civilized Nations" made their continued presence a problem for the expanding cotton-growing South. Joshua R. Giddings, *The Exiles of Florida* (1858).

James G. Blunt. The Maine doctor active alongside John Brown's men became a remarkably successful Union general. From *Harpers Weekly Illustrated*, January 17 1863, p. 45.

Casualties on the field at Honey Springs. From R. M. Peck's "Wagon-Boss and Mule-Mechanic," serialized in *The National Tribune*, 1904.

Lewis Downing. A Unionist Cherokee leader, he served Chief Ross as a Confederate officer and then deserted to the Union Indian Brigade, serving with a commission there; he also represented Ross's government to the Lincoln administration and later was principal chief of the Cherokee.

The loss of a Federal wagon attempting to cross the Arkansas River. The fall of the flooded river exposed the wagon and its driver lost during an attempted crossing in preparation for Honey Springs. From R. M. Peck's "Wagon-Boss and Mule-Mechanic," serialized in *The National Tribune*, 1904.

Coacoochee, or Wildcat. A veteran of the Florida conflict, he joined Cohia in attempting to establish a mixed colony of Native and African descended Indians in Mexico. From Joshua R. Giddings, *The Exiles of Florida* (1858).

Pickets along the Arkansas River near Fort Gibson. From R. M. Peck's "Wagon-Boss and Mule-Mechanic," serialized in *The National Tribune*, 1904.

FOUR

Whiteness Challenged

Contemporaries knew that the campaign they witnessed in 1862 scarcely fit the army's pattern. The volunteers' uniforms seemed either too large or too small, and the typical mounted soldier rode a pony "so small that his feet appeared to always touch the ground." The standard-issue high-crowned, stiff black wool hat of the western armies settled not on their heads but on the mass of long hair falling over the shoulders. As the unit moved along, someone at the head of the column would begin "a prolonged, shrill note" that echoed through the ranks to the rear as "a short, sharp bark like a dog." It would be followed by another from the lead, the sound rippling through the line several times before ending. In combat, these soldiers wore "full war-paint" and gobbled like turkeys in defiance. In a larger sense, the army had launched many an "Indian expedition" waged against Native Americans, but it had no better-fitting term to describe what it was doing when it sent people of color to fight against whites.[1] Perhaps only the flag under which they moved and the color of the uniform reassured some.

The expedition required a rare, if not unprecedented, level of interracial understanding, trust, and cooperation. Union authorities chose to risk white lives and limbs to restore Indians and blacks to their homelands in the Indian Territory. That soldiers of color would find themselves defending the farms and towns of whites in Kansas, Missouri, and Arkansas illustrates the complexities of recasting the United States as an egalitarian liberator. Even as federal policy turned nationally toward emancipation of the slaves, the course of the war in the far West challenged the rigidity of antebellum race relations and raised questions about the extent to which the authorities would be willing to transform the Union in order to preserve it.

~~~

This unprecedented Indian Expedition took place in June and July 1862. On June 6 a brief probe by the Second Ohio Cavalry dissolved Stand Watie's Cherokee force on Cowskin Prairie, in the largely abandoned Seneca lands near the Missouri line, and on June 21 several thousand Federals started south. Alongside the Indian Home Guards and the Ohioans moved all or parts of the Sixth Kansas Cavalry, guns of the First Kansas Light Artillery, and infantry from Kansas and Wisconsin. Command fell to Colonel William Weer, a Wyandotte lawyer associated with Jim Lane. Initially he complained of having to deal with Indians through tribal authorities, but he acknowledged their good behavior and eagerness to fight while focusing his real ire on the whites. Politics had left one of the units "a regiment of officers," and these engaged in "continual intrigues," starting with the attempt some made to stay in Kansas.[2]

Weer became the first Federal officer to complain of "the want of supplies" from Fort Scott, sounding a theme that would re-echo throughout this corner of the war. The Military Road took them through an essentially unsettled area to Baxter Springs, which had one house. South of there, in the Indian Territory, lay farms without towns, "either recently abandoned or occupied only by women and children or negroes." In either area, moving large numbers of troops would require carrying what they needed with them or having it brought down by wagon in long supply trains. Weer noted that commissary officials provided Indians with a parched cornmeal called *sophke*, which loaded their knapsacks for heavy summer marching, but did not give them tents, cooking material, or medical supplies. Everybody ran out of bacon almost immediately, and no one had enough weapons and ammunition to arm all the Indian volunteers who flocked to the Federals' column as it moved south.[3] As Weer learned, the larger and more secure the force and the farther it advanced against the rebels, the more severe would be its shortages.

For their part, the Indians enjoyed a growing official confidence in the enterprise. Experience with the northbound refugees convinced Weer that the Unionists would be "hailed as deliverers from a sad state of most tedious

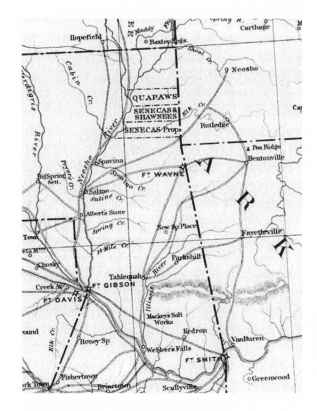

Map 1. The region of Union operations around Fort Gibson. From the *Atlas of the Official Records of the War of the Rebellion*, p. 119.

tyranny." Although originally skeptical about Indian hostility to secessionism, he encountered representatives of the Keetowah among the nominally secessionist Osage. He also secretly wrote Chief John Ross, assuring him that the U.S. authorities realized the Cherokees had acted under duress and that the Indians had acquiesced to the secessionists largely because of the Confederate occupation.[4] Most important, Weer realized that he needed to demonstrate the rebels' inability to hold on to the territory, and he found an opportunity to do that in two enemy encampments close enough to strike simultaneously.

On Wednesday, July 3, the Federals struck. Mounted Kansans routed three to four hundred of Stand Watie's Confederates near his mill on Spavinaw Creek. At the same time, the main body of the Federals surprised Missouri Confederates at Locust Grove, forcing most to surrender. There, Indians such as Su-nuk-mik-ko fought alongside old U.S. Army enemies, and blacks made their first official appearance in Civil War combat—over a year before the assault on Battery Wagner—as members of the Indian Home Guards.[5]

The Union army marked these twin victories with a racially mixed Fourth of July celebration three miles west of Locust Grove, at Cabin Creek. After being resupplied, they advanced to Flat Rock Creek, a few dozen miles up-river from Fort Gibson. Colonel John Ritchie's Indians probed some twenty miles south toward the Grand Saline, giving the residents a good look not only at the old flag but at the blue coats now worn on the backs of their brothers. By July 6 Lewis Downing had led over six hundred men from Drew's Rifles—the official Cherokee Confederate regiment—who crossed over to join the Federal "invaders," and two days later another three hundred, including thirty blacks, passed through Park Hill en route to the Union forces. Kansas cavalrymen reached Tahlequah on July 14, and the next day, Confederate Lieutenant Colonel William Potter Ross and Major Thomas Pegg surrendered Park Hill. There, too, Dr. Rufus Gilpatrick—the brigade surgeon and the uncle of General James G. Blunt—spoke with Chief Ross, who had repeatedly ignored orders from Richmond to force every adult male Cherokee into armed service against the Federals. A Union detachment chased the rebels from Fort Gibson, and got as far as Webber's Falls, where a diarist complained, "The niggers are riding about today looking so saucy."[6]

William A. Phillips rose to authority as the Indians rallied to Union colors. Recruits with Confederate experience, including Captains Pegg, George Scraper, and James McDaniel, filled Ritchie's regiment, but the vast overflow entered a "third or 'impromptu' regiment" under Phillips. The character of its composition later led others to describe it, understandably if erroneously, as "the Third Cherokee." His recruits included such Confederate veterans as Lieutenant Colonel Lewis Downing and Captain James S. Vann, as well as Allen, George, James, and Silas of the Ross clan, while the former second-in-command of the rebel regiment, William P. Ross, became the sutler to the Third. The *Lawrence Republican* urged the party to run Phillips for governor, adding that the state owed him "as much or more" as it did Charles Robinson, Jim Lane, Samuel C. Pomeroy, Martin F. Conway, and other prominent political figures.[7] Phillips, however, chose the unique challenge of leading the only Union regiment composed almost entirely of ex-Confederates electing to bear arms against the secessionists.

Developments in the Indian Territory immediately confirmed Hinton's antebellum predictions for slavery in the region. Not only did the institution tend to disintegrate at the first sight of blue uniforms, but the news of their arrival inspired slaves as far away as Texas "to light out to Kansas and freedom." Regular army teamsters who ignored the provost marshal's orders to buy mounts found a particular windfall in those runaways who had taken horses or mules from their masters to make their escapes. As the large numbers of self-emancipated blacks overwhelmed his camp, Weer found "the negro question . . . a very difficult one," complaining, "Nearly all their negroes are escaping and are very insolent." Rather than send his supply wagons back to Kansas empty, he loaded them with runaways eager to go north.[8]

Blunt, the highest-ranking veteran of John Brown's circle, advised Weer to "accept the services of all persons without reference to color." Even before the mid-July congressional authorization, Blunt and others had already begun to recruit runaway slaves. Officering the effort fell to men who had already confronted the army over slavery while in Ritchie's old Fifth Kansas Cavalry. The determined Colonel James M. Williams raised men around Lawrence and Leavenworth, while Captain Henry C. Seaman—who had also been in Hinton's rescue party for John Brown—recruited at Fort Scott. Other associates of Brown in the effort included Lieutenant Colonel John Bowles and adjutant First Lieutenant Richard J. Hinton, all of whom worked with black recruiters such as "Captain" William D. Matthews in hopes of having at least one company "officered by men of Color."[9]

Not surprisingly, raising black troops to defend Kansas proved initially more controversial than had recruiting Indians for use elsewhere. The abolitionist officers needed to raise enough men to gain their acceptance into service before they would be regularly paid, fed, or equipped, and they had no desire to soften their stance on slavery. Based on little more than faith and political savvy, they offered recruits a certificate of freedom not only for themselves but for their mothers, wives, and children, and one officer summarily ordered the former owner of one of his recruits to send along the soldier's wife and children, maintaining that the runaway's enlistment had "purchased his wife and children" from the slaveholder and adding, "From now on he is fighting for the government, and is entitled to the privileges it now gives—*freedom to all.*" By September 1862 they had collected half the recruits they needed into "Camp Jim Lane" in hopes of mustering the volunteers as a battalion. When the local authorities began arresting and confining his recruits "on the most frivolous charges," Williams took his armed blacks into town and forced their release. Tensions mounted, until the newly elected Kansas governor Thomas Carney insisted that President Abraham Lincoln recall the defiant Williams. In the end, though, the Lane-sponsored black regiment could see little use until Lane abandoned the fantasy of leading his own expedition south into Texas.[10]

Meanwhile, what had materialized of the "Lane Expedition" began getting very hungry in the Indian Territory. On July 17 the officers of Weer's white regiments reminded him that they were 160 miles from Fort Scott, had not been resupplied for ten days, and had only three days' rations "without vegetables or healthy food" for the troops. They insisted on a withdrawal, but Weer remained adamant about remaining and occupying the territory. In response, Colonel Frederick Salomon of the Ninth Wisconsin—who had two brothers in the army and another governing Wisconsin—called a meeting without Weer the next evening and assumed the authority to order a withdrawal of the white troops, leaving behind the unconsulted Indian Home Guards. When informed, Blunt immediately ordered Salomon to keep the white soldiers where they were and to sustain the Indians, warning that retreat "would stampede all the families of loyal Indians who look to our arms for protection." On August 8 Blunt hurried south to take charge, only to find that, contrary to his orders, Salomon had pulled some of the expedition all the way back to Fort Scott. Blunt denounced this "utterly unjustifiable and disgraceful retreat and the abandonment of the Indian country" and rightly described Salomon's action as "insubordination and mutinous conduct," but he filed no charges against the well-connected officer.[11]

A distinct Union Indian brigade stumbled into existence, after the requirements of Indians Home Gurads had been to its own devices. The senior officer, Colonel Robert W. Furnas, was an Ohio-born newspaperman who had become a pioneering journalist in Nebraska before Republican victory resulted in his appointment as the OIA agent to the Omaha. He, Lieutenant Colonel David B. Corwin of the Second Indian Home Guard, and Phillips of the Third dissociated themselves from Salomon's decision and joined OIA agents E. H. Carruth and H. W. Martin in protesting the army's withdrawal, which left them without rations or medical stores. Furnas did persuade Salomon to leave some of the artillery captured at Locust Grove and enough food to keep the Indians on half-rations for ten days. Many of the Creeks and Seminoles of the First Indian Home Guard, then near the Verdigris River, had gone off to check on their homes. In the more mixed Second Indian Home Guard, some of the Osage and Quapaw soldiers—men associated with small-scale communities rather than the larger nations—went buffalo hunting. Fifteen Indian soldiers sent to bring them back fell into the hands of partisans. In the chaos, Phillips's more homogeneous Third Indian Home Guard became a stabilizing force.[12]

Once resupplied on July 27, Phillips took detachments back to Fort Gibson, the Verdigris, Tahlequah, and Park Hill. Confederates near Bayou Menard (or Meynard) ambushed a Union detachment under Lieutenant John S. Hanway—of the Kansas family with John Brown associations—but more Federals soon turned up on their flank, forcing the rebels back to Fort Gibson. There, Captain Panipakuxwe reported, "We saw the enemy, the Choctaw Indians, the half-breed, we play Ball with them, 50 we laid on the ground, 60 we took prisoners, even the Choctaw General, him I took myself alone, he was a big sesesh, 100 Union men he had killed, I brought him to the Cherokees, they killed him." Phillips reported his most serious problem to be keeping the Indians on guard or in reserve during a fight.[13]

Lack of supplies again precluded holding what the brigade had won. Hunger forced Phillips back to Flat Rock and onto half-rations for four or five days, even as scouts returned from the Creek Nation reporting "about 3,000" Confederates under General Douglas Cooper at Fort Davis. In the end, neither the best of intentions nor the strongest of arguments could feed, mount, or equip the soldiers. Having already abandoned Fort Gibson, Major John A. Foreman's detachment followed Phillips's course to Wolf Creek and then back north toward Baxter Springs. Ohio cavalry there had already requested new mounts, arguing that their corn-fed midwestern stock had suffered more from eating simple prairie grass than had local horses; Phillips knew that Indian ponies had hardly fared better and hoped that the army would remount his Indians in the course of formally mustering them into service. Blunt, too, urged the army to provide new mounts.[14] By then, however, new priorities placed a greater claim on resources than did treaty obligations to the nations or military commitments to the Indians in uniform.

The U.S. liberation of the Indian Territory ended in the worst possible way, with a second abandonment. As the Union soldiers moved back north, Blunt estimated that 3,000 more refugee women and children trailed behind, bringing all the belongings and livestock they could manage. Blacks, who had balked at flight earlier, now had to make a choice, and a Webber's Falls diarist reported that "the niggers all cut out." Union withdrawal also meant that nothing would slow the flight of white Arkansans, fearing the desperate rigor of secessionist conscription. All these groups reached Kansas without suitable clothes or shelter. Entire sections of the brigade, disgusted with what they saw as betrayal, simply disintegrated and went home. Panipakuxwe walked off with most of the Delawares. So many Creeks disappeared that Blunt found only about twenty men left of six companies.[15] White Kansas, too, realized that the army had actually increased the number of refugees with which the state had to contend.

In the aftermath Blunt reorganized his own division of the Army of the Frontier, placing one Indian regiment into each of its three brigades, the commanders of which generally detested one another. With neither an investigation nor a vindication of his mutiny in the face of the enemy, Salomon took charge of one new brigade, and Weer, another. Colonel William F. Cloud assumed command of the remaining brigade, after taking 250–300 of Phillips's mounted men on a mad dash to Tahlequah on August 7 to remove to safety Chief Ross, his family, and the Cherokee archives and treasury. Blunt shuttled the chief to Washington, writing Lincoln and Secretary of War Edwin M. Stanton assurances of Cherokee loyalty.[16] None of this would mediate the escalating mess left behind in the Indian Territory.

Meanwhile, developments in Minnesota provided a reminder, though perhaps none was needed, that Indians figured as the traditional enemy of the whites and their army in the West. Through August desperately starving Indians forming eastern tribes related to the Sioux attacked whites around New Ulm, sparking a rapidly spreading rebellion. Just as the Rouge River War made the Oregon farmer John Beeson a prominent critic of Indian policy, the Minnesota rebellion moved the local Episcopalian bishop Henry B. Whipple to take up the cause of the Indian. It made something else entirely of Furnas, who resigned to hurry back to Nebraska Territory, where the former commander of the first Union Indian Brigade took the Second Nebraska Cavalry into a more traditional U.S. Indian expedition.[17]

Distinctions between soldiers and refugees blurred as the Union forces scrambled to respond to renewed offensives by the Confederate army. Later that summer Texas refugees brought the news that rebel units were on the march behind them. In short order four rebel regiments crossed from Arkansas to occupy Pineville, Missouri, with a thousand continuing to Newtonia, six hundred advancing to Big Springs, and recruiters going as far north as the Missouri River. The number of Confederates in Federal reports increased as they went up the chain of command. The 16,000 menacing rebels Salomon reported in August became Blunt's 25,000 in September, and General John

M. Schofield's 30,000. To locate and meet them, General Samuel R. Curtis's department had the 10,800 men of Schofield's Army of the Frontier, 2,500 of whom were needed to protect his supply line from Rolla down to Springfield. Of Blunt's division, the two brigades of Salomon and Weer had 3,500 men nearest the enemy, while 2,000 soldiers under Cloud fanned out farther to the southwest. The authorities called out 6,000 Missouri militia statewide, of whom about 1,800 were moving into the area from the north.[18]

Based at Baxter Springs, Cloud's new brigade—including Phillips's frustrated Cherokees—covered the southern and western end of Blunt's reorganized division, reaching down toward the territory. While Blunt ordered Cloud to guard "against any force that may be in the Indian Territory," he barely had the men or supplies for more than scouting there. Stand Watie's 700 soldiers retook Tahlequah, declared Watie the new principal chief, mandated conscription by their new military "government," and declared "disloyal" any lack of cooperation with the Confederate authorities, including flight to Kansas. Still, the Confederates lacked the numbers and resources to reoccupy the nation, which left vast tracts from the territory back into Missouri's Elk River Valley to guerrillas and bandits, as well as the hundreds of refugee Choctaws and Chickasaws hiding in small clusters along the Verdigris. As well, a newly appointed U.S. OIA agent, the remarkably brave Justin Harlan—a personal friend of President Lincoln—rode through miles of abandoned farmland, homes, livestock, and scattered refugees to visit largely deserted Tahlequah.[19]

Ritchie's Second Indian Home Guard, along with 1,200 to 1,500 civilians, camped twelve miles west of Carthage, at Shirley's Ford on Spring River. (John Shirley himself had several sons fighting for the Confederacy and a gun-toting teenaged daughter, Myra, later famous as "Belle Starr.") One observer recalled that Ritchie harangued "a lot of soldiers and worked himself up to such a pitch of fury in his violent rantings about slavery that he fairly frothed at the mouth like a maniac." Perhaps this intensity gave credence to stories that he encouraged ruthless reprisals against secessionists in the area. On the other hand, his fellow abolitionist Blunt thought Ritchie should be discharged for being "entirely incompetent as an officer." At 8 A.M. on September 20, the Texas Cavalry and Major Thomas R. Livingston's Missouri guerrillas attacked Ritchie's camp, though the Union counterattack drove them off, capturing "their vile flag." Guerrillas continued to show up periodically until the Federals were nearly out of ammunition, and at 3 P.M. on October 1, the U.S. cavalry arrived in the nick of time to rescue the Indians.[20]

Through most of this time, though, the bulk of the troops on both sides probed toward the enemy along the roads farther to the south. Blunt urged Lane to send "all the recruits . . . with any kinds of arms" from Kansas, "on forced marches," while Cloud's brigade eased forward with Salomon's at Sarcoxie. At the same time, Weer's brigade covered Neosho and Granby, its commander complaining to Blunt that "no less than four brigadier generals" were giving him orders while leaving some of his own men "nearly unarmed" and Phillips's Indians without a blanket at Neosho. This last group turned to local blacksmith shops to make their unshod ponies ready for use on the Missouri roads. Meanwhile, Confederate general Thomas C. Hindman concentrated his force in Arkansas, with a strong outpost at the little Missouri college town of Newtonia under Douglas Cooper. Blunt explicitly ordered his division to avoid battle until all the Federal forces had concentrated.[21]

Despite Blunt's explicit orders to avoid a battle until the entire division had concentrated, Salomon initiated the battle of Newtonia on September 30, which permitted his own command of the troops engaged. He began with a "reconnaissance in force" against Cooper's encampment and kept reinforcing that probe until he had about 1,500 men battling a somewhat larger Confederate force. Phillips's men spent several hours of the fight holding a wooded ravine lined by cornfields and stone fences behind plum trees and brush; they repulsed seven charges and withstood concentrated artillery, falling back in good order only after running out of ammunition. Salomon blamed his defeat on the Missouri militia, which he did not inform of his plans; on the other side, Confederate victory did not prevent rumors of Cooper's drunkenness. Official estimates place the casualties in the hundreds, which seems low for a fight in which a single battery reported firing nearly four hundred rounds, many of deadly canister. Several days of Union cavalry maneuvering forced the October 4 Confederate withdrawal to Arkansas.[22]

Once more, Salomon eluded any formal responsibility for his direct disobedience of orders in the face of the enemy, but a certain karmic justice befell him months later. On July 4, 1863, fate presented him command of a wing of the 4,100 Federals who held the heights over Helena, Arkansas, against 7,000 Confederates. Success there might have finally ensured that the governor's brother would receive the kind of fame he sought, but that same day saw the surrender of 30,000 besieged Confederates at Vicksburg, Mississippi, and the retreat from the bloody fields at Gettysburg of what was left of the best of the rebel armies.[23]

Newtonia did mark a political victory for the Indians in Washington. Since the war's start, Indian rights advocates such as Beeson and Whipple had been heard in Washington, and some congressmen, such as Pennsylvania's William D. Kelley, urged a departure from the legacy of corruption, fraud, and deceit practiced on the Indians. After the war, Lincoln told Beeson, "The Indian will have my first care and I will not rest until Justice is done to their and to your Sattisfaction [*sic*]"; he promised Whipple, "If we get through this war, and I live, the Indian system will be reformed." On September 12, the president—then in the process of issuing the preliminary Emancipation Proclamation—conceded to Chief Ross every major point of his argument. At this juncture Phillips's letter on the performance of the Indians at Newtonia reached Ross, who forwarded it to the president through Commissioner of Indian Affairs William P. Dole. In response Lincoln told General Samuel Curtis that Chief Ross "wishes to know, and so do I, whether the force above mentioned [the Indian Home Guards] could not occupy the Cherokee country consistently with the public service." Curtis replied enigmatically that the rebels would soon be "very scarce" in the territory, and he advised Schofield "to move west, eat out the country and operate in the Indian Territory," reminding him of both Ross's and Lincoln's interest in such a move.[24]

Once resupplied Blunt took 1,600 to 1,800 men south in pursuit of the Confederates. After a brief fight at Cross Hollows on October 18, they pressed on to Old Fort Wayne at Maysville, on the border of the Indian Territory. A black runaway guided Blunt's October 22 predawn attack. Prolific exaggerations mark the reports, but Blunt's force likely surprised and routed 2,500 to 3,000 rebels. Phillips's Indians pursued them seven miles into the territory, and scouts later reported that the Confederates did not reorganize before reaching Fort Gibson, seventy miles from the battlefield. The Kansas press and Blunt praised their Indian troops, who had demonstrated their "discipline and deportment" to be "as good as those of other troops and, their services of as much, nay more value to the government, in this section of the country, than those of any other Regiment in the Service." Many of the wagons, mules, and horses seized at Old Fort Wayne went to the Indian Home Guards.[25]

Another Confederate defeat followed within hours, on the opposite end of the Indian Territory. "Captain" Ben Simon, who had been a fur trapper and scout, planned a daring overland raid on Confederate Indian agent Matthew Leeper's Wichita Agency in the Leased District. He recruited seventy Delawares and twenty-six Shawnees, some of the former likely targeted earlier by Leeper's death squads. An estimated 150 southern Kickapoos joined them on the way. On October 23 the Unionists killed Leeper and three or four other whites before torching the agency and turning back to Kansas with about a hundred ponies, $12,000 in Confederate money, and a modest official archive wrapped in a rebel flag, an event one historian oddly called "one of the bloodiest scenes ever enacted on the western plains." The real tragedy came the following day, when the Kickapoos encountered their old tribal enemies along what came to be known as Tonkawas Creek, near the Washita River. They slaughtered 137 Tonkawas there, including Chief Placido and twenty-three women, comprising "roughly half of the Tonkawas nation."[26]

A series of even more serious Confederate reversals in Arkansas ended the year. After Old Fort Wayne, Blunt proposed an immediate move into the Arkansas River valley and against Fort Smith, but Schofield turned back to St. Louis and ordered his entire army into winter quarters at various sites along Telegraph Road, with Blunt's division of 5,000 men farthest south. When the Confederates resumed their activities, Blunt advanced to Cane Hill, closing the passage through the Boston Mountains and, on November 28, fighting a fifteen-mile running battle to push them back into the Arkansas Valley.[27]

The morning after the fighting, trade unionists in blue seized means of production and began turning them to their own purposes. Private John Howard Kitts of the Lawrence Typographical Union found a little cabin containing the equipment of a printing office. Some member of the Third Indian—possibly the old newspaperman Phillips—identified the type as Cherokee and guessed it came from the *Cherokee Messenger,* the missionary publication of the Jones family plundered in the late summer after the Union withdrew from the territory. Kitts and his fellow printers in Company E of the Eleventh Kansas quickly organized a printing office. Officers familiar with the craft worked alongside the enlisted men to revive their prewar skills in the *Buck and Ball.*[28] The break from fighting proved short.

The battle of Prairie Grove constituted the best Confederate attempt to save northern Arkansas. Secessionist authorities there had conscripted 15,000 to 20,000 men to reinforce Vicksburg, on the Mississippi River, but decided to use many of them to drive the Federals from their own state. On December 3 the shivering soldiers in Generals Francis J. Herron's and James Totten's divisions of Schofield's army started south. Hindman started his campaign by warning his army of about 12,000 against the "Pin Indians, free

Negroes, Southern Tories, Kansas jayhawkers, and hired Dutch cutthroats." He then led it by Blunt's flank, hoping to meet and crush the southbound Union column of 7,000 and then turn on the 5,000 under Blunt. December 7 found Hindman's army on the ridge around Prairie Grove Church, with Herron's force attacking around noon and Blunt's winded column arriving about two o'clock. Federal reports cited Tus-te-nup-chup-ko of the Chero-kees and Jon-neh of the Uchees, as well as Su-nuk-mik-ko of the Seminoles. The battle ended in a desperate, almost suicidal Confederate charge against Blunt's batteries, which he had concentrated and loaded with double canister. Total casualties approached 3,000.[29] Once more, Union arms opened the pos-sibility for restoring the Indian nations to their homelands in the territory.

In the days after Prairie Grove, Blunt granted the soldier-printers per-mission to revive the *Buck and Ball* and gave them a good story to report by pursuing the disintegrating remnants of Hindman's army into the Arkansas Valley. On December 27 Blunt's men occupied Van Buren, on the north bank of the Arkansas River, and lobbed shells across the river and into Fort Smith, second only to Little Rock in importance to Confederate Arkansas. Then down to only about 5,000 effectives, the Confederates abandoned the town and even their own wounded.[30] Blunt realized that holding Fort Smith would be impossible without being able to bring supplies up the river through Little Rock, so he fell back through the mountains.

Military success opened the possibilities for radical changes, but these re-mained contingent on their compatibility with any larger plans of greater priority. The Union administration in Missouri depended on local provost marshals, who processed arrests, imprisonments, confiscations, and even ex-ecutions. As does any such system, it invited corruption, extortion, and fraud, which increased tensions with Missouri's civilian government, headed by Governor Hamilton R. Gamble. That regime owed its power to the army and the fig leaf of its constitutionalism to the protection of slaveholding in a state that would be technically unaffected by wartime emancipation. Although Curtis, the department commander, remained a gentleman-professional of the old school, he saw the importance of moving against slavery, while Schofield, his subordinate, had enough allies among Gamble's conservative faction to begin flanking Curtis.[31] This flanking operation seems to have kept Schofield in St. Louis rather than with his troops at Newtonia, Old

Fort Wayne, and Prairie Grove, and the annoying news of victories in the field forced Schofield to disengage from the campaign that mattered most and go back into the field, where he had Blunt arrested.

To the extent that officials such as Schofield intervened in their own interests, those forces tending toward a more radical course fared poorly. A little more than three years after the United States had hanged John Brown, and less than a year after it had arrested officers for freeing slaves in Missouri, it now began to depend on those very abolitionists to lead armed African Americans. On October 17 the authorities formally organized the existing companies of the First Kansas Colored as a battalion at Fort Lincoln, near Fort Scott, but its organizers wanted to muster as a regiment, which posed vexing problems of equal pay and the commissioning of black officers. Using Lane's organ, the *Leavenworth Daily Conservative* and Hinton's contacts with eastern papers, the radical friends of the regiment publicized the determination and deportment of men who "organized and drilled, in camp, for *nine months* before the Government of the United States would recognize or receive them as soldiers!"[32]

Lack of mustering did not keep black soldiers from combat. Stranded after the Confederate withdrawal from Newtonia, rebel recruits resumed guerrilla activities along the Missouri-Kansas line. On the very day the regiment finally organized, 150 guerrillas under William Quantrill sacked Shawneetown, Kansas, and disappeared into the familiar terrain of the border, where a steady stream of irregulars seemed to be working its way south toward Arkansas. To locate it, Fort Scott sent a detachment of 225 of the untried black recruits and other Union soldiers up the Marais des Cygnes and into Missouri. They encountered some 500 newly recruited rebels near Butler, about fifteen miles into Missouri. In "a severe engagement," the eager black soldiers suffered ten wounded and eight killed, including a black Cherokee named Six-killer, who had apparently lived up to his name. They inflicted "severe loss" on the rebels before establishing "Fort Africa" in Bates County and faced sporadic skirmishing around Butler in late November. The *Conservative* declared it "useless to talk anymore about negro courage—the men fought like tigers . . . and the main difficulty was to hold them well in hand."[33] Still, mustering the first black unit to see combat had to wait until several eastern regiments had preceded them.

The unexpected bloodiness of the war created a crisis of military manpower, especially in the far West. A single day's encounter could destroy soldiers by the hundreds, thousands, or even tens of thousands. The successes of early recruitment reduced the number of potential recruits later on, and news from the front made enlistment less appealing. Generally, the high command balanced its massive losses in the Washington-Richmond corridor by drawing troops from west of the Alleghenies, and the West, in turn, reached beyond the Mississippi River for more men. Both Union and Confederate officials in the Trans-Mississippi often balked at cooperating in this process. When General U. S. Grant wanted to replace his losses along the Mississippi River, Curtis dutifully asked his subordinates, and Blunt shrewdly reported having "mostly negroes and Indians," knowing that these would be the least likely embraced by Grant's command at that point.[34]

Early 1863 found the black regiment to be Blunt's key asset. As they prepared to be mustered, the black soldiers celebrated New Year's Day with barbecue and "strong drink." Cheering the official adoption of slave emancipation as part of the Union cause, the soldiers of the First Kansas Colored recalled "the immortal hero whose grave is cradled among the Adirondack Mountains." They belted out "the John Brown Song," declaring that "John Brown sowed, and the harvesters are we."[35]

In mustering the regiment, the high command simply brushed aside the will of its white officers, who wanted blacks commissioned alongside them. On January 9 twenty-one white officers protested the decision "for the sake of justice to individuals, of the principle concerned, and for the harmony & efficiency of the regiment." They particularly made the case for "Captain" Matthews of Company D, "a worthy gentleman and an excellent officer" who stood among "the most thorough and efficient officers" and was "a soldier in every sense of the term, drilled, disciplined and capable." They gave Matthews "a large share" of the credit for holding together the much-abused regiment. That same day both Matthews and Hinton privately wrote Lane on the matter, but the officers accepted for the First Kansas Colored on January 10 were white only. Interestingly, on January 28 Secretary of War Edwin M. Stanton authorized the military to commission black officers, which would not have taken place without Lincoln's approval and support.[36] As with other such initiatives unsupported by the regular army high command, it seemed to be stymied by bureaucratic inertia.

The black recruits in Kansas faced not only the usual issue of unequal pay but also considerable trouble even getting their hands on that. Between January 13 and May 2, the force had to raise another four companies to achieve regimental status. Eighty runaways living with the Sac and Fox Indians turned out to fill Company I. Most seem to have been from the

Indian Territory and of mixed blood, a reporter noting "a very considerable admixture of the Indian in appearance and manners." He added, "Their muster roll is one of the rarest species of literature that has been seen for a long time. What would you think of such names as Quash Bear, Cyrus Bowlegs, Scipio Gouge, and so on to the end of the roll." The men labored on fortifications at Fort Scott through April, yet paymasters arrived with wages only for whites, not for the blacks, some of whom had been in service for ten months without pay. Williams saw their "restlessness and insubordination" as a "natural response" and stopped their manual labor to resumed drill in preparation for the field. He also privately informed Blunt of the problem and insisted that his soldiers be paid.[37] Bringing blacks into the Civil War had clearly stalled, however, and neither Schofield nor anyone like him would move it forward.

In addition, Schofield pulled the Indians from Fort Gibson back into Arkansas. Old Fort Wayne and the Wichita Agency had exposed the Confederate inability to protect—much less to govern—the Indian Territory, and Prairie Grove ensured that secessionist prospects would glow no brighter. As Blunt moved on Van Buren, Phillips probed the Cherokee Nation. On December 26 his "small squad of 250 men" swatted Watie's partisans from their path and briefly reoccupied Fort Gibson. The next day they crossed Frozen Lick Ford into the Creek Nation, chasing more rebels from Fort Davis and "reducing the extensive barracks and commissary buildings to ashes." Unbeknownst to them, these incursions contributed to the Confederate panic at Fort Smith; within minutes of Blunt's attack on Van Buren, rebels turned up with news that the Union Indians had pushed them back toward Skullyville.[38]

From the depths of that winter, members of the Indian regiments told Ross that the army had taken neither Fort Smith nor Little Rock and pleaded its resulting inability to supply troops in the Indian Territory. White Catcher and twenty other officers of the Second and Third Indian Home Guard quoted Blunt as saying that their men were "second to none," but the Cherokee officers also wrote Ross that the brigade was "in some respects . . . like the Chosen People of God": "[We have] been for many weeks upon the very border of our own country and in sight of our own dear homes—for reasons unknown to us—we have not been permitted to possess them." "This Army will go no further South," they sadly wrote the chief, for "everything now indicates a backward move, leaving our families still at the mercy of our Enemies." Some of them suspected a deliberate plan to keep their people refugees, sinking deeper into debts to be paid from the annuities and "enrich Gov't Contractors."[39]

The war's radicalism followed a logic of its own as it reached beyond slavery and even beyond the issue of race itself. During Blunt's approach to Fort Smith, the typographical "Kansas Jayhawkers" acquired newer, more ornate type, apparently from the office of the *Van Buren Press*. Returning to their base, the printers refitted the *Buck and Ball* as the *Arkansas Traveler*, but Schofield shut down the paper and ordered the equipment abandoned when they left Cane Hill.[40] Whites in uniform would have no such voice for long.

Yet Southern whites felt the shift even more clearly. As had John Brown, radicals rejected the depiction of nonslaveholding Southern whites as merely enemies, potential enemies, or future enemies. As has so often been the case in American history, what radicals described as radical would be ignored in favor of a definition imposed by nonradicals. Hinton explicitly complained that "unlicensed spoliation and robbery" by the Jayhawkers "had been construed to mean living off the enemy, and was too often permitted as a 'radical' method of warfare." In fact, the former Ohio land reformer Colonel Edward Lynde ran down those "Red Legs," using the war to plunder Southern whites in occupied areas. An example of a genuinely radical approach was that of the old abolitionist Colonel Edward Daniels, who, after his Wisconsin cavalry secured a Missouri town, would try to engage the residents in a political discussion to show them how "the demagogues and secession leaders befooled them."[41]

Many Southern whites did rally to the national colors, particularly after the dramatic uprisings against the secessionist authorities in Missouri and western Virginia. On January 8, 1863, General Egbert B. Brown's motley little army of mostly armed Southerners in the Missouri State Militia and Enrolled Missouri Militia held Springfield against an attack by veteran Confederates. At the war's inception, a former member of the Arkansas legislature brought a company of his neighbors to Rolla, Missouri, to fight for the Union, and Confederate authorities soon after dissolved a peace society of some 2,500 Arkansans. A group of eighty-three from south of the Arkansas River made it through the Confederate pickets to join the Federals' newly organizing First Arkansas Infantry. Even a small company of Texans made their way to the Union recruiters by way of Fort Smith. The army itself, however, slowed the enlistment of white Southerners to a trickle when—for administrative convenience—it moved recruitment centers from the antisecessionist mountains of Arkansas's northwest corner to Helena, among the eastern and more prosecessionist districts.[42]

Prairie Grove provided dramatic evidence of the extent to which Unionism survived among whites in the Confederate army itself. As his army prepared for that engagement, Hindeman heard that an entire regiment of conscripts on his right had melted into the woods, leaving only a few officers, and later reports indicated that another may have done so on the Confederate left. After the battle many of the hill people of northwestern Arkansas voted on secession the only way they could, with their feet, turning up as deserters approached the Union campfires. Later, as the Federals cleared the field, they found a number of the rebel dead with fistfuls of unfired bullets in their pockets, suggesting these Southerners' unwillingness to fire their weapons for secession.[43] Those devoted Unionists from the North interpreted what they found as an indication that many of those in gray and butternut littering the field had remained fundamentally loyal to the idea of a common American identity.

Radicals participated in the effort to persuade all three groups of Southerners—Indians, blacks and whites—to cooperate with one another in ways they had never done before. Even among the whites, the most reluctant of the three, some defied the racial sanctions of the region's elite, as did a mill owner who ignored death threats to feed Unionist Indian civilians and the Arkansas "Mountain Fed" of whom one officer wrote, "the fear of negro equality never disturbed him." Determined to encourage this, Phillips insisted upon—and widely publicized—the good discipline and order of his multiracial command.[44]

Haunting the course of the war was the antebellum radical sense that the entire nation might be reconsidered as the homelands of a common country, a nation belonging to all. Phillips and others—such as those officering the new black regiment—expected that those fighting for the survival of the nation would emerge with the same freedom and rights under the law as whites enjoyed. The fact that farms and towns in Arkansas, Missouri, and Kansas—once the Indians' and now the whites'—relied on Indian Home Guards for protection must have encouraged the rethinking over whose homelands were being guarded. Certainly most Indians chose to remain in service despite the ease with which they could have disappeared into the territory or among the nearby refugees. In response, whites would fight, bleed, and die to protect people of color in their homes.

The dynamic of the war also turned on the private belief that business was business and should be untainted by political, moral, or personal considerations. In 1862 Secretary of the Interior John P. Usher and Senator Lane piloted a bill to authorize the Union Pacific Railroad. In return for this, the company liberally rewarded them with 10,000 and 9,400 shares of stock, respectively, adding them to a long list of Indian traders, agents, and contractors who had helped pry privileges from the tribes. These included such figures as Robert S. Stevens, who had formed a new partnership with Thomas Carney, "the richest man in Kansas." The fact that Lane had called Stevens a "fraud" did not keep the senator from selecting Carney to replace Charles Robinson as governor of the state in the fall of 1862. So also, Stevens maintained his ties to both Carney and Robinson. Then, in mid-December, Lane introduced a resolution to remove all the Indians in Kansas south into the Indian Territory, something that could be done only by nullifying the existing treaties with the tribes already there. The *Leavenworth Daily Conservative* left matters somewhat open to interpretation when it urged the authorities to retake the territory and "throw it open to the settlement of loyal citizens who will become its protectors, as they have done in Colorado," a move the paper implied would be opposed only by secessionists and their sympathizers.[45] The most immovable obstacle to such "progress" remained President Lincoln, however, who had repeatedly declared that the old treaties remained intact.

However difficult challenging "whiteness" proved to be, challenging the imperatives of the market would prove even more difficult.

FIVE

The Union as It Never Was

In 1863 Richard J. Hinton, the adjutant and self-appointed publicist for the First Kansas Colored, appealed to Senator Jim Lane, saying, "We want to form part of the Indian Division, provided it have a radical chief." He suggested that if William A. Phillips were to take command, "his brains will make any movement successful, while his modesty will not make a success offensive to any one."[1] Hinton, Phillips, and the other radicals planned a project directly dependent on the mutual cooperation and respect of black, red, and white soldiers.

This kind of project obviously assumed an importance both political and military. Even in its initial stages, radicals would number disproportionately among those disposed to risk the ordeal of organizing and managing the restoration of Indians to their homelands. As their superiors distanced themselves from any responsibility for that effort, its dynamic became even more independent, culminating in the construction of a small radical-led triracial Union army that won a remarkable though largely neglected victory at Honey Springs, the largest battle of the war in the Indian Territory. Thereafter the radicals waged subsequent campaigns that reached beyond military considerations toward a general political mobilization of Southerners opposed to secession and the Confederate war effort. The distinctive

Unionism that began to emerge threatened to construct an American nation the likes of which had never been seen.

⌐⌐

Phillips and others regularly assured their Indian soldiers that they would soon reoccupy the territory. These officers, in turn, had assurances from their superiors, who marked the New Year by organizing a new Indian brigade. It comprised the three regiments of the Indian Home Guards, six companies of the Sixth Kansas Cavalry, and a battery of guns captured at Old Fort Wayne, and it totaled roughly 3,200 effectives. Officers around the much-wronged Colonel William Weer objected when its command went to Phillips, but the white and Indian officers, soldiers, and civilians who had served under him wanted no other. Nat Fish and twenty-two others urged his promotion to brigadier general as "a duty we owe to a gallant officer, as well as a brave but weak Nation." Chief John Ross, who had a son and nephew under Phillips, trusted him and wanted him in command of the brigade.[2]

The previous August abandonment of the territory had created an even greater refugee problem. Numbers doubled in the Cherokee camp along Dry Wood Creek, near Fort Scott. Two-thirds of the Seminole Nation huddled at Neosho Falls, and some 300 Choctaws had reached the camps in Kansas, with hundreds more Choctaws and Chickasaws scattered in small groups in the northern Indian Territory. Elsewhere, OIA agent Peter P. Elder cared for some 6,000, mostly from his own Neosho District, though a year of frostbite, measles, mumps, diphtheria, pneumonia, and smallpox had killed at least a tenth of the Iroquois. Seneca chief John Melton protested that the U.S. government failed to pay his people their annuities for the second successive year, and they had never needed it more.[3]

Phillips's brigade positioned itself both to protect the refugees from the guerrillas and to advocate on their behalf in the face of unresponsive federal authorities. After the U.S. government abandoned the Indian lands it had been bound by treaty to protect, its officials continued refusing to pay annuities to the Indians who had been driven from that land, and the army began arbitrarily cutting off food and clothes for the civilians. Blunt and Phillips both protested the "extensive spheres of speculation, not to say fraud," created. The brigade garrisoned the largely deserted town of Neosho, turning a grocery and dram shop on the west side of the town square into a commissary. President Lincoln's new OIA agent Justin Harlan turned up there with goods worth $12,000 and the president's personal acknowledgment of the legitimacy of the Indian grievances, completely contrary to the policy being presented by most of the other military and OIA officials. The brigade itself settled into "Camp Ross," located along the Elk River around Cowskin Prairie, the former stronghold of the guerrillas, who raided the refugee camps regularly. It also established a chain of outposts as far south as Maysville, Arkansas, and began repairing mills to grind corn and wheat for both civilians and the military. Through the winter Phillips reminded the authorities that a reoccupation of the territory was in "the interest of the Government, as well as of these people," who hoped to return in time for spring planting.[4]

Under the brigade's protection, the Cherokees reestablished civilian government. In Ross's absence lesser Cherokee chiefs reorganized the National Council on February 4, 1863. It elected Captain Thomas Pegg as acting principal chief and sent as delegates to Washington the antebellum missionary Rev. Evan Jones. They declared the treaty with the Confederacy coerced and joined Missouri, Kentucky, Virginia, Louisiana, and Tennessee in establishing a loyalist Southern government. The council became the first governing body of slaveholding Americans to abolish slavery voluntarily during the war, taking additional measures to extend citizenship to every male resident of the nation, regardless of the previous condition of servitude. The following month, the Creeks followed the Cherokee lead, acting under the will of the dying Opothleyahola.[5]

The brigade broke camp in an early thaw and moved south to Bentonville, Arkansas, but the smallpox that had already infested the refugees at Neosho now hit the soldiers. Although most of the white artillerists and cavalrymen had been vaccinated before or shortly after enlistment, Phillips rushed in army surgeons to inoculate the rest of his command. On February 22 the disease claimed First Lieutenant Charles Lenhardt. Phillips personally led the funeral procession, and Hinton described their old comrade from the antebellum border troubles as "a faithful soldier of Liberty and union, a devoted friend," adding, "his bravery, generosity and fidelity entitle him to his name—Lion hearted."[6]

After their advanced position proved secure, the brigade resumed its incremental advances, its wagons loaded mostly with corn from the White River. A Kansas visitor described their camp in Maysville as "Fort Blunt," likely the renamed grounds of Old Fort Wayne, an area so deserted that the dead horses and detritus of the previous October's battle still littered the field. On April 3, though, the Indian Home Guards donned their brightest war paint and shouted war whoops with "more animation than usual" as they continued on to Cincinnati, Arkansas, at the border. Four days later, after sending detachments probing as far as Webber's Falls, "two thousand rich Indian voices joined in singing 'America,' 'Hail Columbia,' and other American airs" as they reentered the Indian Territory at Park Hill. The following day the detachment that had been at Neosho arrived with roughly two thousand civilian refugees in a mile-long train of "every sort of vehicle." Dispersing a small rebel garrison, the brigade and refugees entered Fort Gibson, holding an impressive April 13 flag-raising ceremony.[7] At that time the Indian Brigade held—excepting coastal and river waterways and a few isolated little outposts—the thin western tip of that long series of Federal encampments, garrisons, and bases stretching east to the Atlantic seaboard.

The fort, like the country it had protected, would never be the same. Older residents could recall Jefferson Davis's drilling his dragoons between blockhouses and palisades rotting in the marshy bottomland along the Grand River. The surgeon-general had then called that site "the charnel-house of the frontier," claiming that it "invalided more men, for the last ten years, than any other military station in the United States," and the army had moved back up the hill in 1857, starting a number of new stone buildings. Phillips's brigade quickly added a mile of "strong works" that could not be taken, "inclosing 15 or 16 acres—water and strong commissary buildings." They also made three ferry boats to cross the Grand River beneath the earthworks and planned "a floating bridge." Determined not to be forgotten by his superiors, Phillips diplomatically named the new base "Fort Blunt."[8]

The political advantage of holding Fort Blunt could scarcely be overstated. The Federals expected "a very large proportion of the Indians now in the Confederate service" to "lay down their arms and return to loyalty had they an opportunity." As soon as they reached the fort, Phillips negotiated the enlistment of forty rebel deserters and within a few weeks added nearly a hundred to the First Indian Home Guard. Creek Confederates even arranged to signal their desire to desert by wearing a white cloth as a badge or bandanna as they approached the Union lines. Periodic Federal excursions to the west and south returned with rumors of mass disaffection among the Chickasaws and the Choctaws. Phillips assigned these new recruits to fill gaps in the existing three regiments, as he did with officers sent south to lead two new regiments, the Fourth and Fifth Indian Home Guard.[9]

The occupation did not equally benefit all the nations, however, which raised new issues. The Cherokees even had the reassuring presence of an-

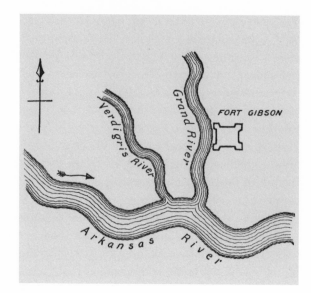

Map 2. Fort Gibson
("Fort Blunt") and
environs. Modified
from Wiley Britton,
*The Civil War on the
Border,* vol. 2, p. 75.

other of their antebellum missionaries, Rev. John B. Jones, who served as a chaplain to the Second Indian Home Guard. Captain Su-nuk-mik-ko and other Seminole and Creek leaders urged the army to advance into their lands to the west of the Cherokee Nation, and even Choctaw Unionists grumbled—without any basis—that the government had diverted annuities owed their nation to the favored Cherokee.[10] In the end, Phillips's superiors permitted the brigades to reenter the territory on the condition that he not attempt to hold more than the Cherokee Nation.

The reoccupation depended directly on white Southern Unionists. Again seeking to resurrect "the Lane Expedition," the *Leavenworth Daily Conservative* quipped that the ways of the army brass at St. Louis and the red tape at Washington were "too slow for Western men and measures." Someone with the brigade reported rumors of mass disaffection with the war behind Confederate lines in Texas, and Phillips was "chafing like a spirited horse . . . to be cut loose and led forward to the Red river country." In fact, Texas Unionist Martin D. Hart led other Southerners in raiding the Confederates near Fort Smith before his capture and execution. More generally, white Arkansans raised Union troops and planned a loyal state government of their own, hosting Phillips to address a mass meeting on March 4. Arkansans garrisoned a series of outposts, such as the hospital at Pea Ridge used by those under Phillips's command, including his brother, Lieutenant Maxwell Phillips. Confederates convinced themselves that white "Tories," like blacks, lacked the grit to stand their ground; on April 18 the rebels launched a four-hour attack on Fayetteville, the telegraphic link to the North only sixty miles northeast of Fort Blunt, but the Arkansans in blue turned them back.[11]

The army's persistent failure to remount the brigade left it with a mobile force too small to protect even the homelands of the Cherokee, especially in the face of other shortages. Phillips reminded his superiors that, for the Indians, the move had been "a question of justice," adding that reoccupation made "the restoration and raising of a crop necessary." He sent soldiers not only to protect farmers but also to assist in planting, posting men at Albertige's salt lick and Hildebrand's grist mill, the only one still working in the Cherokee Nation. The lack of good mounts limited what they could protect, however, so the supplies in the stone commissary at Fort Blunt regularly emptied to a point where the base went on half- or even quarter-rations. Their horses, ponies, and mules would forage on everything available around the fort, forcing the herders to go farther and farther from its safety to find forage.

The brigade always needed much of its mounted force to protect its supply train along the 160–mile trek from Fort Scott, a necessity given the Confederate hold on the Arkansas River. The mounted portion of the brigade that escorted the April supply train down from Fort Scott had to continue on to Webber's Falls, where they successfully dissolved an April 25 meeting of Stand Watie's secessionist Cherokee Council. On their way back, bushwhackers killed General Blunt's uncle, Dr. Rufus Gilpatrick.[12]

Federal horsemen returned from Webber's Falls to a grim reminder that the resources of the brigade had been stretched to the limit. Although the Unionists at Fayetteville had been victorious, they feared another battle with so large a portion of their force without uniforms, so they fell back to Cassville, Missouri. This removed them from Phillips's district to a different command and lost the telegraph link, which added two weeks to communicate with their superiors. Worse, Confederate General William Cabell's brigade marched north from Fort Smith along the now undefended hundred-mile border between the Union-held corner of the Indian Territory and Arkansas. The Prussian-born Lieutenant Colonel Frederick W. Schaurte, a veteran of the regular army, hurried after Cabell with eight hundred men and a section of guns, only to find that the enemy had gone on to Fayetteville.[13]

Underlying the problem of logistics was the reality that Phillips's brigade had almost no real support from any military superiors higher than Blunt. Although Phillips worried of an "untold disaster to these people and their cause," Blunt reminded him that his superiors might feel little sense of duty to sustain the Indians in their homelands but would not want the responsibility of ordering a withdrawal from it. Indeed, General John M. Schofield, of the Army of the Frontier, complained bitterly about having to sustain Fort Blunt, and General Samuel R. Curtis, who had authorized the occupation, wrote the army's chief of staff in Washington, General Henry "Old Brains" Wager Halleck, that Phillips had taken his men "too far down southwest by neglect or disobedience of orders." Worse, Curtis's reluctance to transfer troops east had left him out of favor in Washington, so Lincoln replaced him with Schofield, who cooperated by disintegrating the Army of the Frontier and eventually sending about 20,000 of his 43,000 men to Grant's army at Vicksburg.[14]

This thinly veiled resentment in the high command also encouraged systematic foot-dragging at Fort Scott, which exacerbated the shortages imposed by distance. Officials seemed to delight in subjecting the brigade's teamsters, largely "negroes—slaves of rebels"—who have come within [the] lines," to detours, runarounds, and red tape. Rather than return the April supply train on schedule, the commissary officers had sent it into Missouri to get corn and used "language in the last degree disrespectful" to protesting teamsters. This particular stall forced the base to half-rations, and May left Phillips's soldiers only "two ounces of flour per day." Phillips complained bitterly that that his brigade deserved better "than to be half-starved" and sent officers from his command to inform Blunt in person that Fort Scott had not provided the brigade with a third of the supplies due, doing so "in the dead of winter, before the enemy." Malnutrition contributed to the general declining health around the fort, where smallpox reappeared.[15]

The politics behind the lines had become far more complex than Phillips knew. Blunt made no allies in the high command by blaming Schofield for the fact that Phillips's brigade had yet not been "supported by white troops, as [had] been promised them." In the absence of Curtis, Schofield joined Governor Thomas Carney—himself involved with profiteers such as Robert S. Stevens—to press their investigation of "fraud, corruption, and maladministration" in Blunt's command. Blunt had but one remaining asset, Colonel James M. Williams's First Kansas Colored. Although Brigadier

General Thomas Ewing, the head of the newly autonomous (but logistically dependent) Department of Kansas, thought this regiment "second to none in the service," it remained grossly underrated by much of the high command. With Ewing's support, Blunt moved Williams's men down the Military Road from Fort Scott to Baxter Springs.[16]

Confederate officials protested the introduction of the black soldiers, who found themselves at Baxter Springs without cavalry to scout for threats and armed with two captured cannons "barely able to carry a shell without bursting for three hundred yards." Major Thomas R. Livingston's Confederate guerrillas, who kidnapped blacks to sell them south, regularly raided. On May 18 hundreds of them overwhelmed a foraging party of twenty-two blacks and twenty whites, who "fought desperately both white and black, the latter distinguishing themselves in every instance." Pressing some passing cavalry into service, Williams hurried to the scene, where he found the mutilated bodies of his men, who, after being wounded, had "their brains beaten out with clubs, the bloody weapons being left beside them." As Lieutenant Colonel John Bowles recalled, the Confederates viewed blacks in uniform as rebel slaves and their officers as instigators of slave rebellions, all to be summarily executed, which left "no branching roads ahead leading to prison or hospital—only one highway, which led to *Victory*—or *Death*."[17]

Livingston made further raids on May 24 and 28, but the most documented skirmishing took a literary form. After Livingston permitted the murder of a black prisoner, Williams executed a former Confederate armed in violation of his parole and said to have been involved in the ambush. He then notified Livingston, and challenged him to an open fight. Livingston replied that a Confederate officer would not demean "white men and jentalmen to eaquallize them Selves" with "eatheuoppieons commanded by a lot of low down thieving white men." Williams liked to think his retaliation ended Livingston's "barbarous practice of murdering prisoners."[18]

By then the activities of the Confederate general Douglas H. Cooper had settled the fate of the First Kansas Colored and the Indian Brigade. Cooper's five thousand Texans and Indians advanced to only five or six miles south of Fort Blunt, just beyond the Arkansas River. Cabell had another two or three thousand rebels with a battery of light artillery east along the Arkansas line, and rumors of mounted detachments of Watie's Cherokee Confederates came from all directions. Then, too, the rebels were infiltrating the camp with spies, such as the young white man disguised as a woman who was caught investigating the fortifications. To deal with the menace of these thousands of Confederate troops, Phillips had, as of May Day, only two thousand weakened and hungry Union soldiers, mostly Indians ready to fight.[19]

⌇⌒

The immediate Confederate presence suspended—but did not resolve—the struggle among the Unionists over the kind of nation they wanted, but their military success required a triracial campaign. On May 20, only a few days after the Wisconsin horsemen had left for Kansas, Cooper's artillery began booming along the Arkansas River, and parts of five Confederate regiments emerged from the valley to seize the main road to Fort Smith. The rebel skirmish line quickly swept herders and pickets back to within a mile or so of the fort. Union officers got men into the saddle and led a series of charges to delay the enemy, and Phillips personally brought forward two battalions on foot and a section of guns to cover the retreat of the mounted Federals. When a Union shell exploded among some Confederates moving through the nearby timber, the rebel line began disintegrating or falling back. The war-whooping Federals recaptured some of the livestock and pursued the retreating rebels toward Webber's Falls, while Phillips took cannons down to the Arkansas to drive the Confederate battery from the opposite bank. The official count reported twenty-five killed and twelve wounded among soldiers and civilians, but wagon boss R. M. Peck thought as many as thirty workers were killed, many gunned down after surrendering.[20]

The chronically overdue supply train threatened much worse. On May 23 rebels overran a Union outpost at the Eldridge crossing of the Verdigris, part of the northward movement of a thousand Confederates west of the fort aimed at the train, due to arrive two days later. The next day Phillips made a feint against the Confederate detachments along the Arkansas, to divert any reinforcements earmarked for that raiding column, while sending Schaurte with his five hundred most well mounted men to save the wagons. That night Schaurte's reinforcements woke the encamped train and began moving it to safety. Confederate raiders struck just before daylight several miles from the fort, only to find a large force with artillery defending it. Moreover, Union horsemen fought on foot, turning their mounted assailants into easily targeted silhouettes against the sky. The train reached Fort Blunt at sunrise, and two wagons unloaded and went back to retrieve the dead. The Federals had lost five killed and ten to twelve wounded but had killed a total of thirty-five to seventy and wounded an unknown number.[21] All such victories, however, merely postponed the threat of disaster another month, until the next the supply train.

By mid-June the Federals faced several Confederate incursions. Major John A. Foreman took 325 mounted men to meet a northbound column west of the Grand River, likely to menace the next train, and then turned back to intercept Watie's rebels, then raiding Tahlequah, "now deserted, except for a few families of women and children." Watie had already turned back to Webber's Falls, however, to which Colonel Stephen H. Wattles had marched another 400 Federals. At daylight on June 16, a third, hitherto un-reported rebel force held the timber on the south side of Greenleaf Prairie, barring Wattles's way back to Fort Blunt. Determined to act before Watie's raiders returned, Wattles launched an attack in which old Su-nuk-mik-ko served conspicuously. At about 11 A.M. a fresh body of Confederates ap-peared on the west side of the prairie, and the Federals, withered by five hours of fighting and low on ammunition, waited through the afternoon before heading back to Fort Blunt. Union reinforcements arrived soon thereafter, ending a desperate little battle, official reports of which strain credulity in numbering casualties at only seven killed and seven to ten wounded on each side.[22]

As of June 20 Fort Blunt had received "no mail, dispatch or communica-tions for two weeks." Without rations Phillips's garrison relied heavily on locally foraged supplies, and the vast civilian encampment faced increasing malnutrition and sickness, including "sporadic cases of cholera." Reports from spies, scouts, refugees, and deserters estimated the Confederate concen-tration as high as 11,000, but Phillips optimistically observed that decisively defeating such a concentration might rid the territory of small partisan bands, even allowing Judge Harlan of the OIA to return Tahlequah's former residents to their homes, as he wanted. Phillips reminded Blunt that securing the Cherokee lands would "open the gate to the Creek Nation" and the rest of the territory and perhaps even revive Lane's plan to invade Texas.[23]

Phillips knew that the First Kansas Colored would help secure their line of supply, but his white pickets down on the Arkansas River heard the news from the Confederates. Livingston's outfit had informed the rebels that the fate of the fort rested in the hands of "the First Kansas Nigger." While watering his mules, wagon boss Peck heard the Confederates goading the Federals over captured mail. Soon they began invoking women's names gleaned from the letters, claiming "that Kansas was being filled up with the runaway niggers from the South; and that the young ladies mentioned as sisters and sweethearts of soldiers were having nigger beaux, etc., etc."[24]

For their part, the First Kansas Colored was eager to go where it would not be subjected to relentless mounted attacks. Through early June the six companies of black infantry clashed almost daily with the rebels. Complained Williams, "I have no cavalry, I cannot make much headway in catching them. Indeed they are ahead so far." "I have not had the good fortune to see a dozen rebels since I left Fort Scott," he continued, "but I have seen any amount of *tracks*." Lieutenant Colonel Theodore H. Dodd of the Second Colorado then arrived with six companies of his own, a section of the Second Kansas Battery, and a company each from the Third Wisconsin and Ninth and Fourteenth Kansas Cavalry regiments. On June 24 Foreman rode in from Fort Blunt with a howitzer and 600 men as an escort for the overdue southbound supply train. After consultation, Dodd, Foreman, and Williams added the First Kansas Colored to the escort in hopes of creating a force large enough to deter the expected Confederate ambush.[25]

The Union column started south toward a near certain battle at Cabin Creek.[26] Foremen's Indians found the tracks of Confederate horsemen, and Lieutenant Luke F. Parsons—one of Brown's veterans—took twenty Cherokees in pursuit, returning with prisoners and the news that some 1,600 rebels awaited them at Cabin Creek. They did not know that Cabell had again as many nearby but stranded east of the flooded Grand River. On July 1 Foreman's Indians advanced left and right of the ford at Cabin Creek, which looked formidable even without enemy rifle pits under willow boughs along its sloping south banks. The next morning Indian skirmishers plunged through more than waist-deep water and got close enough to hear the rebels talking before a volley tore into their ranks, taking down Foreman and his horse. The Federals tried another twenty minutes of artillery before the dismounted Ninth Kansas Cavalry advanced, followed by a battle line of screaming black soldiers, whose appearance seemed to break the enemy will, scattering them "like sheep without a shepherd." Kansas horsemen shattered a half-hearted rebel attempt to reform a quarter-mile back from the creek and pursued the enemy about five miles before abandoning the chase. The entire battle had been of only "two hours' duration." Official accounts describe 800 to 900 Federals engaging part of a Confederate force of 1,400 to 1,800, with a similar number unengaged on the other side of the Grand and left to countermarch the 120 miles to Fort Smith. The Federals' reported

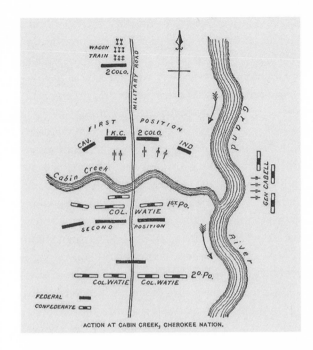

Map 3. The Battle
of Cabin Creek, July
1–2, 1863. From
Wiley Britton, *The
Civil War on the
Border,* vol. 2, p. 89.

casualties stood at three killed and forty wounded, with fifty to a hundred Confederates reported killed or wounded and eight or nine captured.

The fight at Cabin Creek—the first combined effort by units of white, black, and Indian soldiers—proved quite important. The soldiers and civilians at Fort Blunt, bereft of rations for a week, knew that Cabell had moved north, placing as many as 3,000 of the enemy between the supply train and the fort's depleted commissary, but Phillips reminded them that the Grand River would not have fallen sufficiently for Cabell's men to have joined the attack on the train. On July 3—the day after the battle—several Cherokee women rode in from the Grand Saline, opposite Cabin Creek, to report that a battle had taken place.[27] Two days later the escort arrived with the train, ending the "long fast."

Cabin Creek opened the way to save not only Fort Blunt but, perhaps, the general himself. With news of the Union victories at Gettysburg and Vicksburg, the Federals in the far West needed similar successes to maintain their claims on military personnel and resources, and the general needed it to inoculate himself against probes by his superiors. Blunt later claimed that he had heard only on July 4 "from *an unofficial source* that the post, with its garrison, was in imminent danger of being captured" and that he headed off the next day with an escort of "about fifty." Weeks of documented correspondence from Phillips and others on the situation there show otherwise, however, and Blunt's escort actually included all 350 members of the Sixth Kansas Cavalry not already with Phillips, two mountain howitzers, and a section of the Second Kansas Light Artillery—along with a reporter for the *Leavenworth Daily Conservative* and probably an engraver for *Frank Leslie's Illustrated.*[28]

Blunt arrived to take charge of the fort on July 11. He ordered Phillips not to fire the usual salute to avoid informing the Confederates of his arrival, but news spread through the ranks with "lightening rapidity." At an impromptu reception, Phillips recalled the victories of the previous autumn and assured him that the brigade would follow him, after which Blunt announced news of the Union victories at Gettysburg and Vicksburg. The next day Blunt sent orders for his taking command to the post printer, whom he directed to strike off only a dozen copies before scrambling the type. Meanwhile, the Confederates established their main camp some fifteen miles south along Elk Creek and waited for the return of their detached columns, "conscripting everything" in preparation for a move against the fort.[29]

The Federals knew that every day would only increase the enemy's strength. Around midnight on July 15, Blunt "got out of a sick bed with a burning fever" to lead 200 to 250 cavalrymen with cannons on a circuitous route to cross the flooded Arkansas River thirteen miles upstream and sweep the rebel pickets from the main ford to the Texas Road. Leaving about 1,500 men to protect the fort, Blunt's little army spent July 16 in the painfully slow process of ferrying itself across the river. At around 10 P.M. a detail from the Sixth Kansas Cavalry took their position at the head of the column and began moving down the Texas Road. Around daybreak on July 17, some five miles north of Elk Creek, this advancing detail, with Blunt beside them, rolled before it about 200 Confederate Choctaws and Chickasaws. Between 7:30 and 8 A.M. the Union force stopped, posted pickets, and took lunch from their haversacks. "We were all as hungry as wolves," remembered Peck, "and hardtack, raw bacon and branch water tasted fine."[30]

Decades later Lucinda Davis, an aged former slave, remembered that morning. The sky, she said, turned "kind of dark and begin to rain a little, and we git out to de big road and de rain come down hard. It rain so hard for a little while dat we jest have to stop de wagon and set dar, and den long come more soldiers dan I ever seen befo'." She watched as a unit of Texans filed north: "Dey all white men, I think, and dey have on dat brown clothes dyed wid walnut and butternut." They were "dragging some big guns on wheels and most de men slopping 'long in de rain on foot." The Federals recalled that "hard shower of rain" as lasting only about fifteen minutes, but it left enough in puddles to fill their canteens.[31]

The blistering day that followed brought the battle of Honey Springs.[32] Blunt's exhausted 3,000 men, mostly bits and pieces of various outfits, looked down the Texas Road, which was bordered by fields on either side, with periodic clusters of sumac bushes growing toward Elk Creek. Reporting 5,700 men that morning, the well-rested Confederate force blocked the road with a roughly semicircular line running along the uneven line of trees along the creek. The soldiers on both sides left piles of surplus equipment and clothing behind their lines. As the sun climbed over a humid field, many stripped off their shirts for what they knew would be hot work.

The Union army early seized the initiative. They masked their numerical disadvantage by advancing down the road by column, presenting a narrow face to the enemy until they got within a quarter-mile of the rebels, when

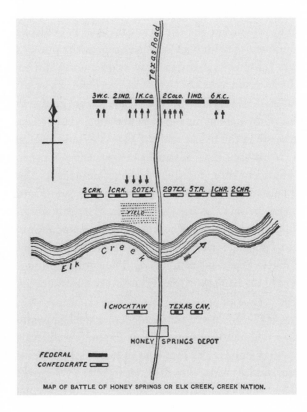

MAP OF BATTLE OF HONEY SPRINGS OR ELK CREEK, CREEK NATION.

Map 4. The Battle of Honey Springs, July 17, 1863. From Wiley Britton, *The Civil War on the Border,* vol. 2, p. 113.

they began filing out to either side of the road. They matched their formation to the length of the Confederate line by denying themselves the luxury of keeping anything in reserve. Phillips's brigade began on the far left, with four companies of the Sixth Kansas Cavalry protecting the guns captured back at Old Fort Wayne, and extended right through Wattles's First Indian Home Guard and Dodd's five companies of the Second Colorado to a couple more guns at the road. To the right Colonel William R. Judson's brigade started adjacent to the road with part of Williams's First Kansas Colored and extended farther right through Schaurte's Second Indian Home Guard to a battalion with four companies of the Third Wisconsin Cavalry covering the Second Kansas Battery. Behind them, Rev. Evan Jones waited nervously to dispatch news of the outcome to Chief Ross while James O'Neill of *Frank Leslie's Illustrated* made hurried sketches.

The Federals fully exploited their only real advantage by opening with their artillery, having a dozen guns against only four Confederate pieces. Dismounted Union cavalry used their carbines to turn back a series of rebel attempts to flank the guns on the ends of the Union line, after which the entire Federal line advanced to engage the enemy. At the center, Williams dismounted almost simultaneously with his Confederate opposite number in the Twenty-ninth Texas Cavalry. As they did so, both men ordered their regiments to open fire. Both commanders fell wounded, breaking the chain of command. Both the Kansas Colored and the Texas Calvalrymen held firm by the sheer stubbornness of the men in the ranks. When the end of Schaurte's line of Indians got between the blacks and the Confederates, Bowles shouted for the Indians to fall back. The Texans heard and saw what they had long expected: the imminent retreat of the mongrel Union army. The rebels then broke cover and advanced into the open from the timber and tall corn until a volley from the unwavering black troops stopped them in their tracks at about twenty-five paces. The Texans made repeated efforts to rush across the short distance, but Bowles had his men lying down and delivering a withering fire that kept the Texans at bay. They dropped a succession of color-bearers until the flag lay on the ground, "a trophy to [their] well-directed musketry."

Fighting at such close quarters deprived the Confederate artillery of any other clear targets, so it opened on the Union guns. As the more numerous Federal cannons replied, they quickly disabled one of the rebel guns and forced the rest off the field or into silence. On the Union left the "incessant gobbling and war-whooping" of the Indians on both sides resounded as Phillips and Wattles pressed the rebels, who later claimed to have been crippled by the poor quality of their powder. At that point the then-undistracted Union guns shelled a unit of white Texans, which fell back, leaving the Confederate Indians unsupported just as Wattles's Indians charged. Bloodied and demoralized, the rebel flanks began to fold back on their center.

The Federal center also pressed forward, with the most injured regiment, the blacks, lagging somewhat. This push sent the Confederate Creeks and most of the Texans tumbling down the embankment into Elk Creek. Part of the Twenty-ninth Texas rallied, found bluecoats pouring past its flanks, and filed off the field to safety, but part of the Twentieth Texas Cavalry found their own line of retreat cut off as the First Kansas Colored bore down on them. Twice the rebels started to surrender but stopped, fearing reprisals because of the past execution of black prisoners; they finally pleaded to Blunt, "If you'll send white men to take us, we'll surrender, but never to a nigger." Blunt sent someone who took the surrender from a sergeant major, the highest-ranking officer left among only sixty standing survivors of the Texas battalion.

After two hours the battle became a running fight back down the Texas Road. Falling back to the south of Elk Creek broke the Confederate formation. Advancing from the Union left, the Creeks and Seminoles of the First Indian Home Guard reached the Texas Road where it crossed Elk Creek, brushing aside a Confederate attempt to hold the bridge and making the Federals' first crossing. The Confederates generally disintegrated into a chaotic flight to the south, passing Cooper's abandoned headquarters about two miles south of the creek and, at three, approaching Honey Springs Depot. Rebels had torched their commissary building and supplies there, but the fires had not taken well, perhaps because of the earlier rain. Various accounts mention fifteen enemy wagons with thousands of pounds of flour and salt and large amounts of meat, sugar, and other supplies. David Griffith—taken to the battle as a slave by his Texas owner and later enlisting with the Union—recounted how the confident Confederates had hauled three to four hundred handcuffs to Honey Springs expecting to make a considerable bounty on the sale of their prisoners. Instead, tired black soldiers joined their white and Indian comrades in making "a bountiful supper" of the captured supplies.

The victory was decisive. Confederates claimed that their powder had turned to paste in the rain, but aside from that brief hard shower in the morning, the real rainfall came only after their line had broken. The slave girl Lucinda watched "de south side making for a getaway": "Dey come riding and running by whar we is, and it don't make no difference how much de head men hollers at 'em," unable to make them stop and return, with behind them "de Yankees, right after."[33] After the rebels scattered into small bands, making their way through the tall grass of the open prairies toward the Canadian River, Blunt called back his pursuit at about 2 P.M. Not only had his men nearly exhausted their ammunition, but they and their horses were simply fatigued. Some Confederate horsemen hovered watchfully, and around 4 P.M. Cabell's footsore Arkansas brigade finally turned up, halting at a respectful distance. Blunt posted pickets at the depot and marched his little army back to Elk Creek. Most had already gathered there by 7 P.M., when the First Kansas Colored trudged onto the field.

The cost of the battle on both sides remains undocumented. The Federals lost between 100 and 200 killed, wounded, or missing; wagon boss Peck remembered a mound of arms and legs at the hospital, adding that "nearly every man who had a limb taken off died soon after." Cooper's report neglected to mention even the loss of two hundred stands of arms, five hundred small arms, two pieces of artillery, a flag or two, and the depot of supplies, so his estimate of casualties may have been even more understated than had been his earlier reports. Given that the Confederate line partially disintegrated in the course of the battle, their losses may been as high as 500 to 600.

Black soldiers gained the stature at Honey Springs that the Indians won at Newtonia. Blunt assured Williams in the hospital that his men had behaved "like veterans, most gallantly," but the blacks bore the brunt of the casualties on the Federals' side. As they brought in the Confederate wounded, "some of our soldiers—even the '——— niggers'—forgetting the fierce hatred with which they had met and fought these men a short time ago were now cheerfully assisting in alleviating the sufferings of the wounded Texans so far as it was in their power to do so." Indeed, the African American soldiers jokingly began calling their proud regiment "the First Kansas Damned Nigger," but those who had first applied the name to them had trouble coming to grips with the result of the battle. On July 19, after Cabell's brigade had marched off, Blunt ordered his little army back to the fort, impressing a slave girl who recalled, "Dey looks purty worn out, but dey is laughing and joshing and going on."

After hearing of Honey Springs, Schofield promised supplies would be "furnished as heretofore" but remained unrelenting in his denunciations of Blunt.

Blunt, in turn, wrote Lincoln directly in an attempt to use his victory to deflect such criticisms. Meanwhile, only days after the battle, the Confederate army reportedly reassembled under the overall command of General William Steele and moved back toward Fort Blunt, with General Richard M. Gano bringing more from Texas. Although the *Leavenworth Daily Conservative* boasted of Blunt's superiority among the Federals' cavalry commanders, the most decisive argument for renewed Federal action came on August 21 with Captain William C. Quantrill's guerrilla raid on Lawrence.[34]

Blunt's subsequent victories should have opened the entire Indian Territory to resupply by river and reoccupation by its peoples. Leaving Phillips and the Indians at their fort, he took 4,500 to 5,000 cavalry south to the Canadian River, sweeping the few thousand rebels there eastward, with fights at Perryville on August 26, Skullyville on August 30–31, and Devil's Backbone Mountain on September 1, the last being the Confederate rearguard effort after abandoning Fort Smith. Earlier the Confederate general Theophilus Holmes had warned that with the loss of Fort Smith, "the Indian country is gone," and desertions subsequently withered rebel Indian units, reducing two Creek regiments to about 150 men. A simultaneous Federal drive under General Frederick Steele, aided by hundreds of white deserters who crossed over to the Federals, seized Little Rock from General Sterling Price on September 10.[35] Three weeks' work left the Arkansas River flowing as unvexed to the Mississippi as did the Mississippi to the sea.

Within weeks, though, the Confederates demonstrated their unwillingness to accept the verdict of Napoleonic strategy. October 6 found Lieutenant James Burton Pond earning a Congressional Medal of Honor by repeatedly rallying a company of the new Second Kansas Colored and some Wisconsin cavalry to defend newly stockaded Baxter Springs against hundreds of Quantrill's men. In the midst of this attack, Blunt and a modest escort blundered unsuspectingly down the road toward the blue-coated guerrillas, who massacred three officers, sixty-seven enlisted men, and ten citizens, including the son of General Curtis and the engraver O'Neill. On October 13 Confederate General Jo Shelby ended his audacious cavalry raid through hundreds of miles of Union territory all the way to Marshall, Missouri.[36] Clearly, securing a new Federal front on the Arkansas River did not mean that such a line could keep Confederate regulars from galloping all the way to the Missouri River or even keep Union generals safe behind it.

Despite Blunt's victories, Schofield and Carney pressed their complaints about him. Lane's tentative alliance with Carney had collapsed, leaving Blunt vulnerable. Blunt wrote Lincoln that he had blocked Carney's plans for the "wholesale plunder of the poor, unfortunate Indians, who had been driven from their homes by Rebels," and reported that Schofield had told him western entrepreneurs and politicians planned to ignore Lincoln's agreement to respect the existing treaties with the Indian Territory in order "to remove the Kansas Indians in pursuance of the Act of Congress of last winter." In fact, officials had secured removal treaties with the Great and Little Osage, and Chief Keokuk's Sac and Fox had sold their land in Kansas with plans to move into the Indian Territory when the rebels were cleared. Lincoln followed his usual pragmatic pattern, however, by removing both Schofield and Blunt—the former by promoting him and sending him east—while placating Lane with the concentration of 12,000 Federals at Fort Smith for a revival of the "Lane Expedition" into Texas; Hinton was likely behind the December 1863 *Chicago Tribune* article, reprinted in the *Leavenworth Daily Conservative*, praising a drive to the southwest.[37]

Despite these maneuvers, the flag flying at Fort Blunt had come to represent values that had been illegal—even treasonable—under the same banner a few years earlier. The brigade made the base a sanctuary for refugees and rebel deserters, blurring the line between soldiers and civilians. Curtis described the brigade as "only about 2,500 very irregular Indian Home Guards." Partly because pay and rations proved to be so irregular, many of the men came to treat their enlistment as something akin to militia service, leaving to revisit their farms, hunt, or even try returning to their old life. Mirroring George Washington in the Continental Army during the American Revolution, Phillips did not treat them as deserters, partly because he believed they would return when needed; he also knew that the base needed to revive farming and stock-raising if it were to become self-sufficient. By then, 7,000 Indians and 500 black civilians clustered under the protection of the brigade, and Curtis estimated that 1864 would see between 15,000 and 20,000 there. One runaway to Fort Blunt remembered reaching an unexpectedly warm welcome by a white officer specially assigned to assist runaway slaves settling into garrison life, that U.S. officer being Luke F. Parsons.[38] Events had placed the authority of the government and the integrity of its flag in the hands of John Brown's comrades.

Based on their military connections and their tradition of autonomy, the governments of the Cherokees and Creeks pointed explicitly toward a radical reconstruction more than did other loyalist governments in the South. Within the Indian nations, the possibilities for transforming the Civil War into a genuinely revolutionary war for liberation seemed a prerequisite for Union victory. Shortly after vanquishing the Confederate Cherokee government, the Cherokees' Unionist Grand Council authorized the confiscation and sale of the property of the "disloyal."[39]

The continuing lack of good mounts confounded the brigade's ability to secure the territory and enforce much of anything. Both the Creeks and the Seminoles pressed for resettlement in their own lands. Captain Su-nuk-mik-ko plausibly claimed to have gotten some assurance from Lincoln (since disappeared) that the government would meet its obligations to the Seminoles; when the old warrior died of consumption on October 29, 1863, his friends Pascofar and Long John took up the Seminole cause. Phillips, however, could not even protect what they had in the Cherokee lands. Watie's rebels looted Tahlequah and burned Chief Ross's Rose Cottage on November 12. On December 19 a Federal force at Barren Ford drove off an attack by Watie but could do no more than watch as the rebels rode off into Missouri. That winter—"the coldest within their recollection"—allowed for repeated raids, especially around Rhea Mills, an essential source for processing the food needed in the territory.[40]

Phillips sensed an opportunity among the thousands of refugees behind Confederate lines on the Boggy Blue and Kiamichi Rivers, clustered around small Confederate garrisons at Fort Washita, Boggy Depot, Fort McCulloch, and Doaksville. While Blunt estimated that there were nearly 9,000 Confederates soldiers in the territory, only 2,236 actually wintered there. Months after witnessing the battle of Honey Springs, Lucinda described conditions around Boggy Depot, where Confederate Indians "jest quit de army and lots went scouting in little bunches and took everything dey find." Out of a force ostensibly numbering 6,200, Cooper had only 659 present for duty. Confederate Colonel Jackson McCurtain of the Third Choctaw Cavalry secretly wrote the Federals, reminding them that his people, like the Cherokee, had wanted neutrality before their military subjugation by the secessionists and stating that they now wished to follow the Cherokee course as soon as the Union army could protect them. As Cooper's replacement, General Samuel B. Maxey, reassured the Choctaw General Council of its security, Phillips decided to demonstrate that Maxey could deliver nothing of the sort.[41]

During the hardest freeze of that winter, Phillips mounted the largest force he could. On February 1 he took to the Canadian River, deep into rebel territory, leading a thousand men from the First and Third Home Guards and the Fourteenth Kansas Cavalry (also partly composed of Indians from that state), as well as some howitzers under Captain Solomon Kaufman. A few days later Kiziah Love, living in one of the Confederate refugee camps, quickly hid her chickens and scurried off to her master's home. "Them Yankees clumd down the chimbley and got every one of my chickens and they killed about fifteen of Master Frank's hogs. He went down to their camp and told the captain about it and he paid him for his hogs and sent me some money for my chickens." After the Union horsemen fought daily skirmishes from February 5 through 8, the Confederates concentrated at Middle Boggy to demonstrate that they could prevent the raiders from passing, but it took less than half an hour's fighting to kill fifty of the rebels, driving the rest back to Fort Arbuckle. At this point Phillips turned back to Fort Blunt, assigning foraging patrols to sweep the territory up to fifty or sixty miles on either side of the column. The raid demonstrated that, properly mounted, his brigade would "crush and end the rebellion in the Indian Nation." On February 13 he led a smaller raid west through the Creek and Seminole lands.[42]

Everywhere in these ostensibly enemy districts, Phillips armed his men with bundles of the president's December proclamation of amnesty. Between skirmishes his soldiers freely distributed Lincoln's offer of peace to all who would down their arms and resume allegiance to the Union. After one of these raids, Private James Lemuel Clark and about forty white Texans decided to cross over to the Federals. Clark remembered reaching Fort Blunt in May, when, he said, Quartermaster Peck and Phillips "took us in at once." Clark became a scout under the Creek Bill Childress. All the while, Phillips corresponded with the Choctaw, Chickasaw, and Seminole rebel chiefs, urging them to accept Lincoln's generous terms.[43]

⌒

A handful of veteran abolitionists and other radicals—some directly associated with John Brown—demonstrated the possibility of military victory in the Civil War through the political mobilization of native, black, and white Southerners against the secessionist elite. This approach fueled Federals' achievements in the Trans-Mississippi, from the revolution of Missourians against their secessionist state officials, through the de facto early adoption of an emancipationist policy, to the Unionist successes in convincing soldiers from the Indian Territory and Arkansas involuntarily serving the Confederacy to turn to the Union cause. The extent to which such dramatic developments could reshape Union war goals remained to be seen.

A genuinely radical strategy certainly faced immense obstacles. In the long run, such an approach would place the future of a reconstructed United States beyond the hands of those who owned and governed exclusively by right of habit. More immediately, though, the wartime structure of federal institutions gave priority to those forces directly invested in keeping the power structure in "the Union as it was." In the same way that the course of Confederate government in the Indian Territory presaged the fate of Southerners everywhere under that regime, the ascendant federal power in the territory offered an eerie view into the future of Indian relations, Reconstruction, and the priorities of postwar federal authority.

SIX

Beyond the Map

A year after the victories at Honey Springs—nine months after driving the rebels from Fort Smith and Little Rock—the Federals' authorities issued orders to evacuate the Indian Territory and Arkansas. Astonishingly, military officialdom found that the vast expanses won at by blood and sword had become administratively inconvenient and logistically cumbersome. Indian, black, and white Southerners who had risked all to deny these lands to the Confederacy now faced plans to abandon them and their homes. At almost the same time, General Francis J. Herron, a veteran division commander in the old Army of the Frontier, clandestinely reported to Washington that those same authorities planning the abandonment of the region were holding Colonel William A. Phillips "under court-martial at Fort Smith, where he now is."[1] Phillips and his Indian Brigade had clashed with his superiors over nothing less than the meaning of the Civil War.

The emergence of a racially mixed army of Indian, black, and white soldiers on the western border required decisions that reflected predispositions about the future of a reconstructed nation. Relatedly, antebellum southern and Democratic cultivation of profitable, if piratical, Indian policies proved to be no less attractive to wartime federal officials, particularly given the especially vulnerable position to which the conflict had reduced the Indian nations. In the end, though, the prospect and promise of triracial Unionism proved too powerful and popular to be simply dismissed in the course of the war.

⌐⌐

If the Civil War was going to free anybody from anything, it would have to liberate Southern peoples from the control of their masters and rulers. Obviously, methods for doing so would depend largely on the culturally constructed category of race. Issues of race not only went beyond slavery but involved more than relations between African Americans and Caucasians and reached beyond the immediate regional questions to the identity of nations and the meaning of liberty itself.

Interest in a discussion of Indian rights reached new levels back east. Chief John Ross secured allies such as the sixty-year-old Presbyterian minister Thomas Brainerd, a veteran reformer, and agitated for the government to supply the territory by river through Arkansas. The friends of Indian reform occupied the U.S. capitol on March 9, when a spokesman for Ross presented "the deplorable and almost starving condition" of Indians in the territory and their "suffering both at the hands of the rebels and the Union troops." He depicted the wasted fields of the Indian Territory and an impoverishment that left the women and children scavenging for food among the grains of corn and oats used to feed the army's horses. The rally urged forming four councils to investigate "the most cruel and unjust war of extermination" taking place in the Pacific Northwest, the northern plains, New Mexico, and the Indian Territory and to prosecute the guilty parties.[2]

Agitation around the issue continued in the background. In the wake of this meeting, U.S. senators asked for and got "copies of reports made by a commission appointed by the Secretary of the Interior, or by the Commissioner of Indian Affairs, in 1861, consisting of Messrs, Day, White, and Wattles." As John Beeson carried the struggle back into the embattled West, a national convention of spiritualists discussed how the North's "indolent forgetfulness of the rights of human brotherhood permitted the exile for the red man from his native lands, his extermination upon our boasted soil of freedom." It denounced corruption in the OIA and the government. The spiritualists opposed "further infringement of the Indians' rights, in solemn vindication of those rights, side by side" with those of white and black Americans.[3]

Yet such rethinking took place alongside the continued U.S. war against Indians generally, not just those engaged in hostilities. Officials at Crow

Creek, directing the reactions to the 1862 Minnesota uprising, detained the Winnebagos as well as the tribally associated Dakotas and in 1863 launched a crusade against the hitherto uninvolved Sioux west of the state. Indeed, the commander of the first Indian Brigade, Robert W. Furnas, led the Nebraska regiment that waged the "battle" of Whitestone Hill on September 3, the shameful slaughter of over two hundred Inkpaduta men, women, and children, and enforced the survivors' long death march to Crow Creek.[4]

A succession of even bloodier Indian campaigns ripped through 1864. General Alfred Sully's expedition into the Badlands crushed a large Sioux force at Killdeer Mountain on July 28. It then swept westward to the Yellowstone River, killing those Sioux who decided to stand and fight, before returning to the newly established Fort Rice, near present-day Bismarck. In western Kansas James G. Blunt made the transition from advocate of the Indian to the leader of a military force clearing the Santa Fe Trail. As part of that effort, on November 25 Colonel Kit Carson, the famous scout and mountain man, faced the largest Indian battle of the period at Adobe Walls, along the Canadian River in north Texas. Only four days later, on the morning of November 29, Colonel John Chivington led his troops into the massacre of Chief Black Kettle's virtually defenseless village at Sand Creek.[5]

In fact, even allied Indians proved to be far less manageable and more savvy than the U.S. authorities had expected. Creek refugees who met with OIA superintendent William G. Coffin in Kansas on May 3, 1864, agreed that the rebel chiefs deserved "no water, no trees, no grass, no game, no lands, no sunshine!" Yet they flatly rejected any confiscation scheme that threatened the "perpetual inheritance" of the land they had been promised. One of them told Coffin that there had been a time back east when "lo, the poor Indian, whose untutored mind clothes him before and leaves him bare behind," accepted the promise of holding western lands in perpetuity from a Great Father who assured the Indians that he "would shed his last drop of blood for their protection." This meeting of "only . . . the old men, the women and children" indicated that the war had exploded such a faith among the Creeks.[6] These Indians clearly understood the difference between federal encouragement of confiscation plans to foster social revolution or democratic land redistribution, on the one hand, and official connivance with business interests, on the other.

While radicals expected the federal embrace of an emancipationist policy to improve Indian relations, it actually seemed to give officials something of a psychological tool for displacing Indians in the Unionist coalition. Williams may have been ignorant about events in the territory for a year before Cabin Creek, when he described the fight as "the first in the war where white and colored troops were joined in action," but his comments essentially rendered invisible the existence of the only genuinely integrated units in U.S. service. Reporting views from the field, the *Leavenworth Daily Conservative* noted praise of the Indian troops, alongside the blacks, but interestingly added in the same report—which likely means it was an editorial change back in Leavenworth—that Indians on both sides "disappeared in the brush. Not one of them was killed or wounded, and not one was seen again on the ground." Ignoring the contradiction, the *Conservative* editorialized that "Indians won't stand in a fair stand up fight" and that the Union would "*have to rely mainly upon the colored soldiers.*"[7]

Wagon boss R. M. Peck, a teamster of the old regular army, had no love for either. He distinguished between the civilized conduct of whites and blacks, however, and that of the Indians. "It is presumed that there will be few prisoners taken on either side when Union Indian meets Rebel Indian in war." He found it "a redeeming feature of the war" that "the true American soldier," white or black, tried to treat prisoners decently, whereas Missouri bushwhackers and Indians were "almost as cruel and relentless as the wild Indians on the frontier."[8] The white guerrillas were bushwhackers by circumstance, while the implication was that Indians were what they were by their nature as Indians.

Of course, the sheer numbers of blacks entering the Union army nationally overwhelmed the relatively small numbers of Indians. In the spring of 1864 the army formally reorganized the United States Colored Troops (USCT) into a force that would recruit at least 180,000 soldiers. The raising and combat use of such regiments of "African Descent," initiated in the Trans-Mississippi and the West, became acceptable across the country. By May 1864 Union troops consisting largely of USCT units moved on the Confederate capital itself. At Fort Blunt the Federals separated the black and white soldiers from Phillips's brigade and moved them to Fort Smith, reflecting an emergent alliance from which the U.S. authorities found it convenient to leave the Indians behind, unmounted, unfed, and uninvolved.[9]

African Americans enjoyed a pride of place—at tremendous cost—in the new incarnation of the Lane Expedition, while Indians had no place at all in it. Lieutenant General U. S. Grant's strategy of bleeding the rebellion to death precluded paroling prisoners, offering grand amnesties, or promising a radically new social order in the South. Partly as a concession to textile interests at home, the Union army planned to move up the Red River to seize vast stockpiles of cotton in Louisiana, while General Frederick Steele advanced from Little Rock through southwestern Arkansas, joined by a column from Fort Smith under General John Milton Thayer, a New Englander who had built his reputation as an Indian fighter. Moving over 10,000 soldiers through a scoured countryside, this Camden expedition required trailing a very long and vulnerable supply line and halving rations. On April 10 the Confederate general Sterling Price blocked their way at Prairie d'Anne, 110 miles short of their goal at Shreveport, and the Federals' retreat left vulnerable bulky supply trains largely protected by the First and the new Second Kansas Colored. Revenge for Honey Springs came on April 18, when the Twenty-Ninth Texas Cavalry overran an outnumbered escort for one of the trains and slaughtered the wounded. "Where is the First Kansas Nigger now?" asked one. "You First Nigger now buck to the Twenty-ninth Texas," said another. Thereafter, black soldiers began using "Remember Poison Springs!" as a rallying cry, but they and white "Tories" suffered further disproportionate losses at Mark's Mill and Jenkin's Ferry.[10]

Meanwhile, the high command left the Indians to languish in the territory, ill-supplied, unmounted, and isolated from the rest of the army. Phillips's spies in Texas reported rebel plans to retake Fort Blunt and Fort Smith, and scouts from the latter reported an unexpectedly large concentration at Fort Towson. The same lack of mounts that left the black soldiers blind to possible dangers back at Baxter Springs a year earlier began to afflict the entire Indian Brigade. Phillips's men could usually do little more than monitor Stand Watie's raiders or William C. Quantrill's guerrillas as they passed through the territory. To keep the rebels off balance, Phillips raided as far as Skullyville and kept patrols as far as Perryville. In late June Phillips told Ross that the brigade's very success at discouraging raids seemed to provide his superiors with an excuse to deny his men horses, which would likely "embolden the enemy" that fall.[11]

Neither did official policy greatly encourage Southern whites. After all, they had long enjoyed a much greater freedom of action that might well carry Unionism into channels of their own choosing. As they had for blacks and Indians, war and secession had driven thousands into exile and hiding. Refugees doubled the size of Fort Smith, with more turning up at Helena and Little Rock, as well as Pine Bluff, DeValls Bluff, Van Buren, Clarksville, Fayetteville, and smaller outposts. Officials talked about getting such people back to farming, self-sufficiency, and civilian government. Since

Prairie Grove, Confederates from northern Arkansas had been deserting and coming home and were "readily enrolled into militia for home protection and to hold the country." Still, it took four months from the fall of Little Rock before a constitutional convention, and voters did not ratify the results until March 1864, electing as governor Isaac Murphy, the sole antisecessionist from the state convention three years earlier. By that summer loyal white Arkansans adopted their own military version of land reform. The First Arkansas Cavalry resettled loyal families on rebel estates in groups of about fifty, the able-bodied men of whom functioned as something like the enrolled militia in Missouri.[12] For many reasons, these "Military Farm colonies" proved to be very limited experiments.

It seems natural enough, then, that one of the grand strategists struck on the most obvious solution to the administrative trouble of keeping troops in hard-won territory and defending the civilian population against enemy bushwhackers, raiders, and regulars. "Why," asked one of them, "do we continue to occupy the interior of Arkansas?" After the Camden expedition, officials proposed abandoning virtually everything beyond the Mississippi River but Little Rock. The Unionist governor Isaac Murphy pleaded with Lincoln to prevent the abandonment of Fort Smith, after which the high command agreed to keep Fort Smith as well as Little Rock while still planning to leave the rest of the state to its own devices.[13] The high command could hardly have found more direct ways to give away what their men had purchased in blood and to ensure the slaughter of Southern Unionists.

The extent to which the military high command and its allied businesses might foster any racial equality became evident in the differences and similarities in its approaches to managing Southern Unionism among whites, Indians, and African Americans. Keeping Indians dependent on the government and its licensed traders allowed the latter to profit immensely from their monopolies, selling needed goods to the Indians and having the government deducting whatever they claimed to be Indian indebtedness from the annuities and subsidies. In contrast, white Arkansans generated no such revenues, and their abandonment would cost the people who counted even less than would that of the Indians.

⌐⌐

Perhaps the most powerful figure looming over the Union-held Indian Territory wore no uniform and had long remained indifferent to the politics of the sectional conflict. Alexander McDonald, the Fort Scott dry goods merchant, had shunned the antebellum border conflict to pursue his business. During those years the "principal citizens and officers of the fort became quite intimate," and as previously mentioned, Charles Jennison had even taken a shot at him before the war. McDonald had raised a company of fourteen-day volunteers in the fall of 1861, but his closest military connection came through his long association with Charles W. Blair, who had become the colonel commanding at Fort Scott. Fueled by the war, Fort Scott grew to 3,000 and saw the construction of not only a stockade and a large earthen fort but also a city hall and a succession of local "firsts"—including a flour mill, wagon scales, a block of stone business structures downtown, and a stone church. All this local growth came from generous government spending and McDonald's prosperity. His company had sold $175,000 in dry goods during 1862, but other business investments brought in another $100,000. By June 1863 the company moved as much as $35,000 worth of goods in twenty-four hours and had enough clout to get Blunt to select it as the sutler at Fort Smith without taking bids; even as the general got news of his own removal, he was assiduously pursuing his duties, loading three hundred wagons of company supplies.[14]

Once secure at Fort Smith, McDonald's company expanded into the even more lucrative monopoly over the Indian trade. At the time of Honey Springs, Phillips had designated the antebellum Cherokee storekeeper, Keetowah, and former Confederate officer William P. Ross to be the brigade's sutler at Fort Blunt. A fire consumed Ross's store, however, including $30,000 in stock, and his capture by Watie's raiders ended plans to reopen, both nicely timed for the arrival of McDonald's company. In Ross's convenient absence, McDonald got an exclusive license to do business among the refugees in the territory, though the firm sometimes did so using names such as McKee and Company, "the branch establishment." Officials also authorized the company to purchase flour, livestock, and other goods for the government.[15] The war paradoxically extended the abusive antebellum monopoly over supply into a de facto control over both supply and demand.

One soldier complained that the company reshaped the priorities of high-ranking officers in favor of those "interested more in their own financial success than in the success of the government," and the company obtained a monopoly in both buying from and selling to the Indians. As the Keetowah pointed out, this allowed the company to place its own price on the "considerable corn growing" done at places under the brigade's control while charging its own prices for whatever the Indians needed to buy, including corn. When President Lincoln authorized $200,000 for the purchase of additional corn, the government paid company prices, with the proceeds going to both the officers and "the worthless soreheads caucus in McDonald's and McKee's Store." A similar sweetheart arrangement prevailed in buying and selling beef.[16]

The arrival of McDonald's new partner, Perry Fuller, took the firm's horizons beyond dry goods. A freelance facilitator and quasi-official liaison, "Major" Fuller had been fleecing the Sac, Fox, and Chippewa back in territorial Kansas before the tides of war washed desperate refugee chiefs from the territory into his hands. Ignoring the Lincoln administration's policy, officials in Kansas told the Creeks that they had nullified their treaty with the United States and instructed them to hire Fuller as their chief negotiator for a new treaty. Then, government officials once eager to purchase the Neutral Strip from Cherokee leaders refused to discuss the matter with anyone other than Fuller, who made a take-it-or-leave-it offer to broker the sale for a commission amounting to one-third the price to be paid to the Cherokee.[17] Official unwillingness to deal with some Indian groups without Fuller's mediation and the cost of his services became notorious.

Fuller's activities demonstrated the association of the company and its allies with the much broader capitalist interest in abnegating the Indian treaties, which Lincoln had said he would not do. These vested interests had enough clout in Washington to mount a threat to Lincoln's 1864 renomination. When the Kansas-Pacific Railroad requested $640,000 for laying forty miles of track, even though it had not even placed a roadbed, authorization came from the Treasury Department under Salmon P. Chase. Shortly after, the "Pomeroy circular" of U.S. senator Samuel C. Pomeroy of Kansas rewarded Chase by calling for Lincoln's replacement as the Republican candidate, a move masked as a "radical" one. On March 9—the very day that the Indian rights meeting was held in Washington and Grant took supreme command of the army—Chase himself ended "the Chase boom" by announcing he would not run.[18]

By then, the scale of McDonald and Fuller and its various manifestations reflected the pervasive official complicity. The Keetowah complained that "the Combination is a large, well-regulated and wealthy one" that involved Blair, commanding Fort Scott; Superintendent Coffin; and Blunt, their one-time champion. All this seriously implicated Jim Lane, who had been involved with Fuller in the Mineola land fraud before the war. When the new Republican OIA agent to the Pottawatomie protested official connivance with the company, Lane arranged his removal. Such influence was impressive, even if inadequate to intimidate Lincoln's old friend Justin Harlan, who wisely advised Indians to ignore the company as much as possible and do business with one another.[19]

Tragically, Blunt had become an owned man. After General John McNeil arrived to relieve him, Blunt chose to stay at Fort Smith, caught between not only the conflicting jurisdictions of the Missouri and Kansas military departments but also the military and civilian business authorities. McNeil believed that Blunt operated "hand-in-glove" with the speculators, and Thomas Ewing noted the previously mentioned no-bid sutler contract Blunt had awarded McDonald and Company. The following spring, Colonel William R. Judson described his old commander as working so assiduously for "McDowell" (i.e., McDonald) that Judson asked rhetorically whether the army existed simply for the benefit of the company. Although an old critic of Blunt's nemesis, Schofield, a chaplain at Fort Smith described Blunt as a "military poltroon" overindulging in food, drink, and women and planning to steal Confederate and private property for sale to the U.S. government.[20]

After the collapse of the Camden expedition in April 1864, Judson formally complained that Blunt had refused to release supplies to him. Officials at McDonald and Fuller openly boasted of having spent $50,000 in order "to bring Blunt to time," and the general then horrified the men he had earlier led with his proposal that Indian units be "broken up." Worse, on April 16 Blunt's Special Order Number Seven (which is not included in the *Official Records of the War of the Rebellion*) made the responsibility for arresting thieves a military matter. Coupled to the deliberately crippled state of Phillips's brigade, the order virtually turned the territory over to the company. As officers, soldiers, the civilians protested in vain, Phillips tendered his resignation, though Chief Ross reported that the army refused to accept it.[21]

The same military officials who prevented the remounting of the Indians made contracts to capture and remove usable horses and ponies from the territory. A company representative then offered Phillips a partnership to "supply the horses necessary for the cavalry service in the same way, and proposed to divide the profits, which would be very large, as it would be all profit." Phillips threw him out and threatened to arrest him should he make another such offer. A Cherokee officer described Phillips as a notable exception to the "weak, subservient or corrupt" officials, crediting him also for trying to keep "his own officers unpolluted by crime or untainted by suspicion." The chaplain of the First Kansas Colored confirmed that Phillips refused to accept bribes "or to permit officers or others in his command to do so," which likely caused problems, as "the opportunity for making money in this command was perhaps greater than in any other."[22]

As surely as Phillips rose to the occasion in dealing with repeated Confederate advances, he repeatedly defied, confronted, and publicly denounced the "ring of conscienceless men who sought to steal themselves rich by gigantic frauds and peculations." Observers confirmed that Phillips believed "the Government's Indian policies should be based on principles of justice and honor." The army, he told Blunt, had an obligation to those "sent [from their homes] by the Government." The Indians, in turn, saw him as an officer who had kept his word to them, even at the risk of displeasing his superiors, and described him among themselves as "fully understanding" the Indian position with regard to the United States. One white who served with him thought he would "become as illustrious as the Gracchi," the great land reformers of Roman antiquity. So entrusted by his command, Phillips determined that "their confidence should not be abused."[23]

Phillips's voice could not be stifled with impunity. He had been a delegate to the convention that had nominated Lincoln and had been mentioned for a gubernatorial nomination himself. He represented Kansas on the National Executive Committee, which signed the February 22 call to the "National Union Convention" that renominated the president, and the Republican State Convention at Topeka elected six delegates to attend that national convention; and Philllps came in seventh, although he held no civilian office and was absent in the army.[24]

For a brief time, then, the proponent of "free labor" unshackled by corruption and monopoly as well as slaveholding defied those motivated by a more mercenary patriotism. Taking his position in stride, Phillips told Ross that the company had "a thousand wicked schemes of plunder on foot," adding, "As they expect my steady hostility, it is fair that I should expect theirs." He also solicited all the help he could muster in addressing the related problem of remounting his brigade and curtailing the rustling of Indian cattle and horses "chiefly by Contractors and Officers of the United States Army."[25] The silence of his direct superior, General Thayer, on both matters was indefensible, inexcusable, and negligent, if not criminal.

On paper Phillips won this argument in March 1864. When General Grant assumed command of the Union armies, he approved remounting Phillips's men, but that order went the way of the previous year's War Department directive to commission black officers, willfully stranded through bureaucratic inertia. As warmer weather renewed rebel raiding activities, Phillips hoped "to get 1,000 men mounted before the summer passed away." "I have no cavalry," he complained, and he had "to borrow and hire horses even for scouting purposes."[26] Keeping the brigade effectively unmounted meant that contractors rustling Indian cattle, the criminal activities of the company, and the cozy business arrangements of the high command could go unchallenged.

Getting new mounts touched on the standing problem of logistics and supply that dated from the Federals' first attempts to reestablish control in the Indian Territory. At the time participants expected that the people, once restored to their homelands, would resume farming and raising livestock, becoming self-sufficient once again. After the soldiers retook part of the territory, however, the authorities failed to supply what was needed to defend such activities, which left everything there dependent on those long supply trains coming down from Fort Scott. At that point participants still looked to the Federals' seizure of the Arkansas River to open a river route for supplies moving through Little Rock and Fort Smith to Fort Blunt. After this happened, though, the authorities noted that the river would not be deep enough to use until spring. Of course, nothing prevented bringing the supplies by river to Fort Smith and supplying Fort Blunt overland with a much shorter and less vulnerable supply train, but such a course would have required interdepartmental coordination and cooperation.

The river's failure as a route of supply provides a fascinating tale. As early as May, the *Fort Smith New Era* reported the upriver passage of the steamer *Sunny South*, "loaded principally with Indian and sutler goods, belonging to McDonald & Fuller, who have a contract to furnish goods to the Indians up there." While there is no report of any attack on the company supplies, the military goods that would have minimized the Indian dependence on the company never quite traversed the route. Of course, the army did not attempt the passage until mid-June 1864, when it then assigned a mere twenty-six soldiers to escort the *J. R. Williams* and its cargo of flour from Fort Smith to Phillips's brigade. At Pleasant Bluff, near the mouth of the San Bois Creek, Watie's rebels disabled the ship with artillery. Although the Confederates scattered the guards, they lacked wagons to get the supplies safely back to their lines, so they torched the boat with its cargo. Black infantrymen arrived too late to do much more than watch the fire, and the fleeing guards alerted John Ritchie's two hundred Indians at the nearby Salt Works. After this half-hearted and clearly sabotaged attempt, the army authorities declared it "unsafe to attempt to ship supplies to the troops at Fort Blunt by steamboat."[27] The military would renege on its most elementary obligation to its own soldiers in the Indian Territory in order to leave them at the mercies of the company.

The fate of the *J. R. Williams* makes no sense without Confederate foreknowledge. Watie's raiders made quick strikes and almost never burdened themselves by bringing along the big guns. In this case, they dragged them to the right place and the right time to cripple a military supply boat without any apparent concern that unencumbered enemy cavalry might overtake them. In addition, no report of the raiders ever hitting any company boats raises a related set of questions. Whatever the reasons for which others waged the Civil War, for the company and those it had purchased in the military command structure, the conflict had become a struggle to turn the biggest profit. In a setting that fostered black marketing and doing business with the enemy, the capitalist ethos made strange bedfellows.

In terms of the brigade, the issue came to a head in July, when Phillips actually had enough mounted men in the right place to test Blunt's order making rustling a military matter. Even as the army planned its abandonment of Arkansas and the Indian Territory, Captain Henry S. Anderson and a detachment of the Third Indian Home Guard had encountered eleven men, "part Indians, part white men caught with a herd of stolen cattle sixty miles up the Verdigris." Nine of them, hired at five dollars a day, surrendered, while their two bosses tried to escape and were killed. On July 10 Phillips reported that "herds of cattle have been driven out [of the territory] by U.S. soldiers into Kansas."[28] Blandly he informed his astonished superiors that under his orders Indians in army uniform had shot and killed white government contractors or subcontractors.

The very next day Thayer passed on Phillips's request for new mounts to the desk of General Frederick Steele. Thayer's annotations argued that the brigade had been appropriately mounted on ponies, that the army could supply horses only, and that other units had priority on these; he also argued against spending $160,000 to mount the regiments on the verge of being mustered out. With coldly cynical sophistry, he added that the brigade had not demonstrated that they could protect the forage for their mounts.[29] Lacking the courage to buck the trend, Steele simply returned Phillips's letter without comment.

Meanwhile, Captains Anderson and Ta-ma-tus-ta-nuk-ka trailed more rustlers to the supply depots of the U.S. Army at Fort Scott, where they intercepted a Union officer with a group of Osage bringing in 150 head of cattle with Creek brands. After a survey of the herds at Fort Scott, Anderson estimated that contractors had 6,000 to 7,000 head of Creek and Cherokee cattle, more than could have been possible without official army collusion. Witnesses also described the rustlers as being escorted by two cavalry companies under a "Captain" David S. Vittum—though Vittum's rank was actually lieutenant colonel. Phillips surely knew that such a rank and his appointment as provost marshal by Blunt could not have been possible without the involvement of others higher up the chain of command. Much seemed to point to Colonel Charles W. Blair, McDonald's old friend and Fort Scott's commander, who had also been the man ultimately responsible for the systematic tardiness that plagued Phillips's supply train.[30] Perhaps army officials began cooperating with the company to supplement seasonal shortfalls, but the policies served also to accumulate surpluses, as did skimping on the rations sent into the field.

Phillips placed the entire matter before the Lincoln administration. He hoped to get the War Department to remove McDonald and Fuller and force the repeal of Special Order Number Seven. Daniel Ross urged Chief Ross to "second Colonel Phillips in his effort to protect [their] People and Save the Gov't against the greatest fraud of the war" and assured him that that the issue represented "a Fraud such as will startle the world." Back east, Ross made the case and put the matter of official rustling before Edwin M. Stanton and John P. Usher, respectively the secretaries of war and the interior.[31]

Serious measures were needed immediately to make the frontier free for rustling, land fraud, and contract monopoly. On July 30—within a week of Phillips's report on Fort Scott—Thayer's Special Order 117 instructed him to turn command of the brigade over to Stephen H. Wattles and "report in person to . . . head-quarters immediately." Phillips subsequently dropped from the record of the war, clarifying the real lines of authority up through the generals to McDonald and Fuller.[32]

On the heels of Phillips's removal, Wattles got orders to abandon Fort Blunt and the Indian Territory for the third time since the start of the war. The Unionist Arkansas governor Murphy's agitations proved sufficient to thwart army plans to turn his state completely back over to the rebels, however, and Chief Ross went directly to Lincoln over these plans for the Indian Territory. Astonishingly, it seems as though only the last-minute intervention from Washington prevented the abandonment of that vast expanse for which thousands of white, African, and Native Americans had risked all.[33] The army's willingness to throw away its victories in the interest of managerial convenience reflects its institutional disinterest in preventing corruption in its administration of the occupied South.

⌒⌒

With Phillips's arrest all sorts of information about army complicity with private fraud began surfacing. Government contracts were supposed to change every six months, and McDonald and Fuller had supposedly yielded its place to Carney, Stevens, and Company, of Leavenworth, a partnership that included the antebellum enterprise of Robert S. Stevens and Governor Thomas Carney. Reports from the territory and elsewhere, however, indicated that this represented no more than a new name for McDonald and Fuller. Observers had "no question but that the contractors and the Indian agents" had "committed great wrongs against these refugees" and that they were "doing so yet." The rustling of Indian cattle became an open secret: the contractor hired "different operators from Kansas, and several officers" for the enterprise, and the Union general George Sykes thought the involvement of government officials "beyond question," adding that McDonald and Company had gotten control of "all the corn in Southern Kansas" and charged the army between "75 to 100 per cent. above the market." In the elections of 1864, the firm financed and helped elect a number of prominent Kansas Republicans.[34] Once competitors, McDonald and Carney had now become partners, functioning under the protection of the civilian and military authorities.

Keeping the territory vulnerable to profiteering carried with it a high military price. On September 19, in the second battle of Cabin Creek, the Confederates finally seized and burned an insufficiently defended supply train, massacring isolated details of black soldiers along the way. At the same time the Confederate general Price led over 12,000 rebels back into Missouri, forcing the recall of Blunt from western Kansas and leading to a situation involving many of the figures who had fought together along the border and in the Indian Territory. In late October Price's nearly disintegrating army hurried south ahead of Blunt's pursuit, leaving a trail of exhausted livestock and discarded booty into the Indian Territory, where the Confederates forded the Arkansas River near Webber's Falls. Not far away the Federals' Indian Brigade sat helplessly, without the numbers, mounts, and commander needed to delay the rebels until Blunt's arrival.[35] Had it been otherwise, months before Appomattox Blunt himself might have accepted the surrender of the most active Confederate army west of the Mississippi.

General Grant, to his lasting credit, took action when he heard rumors that any of his soldiers were not being regularly fed and supplied. After consultation, Secretary Stanton's War Department sent a trustworthy observer, General Francis Herron, to investigation conditions in the territory. Herron avoided suspicions by sending his reports as personal letters to New Orleans for forwarding to Washington. He reported Fort Smith to be in the hands of the contractors and, "after a tedious trip of three days," found at Fort Blunt "the same influence" that governed at "Fort Smith, and indeed . . . the entire District of the Frontier." (Within days Dick Hinton passed through on his way back to Kansas and testified as to the efficiency of the arrangement, noting the brigade to be "on quarter rations.") The colonel's brother, Major Maxwell Phillips, was present, but Major Foreman had gone north toward Fort Scott, hunting for yet one more inexplicably delayed supply train. Herron thought that, since Phillips's removal, the government had provided "the next thing to nothing" for Fort Blunt, which had been reduced to 1,800 soldiers and "about 6,000 loyal refugee Indians, mostly Creeks."[36] The fall of numbers reflected the desperate decision by Indians, particularly among the Cherokees, to risk returning to what remained of their homes, where they might scavenge for more food than they could get at the fort.

Herron found their old commander back at Fort Smith under arrest. The general wrote that Phillips had been "kept off duty for a month." During that time residents of the territory joined officers of the Indian Home Guards in petitioning to restore him to his command. They charged that Thayer had removed Phillips for spurious reasons in the face of "a large rebel force" at the edges of the territory. Shortly thereafter, noted Herron, Phillips had been "placed under court-martial."[37] Those events further confirmed that well-placed officials in and out of the military had conspired to defraud the government and to betray its most vulnerable peoples.

Behind the scenes, the move to restore Phillips to command gained ground. Herron concluded that business interests had arranged to remove "the best officer they [the Indians] ever had," a man who had "managed matters admirably both for the Government and the Indians." "In my opinion," continued Herron, "he should be ordered back without delay." The former secretary of state William H. Seward, apparently having outgrown some of his earlier positions, praised Phillips's efforts to force the United States to meet its obligations to the Indians in defiance of the contractors. Horace Greeley sent documentation on the case to Lincoln's secretary and added, "I pray you to see that justice be done in the matter of my friend Col. W. A. Phillips." Doing much the same was John L. Scripps, of the old Chicago National Reform Association, who had probably known both Lincoln and Phillips for years. In late October Phillips placed the entire matter before Secretary Stanton, apparently specifying the officials responsible for his removal.[38]

Lincoln concurred but chose to do nothing until he ensured his own reelection. The army restored Phillips to his command on December 29, inspiring Chief Ross to redouble his efforts to remount the Indian Brigade. Phillips "could scarcely get an escort" back to Fort Blunt and feared that his release would allow the grievances to be ignored. He wrote, "I would have preferred to meet and expose the powerful organization that I fear is not dead yet" and "to make needful rules to protect the rights of the Indians."[39]

Phillips returned to duty to find that some of those who had struggled with him to defend the territory against federally licensed thieves as well as Confederates had disappeared. While he had been at Fort Smith, the army had cashiered his Indian detective, Captain Ta-ma-tus-ta-nuk-ka of the First Indian Home Guard. So, too, Captain Anderson of the Third seems to have been driven from the base.[40]

The colonel himself took up where he had left off, sending written protests to any of his superiors he thought might read them. After the July incident when Indian soldiers shot the government's rustlers, Curtis apparently superseded Blunt's order making cattle theft a military matter and referred it instead to local civil courts, which were never going to exist in the territory until they could be protected. Then, too, the Treasury Department declined to exercise its prerogative of investigating the flow of government money. Phillips described the "systematic and wholesale" robbery of Indians by the company as "encroachments on the rights of the people of the Indian Nation." "The Indian soldiers," he suggested, were "more to be trusted for their own protection than others." He insisted, however, that they could not stop rustling "without a cavalry force" and added, "as the country to be protected is very extensive, it appears almost impossible to put a stop to it without some co-operation from the department above."[41]

While required to use the McDonald firm for supplies, Phillips persisted in exposing its doings. Confirming Sykes's impressions, Phillips traced the flow of corn back and forth between the territory and Kansas, sold and resold at ever higher levels of profit for the contractors. He also resumed documentation of the rustling, which directly implicated government officials. Finally, on February 13, 1865, his efforts brought about an order that both acknowledged widespread thievery and again remanded rustlers to the military authorities.[42] This rather belatedly vindicated the conduct of the Indian soldiers and their commander who had confronted rustling contractors the previous year.

As conditions improved, Phillips responded to the Creeks' long-standing agitation for military protection in their own nation. With the active support of the Cherokee leaders, he gathered the Creek refugees not already at Fort Blunt. As the winter ended, detachments of the brigade escorted the Creeks across the Verdigris and the Arkansas and into their lands, and they established a permanent garrison at Tullahassee Mission to protect the returnees.[43] Having suffered immensely, the people of Opothleyahola had, at long last, come home.

Under the protection of the brigade at Fort Blunt, plans for something like the "Lane Expedition" reappeared in its final form. In March 1865 Phillips sent the Union scout (and former Confederate) James L. Clark south with a detachment of men to recruit Unionists in his native Texas in preparation for an invasion by Federals.[44] Before the Texans were in a position to raise the specter of revolution in the state, the war ended.

Chief Ross and the Indian leaders in Washington clarified conditions as well. On March 12 Secretary Usher responded to Ross's claims on the Cherokee annuities by citing alleged Cherokee indebtedness to McDonald and Fuller, which opened the door for Ross to introduce evidence of the company's misconduct and its links to high-ranking Union officials, evinced in Herron's report implicating OIA superintendent Coffin. Ross confided to allies that the last particularly caused "much *alarm* and *excitement* in the wigwam." The chief also petitioned the Senate and the House and aired Indian grievances to Secretary Stanton, Secretary Seward, General Grant, or anyone who might listen. With other Cherokee leaders, the old chief urged the military removal of the company in all its manifestations, the reorganization and remounting of the brigade, the establishment of a military department separate from Kansas, and reinforcements sufficient to reoccupy the entire territory.[45] Officials ducked these discussions, likely concerned that they might come to the attention of President Lincoln, who had been preoccupied but never indifferent to the Indians' appeals.

Far greater plans were afoot. Railroad investors, particularly, wanted the treaties set aside and boundaries within the Indian Territory renegotiated so as to remove Indians in their way, settling them elsewhere in the West. Many prominent Kansans, including Lane and Blunt, had invested heavily in questionable titles to what remained Indian lands in Kansas. In a congressional discussion of Indian appropriations, Lane urged adoption of the "British system" of reservations used in Canada. This would allow the removal of Indians from Lane's own state and charter what a Minnesota colleague rightly called "a great monopoly" like the Hudson Bay Company. "The sectional conflict," as one historian wrote, "masked motives of land sharks and politicians who lusted after the nearly ten million acres of Indian land in the eastern part of Kansas."[46] Fashionably chalking up Lane's proposal to some kind of generic racism minimizes its direct implications for his state, his entrepreneurial friends, and his own pocketbook.

As previously explained, removing the Indians from Kansas required annulling the antebellum treaties defining the boundaries of the nations within the Indian Territory. The Confederacy provided the necessary pretense by imposing its 1861 treaties on those peoples. A compliant U.S. Congress had authorized the president to declare the antebellum treaties abrogated by the Indians; although Lincoln repeatedly stated such a course to be unjustified, he would not remain president forever.

Nevertheless, the proponents of the new policy had proceeded for several years as though the president had never said anything on the subject. The OIA commissioner William P. Dole had been negotiating treaties to move the major tribes from Kansas to the Indian Territory, assuming that the boundaries there would be redrawn. Worse, Iowa's Senator James Harlan, who agreed with Lane's reservation strategy, became the new secretary of the interior on March 9, 1865, and soon replaced Dole with Dennis N. Cooley, an even more ruthless functionary.[47]

The triumph of the Federals' arms in April and May 1865 ended any pressing need to "think anew," as Lincoln had advised. The largest Confederate forces began surrendering on April 9 in Virginia and continued until the Trans-Mississippi gave up on May 26. Even then, General Jo Shelby took the remnants of his Missouri brigade across the Rio Grande into Mexico on June 3, while Watie's withered command remained at large until his July surrender at Doaksville. By then Lincoln was dead, the fate of former slaves preoccupied Congress, and the future of the people of the Indian Territory concerned very few with any real power. The most prominent of those few tended to be capitalists, investors, and speculators.

During September 8–21, 1865, a hit squad of U.S. functionaries hosted a conference at Fort Smith. Without any discussion, the authorities presented to the assembled chiefs of the Osage, Quapaw, Seneca, Shawnee, Wyandotte, Creek, Cherokee, Seminole, Chickasaw, and Choctaw the government's decision that the Indians had nullified their treaties. This essentially celebrated the North's defeat of the secession by declaring the chiefdoms of its allies illegitimate and those of the secessionists legitimate. The U.S. officials collectively specified that they wanted the new treaties to include concessions of land for railroad rights-of-way, as well as for the relocation of Indians from Kansas. As they had with removal and secession, Watie and his kindred spirits readily accepted the new edicts of the white government and joined together in brushing aside their rivals—that is, the very Indians whose sacrifices in lives and property for the survival of the United States had been proportionally greater than those of any other Americans. Now, however, having given so much to protect the Union and destroy slavery, they found themselves repudiated by the federal government in league with the former secessionists.[48] The Fort Smith directives, which were said to have left old Chief John Ross to die a broken man, broke the promise and the very existence of entire nations.

An egalitarian vision of what an American civilization without slavery might become contributed to the survival of the United States and had made that survival significant in universal human terms. Nevertheless, the U.S. authorities who could not keep faith with Indians would not do so fully over the next decade with the newly freed black people across the South or, ultimately, with any Americans unable to pay the price for it. In the absence of that vision of universal human significance, the American republic deferred the basic decisions about its future to sterile interests defined simply by the imperatives of the soulless marketplace. That can accord no worth to what is genuinely and literally priceless.

Conclusion

Years after the war, a former slave named Tom W. Woods explained its outcome, visible in the possibilities posed by the presidency of the railsplitter Abraham Lincoln. "Lady," he told a WPA interviewer in the 1930s, "if de nigger hadn't been set free dis country wouldn't ever been what it is now! Poor white folks wouldn't never had a chance. De slave holders had most of de money and de land and dey wouldn't let de poor white folks have a chance to own any land or anything else to speak of." He continued, "White folks as well as niggers profited by emancipation. Lincoln was a friend to all poor white folks as well as black ones and if he could a' lived things would a' been different for ever'body."[1] Arguing that Lincoln's war had broad social implications, Woods could have added that the president, who repeatedly declared that the Indian nations had not broken their treaties, was replaced by those, North and South, eager to declare old arrangements abrogated and open a new round of expropriations.

Historical memory results from a consensus among those with power enough to shape it and vested interests great enough to exercise that power. The experiences of John Brown's body of followers in the Civil War demonstrate how that power fell unevenly on different peoples. In racial terms, ruling circles aimed most immediately at extracting more resources from those nonwhites who had them, the Native Americans of the Indian Territory. Having long-standing experience at pitting groups against one another, they offered expanded rights to African Americans partly at the expense of the Indians and ultimately dependent on white capitalists. In the end, black empowerment in the territory would be no more permanent than elsewhere in the South, while creditors and the railroads gained everything they needed.

⌐⌐

Constructing the historical memory of the Civil War as a sectional conflict represented just such a consensus of the powerful. Clearly demonstrating this was the fact—evident in everything from representation in the Confederate government to the number of stars on its flag—that the secessionists claimed thirteen states, contemptuously disregarding the will of Missouri's and Kentucky's white citizens. In the end, elite interests, North and South, shaped memories of a sectional conflict that regularly and systematically misrepresented the Confederacy as consisting of only eleven states, which both minimized the apparent scale of the rebellion and made its legitimacy more plausible.

Our understanding of the Civil War also largely ignores the importance of the sectional differences of East and West. Something like Tom Woods's sense of the way historical memory belied experience may have flickered across the mind of the former Confederate general Jo Shelby as he rubbernecked his way through the streets of Richmond in July 1896. The authorities were dedicating a monument to Jefferson Davis, beginning what became Monument Row, commemorating the leading figures of "the Lost Cause." Within that mythology, Virginia and eastern memories prevailed; the acknowledgment of anything west of the Shenandoah Valley seemed pretty much an afterthought. Shelby and his Missourians, who had gone into Mexico rather than surrender their allegiance to the Confederacy, found themselves virtually lost not only in the streets of its capital but in the byways of its memory.[2]

This historical memory of a sectional conflict between North and South—centered on the romantic clash of professional military leaders in the East—became as essential to the chest-thumping triumphalism of the Grand Army of the Republic as to the dewy-eyed romance of the "the Lost Cause." Official realities aside, the shooting war actually began in the West, among civilians, and events in the Indian Territory had determined its nature as "total war" from its inception. The postwar federal betrayal of the loyal Indians foreshadowed the fate of all other Southerners not in—or allied to—the planter class.

Most essentially, this constructed memory of a clash between geographic coalitions of states missed the social dimensions of the conflict. Even within the officially sanctioned total of eleven seceded states, official and quasi-official policies denied Southern Unionists the postwar honors lavishly bestowed on their formerly secessionist masters or on conscripts of either sides. Governments denied pensions, and the Grand Army of the Republic denied memberships to Union veterans who had earlier performed any Confederate service, including members of home guard or militia units or conscripts. Even acknowledging the decisive contribution rebellious slaves made to Union victory required recasting them as dutiful soldiers. Southern communities that had produced more Union than Confederate volunteers—something with no parallel in the North—raised statues to the mythological "Lost Cause" and today may find their Civil War reenactments crippled by shortages of people willing to wear the blue, even for a day. This memory of a sectional—rather than a social—conflict made possible a later and more fanciful revisioning of the Confederacy as a celebration of geographic multiculturalism, reflecting the will of nonwhite Southerners as well as whites.

In reality, no other group sacrificed as much for the survival and triumph of the United States as did its Indian allies. A reasonable estimate suggests that of the 3,530 known members of the Federals' Indian Brigade, fully 1,018 died. Although the Cherokee had begun to recover from the devastation of forced removal, the Civil War probably halved their population to roughly 14,000, and the proportional loss among other groups generally exceeded that of the Cherokee. The war in the Indian Territory widowed most adult women and orphaned most of the children.[3] The regular ignoring or slighting of such a level of loss should certainly raise questions about the perspective from which we shape and process historical memory.

Postwar Indian reform offered some initial promise that the Native Americans' contribution might not be entirely smothered. The scandalous massacre at Sand Creek had moved radical congressmen such as Ignatius Donnelly and George W. Julian to take up the cause, and in March 1865 Senator James Doolittle secured the appointment of a committee to review various plans. Indian reform became a point of agitation for figures as different from one another as were John Beeson, Henry Whipple, Wendell Phillips, Henry Ward Beecher, and Peter Cooper. After a few more atrocities under the administration of Andrew Johnson, U.S. Grant came to power with a "peace policy" that smoldered into a "humanitarian" and "philanthropic" paternalism.[4] This offered a reservation version of the "settlement house" to ease personal assimilation into white society, which suited the fantasy that the brutalization would be temporary and that its duration would be in the hands of individual Indians.

In the end, the opportunities for further postwar dispossession made the Civil War seem like little more than a brief hiatus in the centuries-long subjugation of the Indians. Some who had served alongside Indians in the war turned their skills at conquest toward resolving "the Indian problem." These included not only James G. Blunt but also John M. Schofield, Samuel R.

Curtis, and Francis J. Herron, as well as John M. Thayer, who went back to Nebraska, where he became one of the state's first U.S. senators and later its governor, a position he held in the Wyoming Territory, too.

Robert W. Furnas, the commander of the first Indian Expedition, became the governor of Nebraska after commanding at the "battle" of Whitestone Hill. What he called "the severest chastisement ever inflicted upon Indians" later inspired his recollection: "The battle now raged with great fury for some time on both sides, the enemy successively by a desperate charge attempting my right and left flanks, but they were repelled with slaughter. They fell in every direction in front of my line by the unerring aim of my brave soldiers, who, both officers and men, fought with the coolness and courage of veterans, exposed as they were to a galling fire from the enemy the whole time." He recalled the butchering of a village in a language more appropriate to an account of Gettysburg. Having resisted the imperial and racial imperatives of King Cotton, he famously declared "Corn is King," and this new monarch of the market had racial imperatives of its own. Governor Furnas predicted that irrigation and new crops would virtually reengineer climate on the plains. As if in a biblical response, clouds of grasshoppers descended on the state, consuming everything, including Furnas's nursery, and were not particularly helpful to his administration's prospects for reelection.[5]

The logic of conquest generated over centuries became evident in the career of Joseph K. Hudson, one of the old John Brown League. After serving as a major in the First Missouri Colored—the Sixty-second USCT—Hudson found himself torn in civilian life between the concerns of the farmers in the emerging Grange movement and his loyalty to the Republicans, with the latter ultimately prevailing. Hudson reentered the army during the Spanish-American War of 1898–99, later served in the Philippines, and rose to brigadier general in the service of the new American empire.[6] So it was that the reunified nation embraced the antebellum aspirations of Harry Titus and the *filibusteros*.

Ironically, the victims of historical memory are often conscripted to help lock the mythology into place. The postwar betrayal allowed the relocation of many Indians into the territory, creating a constituency whose legitimacy rested on the betrayal. Then, too, opening the territory to white settlement in 1889 and its 1908 admission to the Union as the state of Oklahoma brought legions of southern whites and organized Confederate veterans into the area. Responsibility for antebellum injustices to the Indians was ascribed to a Union leadership that had never actually held power, a move that recast individuals such as Stand Watie and John Jumper as the real "rebels," fighting the injustices of the white power structure alongside Douglas Cooper, Jefferson Davis, and others. Mythologies about the Indians became integrated into the Lost Cause long before those about "black Confederates."

In many respects scholars otherwise sensitive to the plight of the Indians contributed to this bizarre posthumous integration of Indians into an imagined multicultural Confederacy and the vilification of the Union, particularly in the treatment of the refugee problem. Regardless of her intentions, in 1914 Annie Able described the refugee encampments in Kansas and Missouri as "concentration camps," which implied they were something like the forced British internment of Boer civilians during the then recent war in South Africa, which they were clearly not. Despite the fact that usage in the Nazi era and World War II further redefined the term to mean extermination camps, later students of the subject have repeated its use, with no caveats against its almost certain misunderstanding, one actually describing the Creek refugees as being "herded into death camps" by wartime Union authorities. To clarify this academic bid for Indian integration into the Lost Cause, scholars have asserted that Unionists engaged in greater depredations upon loyal Indians than did the Confederates and seized on Indians—as well as "black Confederates"—to assert a multicultural secessionism so more acceptable to the modern admirers of the Confederacy.[7]

Concerns about the former slaves and freed blacks became the vehicle for further dispossession of the Indians and a vigorous new racialization of postwar American life without slavery. It seems terribly dishonest and negligent not to question the sincerity of many political leaders. One of the loudest of these, Jim Lane—an overtly racist Democrat won to the antislavery cause—once suggested that his white constituents back in Kansas would benefit from the aspirations of black runaways by using them as cheap farm labor, "if the contrabands hereabout could be distributed throughout Southern Kansas."[8] Such a "distribution" scheme shows freedom fostered on one side of a surveyor's line only in order to impose cheap, implicitly forced labor on the other.

Still, the Lane organ—the *Leavenworth Daily Conservative*—realized the merits of distinguishing (however inconsistently at first) between Indian and black soldiers, to the great detriment of the former. Political necessity moderated the extent to which wagon boss Peck would have to limit the racism of the antebellum regular army. Blacks, like whites, would be regarded, at least temporarily, as "the true American soldier," while the Indian would not be. In short, Lane's solution allowed for the elevation of blacks while sustaining the treatment of Indians—all Indians—as conquered enemies. Because of this, the elevation of blacks was only a temporary means to an end.

Federal authorities forced the Indian nations to cede citizenship to African Americans with a rigor never evident in their dealings with the white planters and required land and material concessions never demanded of whites. This should, at least, have been a great assistance to little Mary Grayson and her family as they sought to rebuild their lives (as they made their way north through the Seminole Nation to the Creek Agency, Jake Perryman, now a discharged Union veteran, rejoined them).[9] For the most part, however, blacks in the territory tended to become indebted to white investors, increasingly sinking into the general impoverishment of their Indian neighbors—for which frustrated Indians often came to blame blacks.

This can hardly be disentangled from the general terror about the dynamics of the war. Certainly the generally misnamed *Daily Conservative* mocked those more reluctant to put down treason as fearful that the process might "make a disturbance, give us a bad name and—'hurt the sale of property.'" Nevertheless, the *Conservative* assumed that a war for freedom would not have a priority over economic development and profit making. When wartime conditions seemed to do so, it began to fret, editorializing, "The relations of capital and labor in the United States are completely reversed. Capital is the slave of labor and a condition of things results which threatens serious detriment to various important interests." Wage demands might be justifiable, the paper conceded, but unionism tended "to dictate to the employer a series of rules for the mechanical operation of his affairs, independent of that which . . . immediately relates to themselves, and directly interfering with the natural rights of others." Lane's people even portrayed labor militancy as threatening violence to the imperatives of the marketplace comparable to that of "the present fiendish rebellions." With notable inconsistency, respectable views inspired military interventions against strikes, which Lincoln had frankly ascribed to the "social influence" of businessmen on his generals.[10]

Following the official betrayal of the Indians, when the Reconstruction teetered on the fate of President Andrew Johnson's administration, Lane simply switched sides again, pretty much as John Brown had warned he would. Lane had voiced radical concerns very well when he thought they served his purposes, but no principle ever carried more weight with him than did his own ambitions. He proved quite willing to ignore the rights of blacks as thoroughly as he had earlier ignored those of the Indians or white Missourians. When he found that his abandonment of the radicals did not purchase his reintegration into the ever more moderate power structure, he made pointless overtures to the betrayed radicals, who ignored him. After sinking deeper into depression, Lane twice attempted to take his own life, succeeding on the second try, July 1, 1866.

Lane's old ally, Congressman Martin F. Conway, a former founder of the national printers' union, also repudiated his wartime radicalism to support Johnson. As recompense, he won an 1866 appointment as U.S. consul to Marseilles. Thirteen years later he returned to a Washington that neither appreciated his achievements nor concerned itself with his motives. On a public street he shot and wounded former senator Samuel Pomeroy, who, Conway ranted, had ruined him and his family. Having long lost touch with who he was, Conway entered St. Elizabeth's Hospital Asylum for the Insane and died there in February 1882.

James G. Blunt should have emerged as one of the great radical heroes of the war. An ardent advocate of John Brown's egalitarian principles, he had helped to arm and organize nonwhite regiments, led them into desperate battles against long odds, and despite his lack of professional military training, established a brilliant military record. His personal loyalties to Lane, however, required his turning his back on the "civilized" Indians in the territory, ultimately becoming involved in extending the railroad into the area. After helping to inaugurate the wartime slaughter of the "savages" on the Plains, he apparently became so adept at the butchery of war that he forgot why he had begun to engage in it. The logic of his position moved him quickly. While he continued to advocate black suffrage, he reversed himself on many matters, even participating in a Kansas meeting against woman suffrage.[11] Mercifully spared much self-awareness, Blunt died a year before Conway, but also as an inmate at St. Elizabeth's.

The failure of radicalism in wartime Unionism and the triumph of racism proved profitable. Military officers such as Charles W. Blair and civilian officeholders such as Thomas Carney worked with businessmen such as Alexander McDonald, Robert S. Stevens, and Percy Fuller. As one historian wrote, "To say there were conflicts of interest is merely to scratch the surface." They arranged to rustle cattle from hungry Indians only to ration a portion of that beef back to its robbed owners, grudgingly, irregularly, and at exorbitantly fixed prices.[12]

The results proved very lucrative. McDonald had become involved in banking in Arkansas in 1863, which put him in a position from which he could later reconstruct banking in the state. Upon Arkansas's readmission to the Union, the state's legislature sent him to the U.S. Senate; by the 1880s he was involved in the railroads and moved to New York. Stevens got 52,000 acres of Sac and Fox lands and 500 tracts in what had been the reserve of the New York Indians before shifting his operations to the Indian Territory, acting as the general manager for the Missouri, Kansas, and Texas Railroad, which plowed its ruthless course through what had been Indian land. By then Fuller had moved on to a promising new field of operations in the Southwest, where he began vigorously fleecing the Navajo.[13] The wartime concerns of the business community simply dragooned the government and the army into their service.

Phillips believed that, under these circumstances, "the interests of the government and the interests of these people fall at once into the hands of those rapacious devourers." As it had with slavery, officialdom simply set aside the claims of justice or, more accurately, redefined justice to serve what Chief John Ross called the "mercenary interests of the Great Combination, of Capitalists." The "influence of the great monied Capitalists," said Phillips, formulated the "unrighteous Policy" imposed on "loyal Cherokee People and others on the western frontier." Phillips listed the activities of "an official or moneyed aristocracy" along with those of a slaveholding one as "crimes against the Republic."[14] Moreover, Americans such as Phillips or Ross predicted that the institutions, policies, and procedures developed for the exploitation of nonwhites would invariably be used for the exploitation of all.

⸺

Perhaps most striking is the number of participants in the events along the wartime border who did not abandon their earlier principles. After the war, the aging individuals who had lived through the border troubles had become as concerned with their assessments of their past as with the future they would never see. Their failures to shape historical understanding began with John Brown himself, who left a record of his purposes and plans with Augustus Wattles and James Montgomery. When Montgomery died in the winter of 1871–72, Wattles remembered the unofficial archives kept in a bearskin trunk and hurried to Montgomery's home, where he found that Mrs. Montgomery had burned the contents of the trunk, along with other of her husband's papers. Wattles himself followed Montgomery to the grave a few years later.[15]

John Ritchie involved himself in philanthropic pursuits in later years. At Topeka he donated land for Washburn College, a free cemetery, and homes for blacks. He also helped to revive the agitation for woman suffrage and to launch the Greenback-Labor movement in the state, in which former wartime governor Samuel Crawford participated. At his death in 1887 Ritchie left behind a well-developed and prosperous community that tended to forget that his idea of progress ran deeper.[16]

There were many other examples. Edward Daniels resettled in Virginia; joined the International Workingmen's Association, which Hinton organized out of Washington; and battled first for radical Reconstruction and then for Greenback-Labor politics. The Indian agent Peter P. Elder also helped launch the Greenback movement, established ties to the socialists, and became the Kansas representative in the leadership of the International Working People's Association, an anarcho-communist group of the mid-1880s most famous for its involvement in Chicago's Haymarket affair. Old William Vanzandt Barr later moved to Chicago, played an active role in the Knights of Labor, and ran on the United Labor Party ticket after Haymarket.

The more famous successor to this third party among the farmers, the People's or Populist Party, found leadership among the four Vincent brothers, the scions of John Brown's antebellum Iowa hosts. The grasshopper problems that plagued Furnas created a political movement in western Nebraska headed by Thomas H. Tibbles. In the course of touring to solicit relief, Tibbles found himself stranded in Omaha, where striking printers hired him to edit their cooperative newspaper. His subsequent work on the pro-Greenback *Independent* eventually led to his 1904 nomination for vice president on the Populist ticket. Nonetheless, history most clearly recalls Tibbles as the tirelessly militant and somewhat successful proponent of Indian rights.[17]

By the end of 1874, three of "the Secret Six" who had supported and nurtured John Brown's schemes had died. After a virulent defense of John Brown, Theodore Parker had succumbed to consumption in 1860. George Luther Stearns defended Brown's actions before the Senate committee investigating Harpers Ferry and worked tirelessly for emancipation through the war, his efforts contributing to his death in 1874, the same year in which Gerrit Smith died. Parker's association with a range of antebellum reform movements was well established, but Stearns's ties to the Fourierist movement and Smith's ties to the working-class land reformers were particularly strong. Samuel Gridley Howe, who focused on the education of the blind, deaf, and mentally ill, died in 1876; his wife, Julia Ward Howe, penned "Battle Hymn of the Republic," which carried the abolitionist "John Brown's Body" into the institutional heart of American music. The two men remaining of the six, Thomas Wentworth Higginson and Franklin Benjamin Sanborn, lived well into the twentieth century. In addition to advocating many other reforms in their long lives, both became associated with the socialist Nationalist Clubs of the early 1890s, inspired by Edward Bellamy's novel *Looking Backward*.

Hugh Cameron, the Kansas radical in the Second Arkansas Cavalry, later explained, "I wanted to be a seer so I buried myself here in my work. Some day the vision may come." In 1870 he helped to organize the state's Workingmen's Party, over which William V. Barr presided. Cameron also published the *Useful Worker* and periodically turned up on the fringes of the farmers' movements before he moved into a dugout shelter in the bluffs outside Lawrence and took up the life of a hermit. Before his death in 1908, the old Republican had seen bids for political power by the Greenbackers, the Populists, and the Socialists, but it seems he never quite saw his vision taking form.[18]

Richard Josiah Hinton remained a harsh critic of government-sponsored exploitation of western lands for profit and warned of the long-term impact of capitalist development in the West. He ended the war a lieutenant colonel of the Eighty-third USCT, and he immediately resumed his journalistic crusades. After touring the defeated former Confederacy, he agitated for unrestricted black suffrage and the impeachment of President Johnson before performing various assignments to assist the administration of President U.S. Grant. He also organized American sections of the International Workingmen's Association, or the "First International," which Karl Marx and others had founded in London during the war. He later said, "The efforts of the Liberty Leagues and Party, of Free Soilers, Conscience Whigs, etc., can be run parallel with the struggle of Greenbackers, Silverties and [Farmers] Alliance nominations."[19] Groping toward a solution to the problems posed by a system centered on the needs of firms such as McDonald and Fuller to turn the greatest possible profit in the shortest time, Hinton went on to become a leading spokesman for American socialism.

The fate of William Addison Phillips mirrored that of the cause he espoused. After obtaining his commission, he had repeatedly led his regiment into battle, been wounded, and had horses shot from beneath him. Along with his brigade he had advanced deep into enemy territory, captured key installations, won entire enemy units to the Union army, and defended them with brilliance and originality, confounding forces much larger than his own, never losing an engagement, and rarely retiring from the field before the enemy. To all this should be added his recruiting work, his construction of a civilian intelligence network extending over hundreds of miles, and his subverting the allegiance of thousands of enemy soldiers. The army and the government, which generally awarded promotions, medals, acknowledgments and encouragements for accomplishments such as these, accorded none of them to Phillips, who did not even receive one of the largely pro forma brevet brigadierships doled out at the war's end, as did Stephen H. Wattles and John Ritchie.

Phillips, perhaps like old revolutionaries anywhere, tended to cling to the party he had seen make a revolution despite what he acknowledged to be its failings. Serving several terms in Congress, he continued to espouse the old social reformism of the antebellum and war years. Despite his persistent radicalism, Phillips mistrusted the Kansas Greenbackers and Populists, many of whom hypocritically urged the federal government to pry open the Indian Territory to white settlement. Having served as legal counsel to the Cherokee Nation, he drew closer to it after his wife's death and eventually remarried into it. By Cherokee law, his marriage to Anna B. Stapler, a relative of the Ross and Hicks families, made Phillips a member of one of the Indian nations he had sought to protect in the war. When Henry George's *Progress and Poverty* appeared, Phillips and his new wife set to work on *Labor, Land, and Law*, published in 1885. A solid restatement of old land-reform arguments, it bore the subtitle *A Search for the Missing Wealth of the Working Poor*. As did Hinton, the Phillipses echoed the traditional Indian concern for the impact of commerce on the natural world of the West.[20]

Hinton and Phillips—the revolutionary socialist and the Republican congressman—seem to have remained friends after the war. They had confidence that each shared the other's fondest hopes for the country, and for each, like so much they had learned to look beyond, the label the other chose was only skin deep. Phillips, who had challenged the immutability of "color caste" decades before, remained interested in Hinton's pointed question asked of their century: "Have we still to learn that Freedom belongs to Man—to Humanity—and not alone to favored portions or races thereof?"[21]

In 1893 the generation that most readily praised the strivings for freedom would impose Jim Crow laws and invent social sciences to define the boundaries of freedom. That year Frederick Jackson Turner, one of the new professional historians, issued his famous thesis emphasizing geographic and environmental considerations as determining factors that create racial injustice and social inequalities as matters of course.

Both Phillips and Hinton had long realized that the ongoing struggle over the future of that expanding frontier had led the nation to the brink of self-destruction. Phillips died at old Fort Gibson in 1893, while visiting his in-laws amid the sights of his wartime brush with real power. Published during the same year, Hinton's *John Brown and His Men* retraced the western frontier's road to Harpers Ferry based on his recollections and interviews with Phillips and others.

Hinton survived another eight years and spent considerable effort trying to preserve the memory of those who had gone before. In 1899 those who had secretly buried John Brown's comrades almost forty years earlier helped quietly to disinter the bones, moving them in trunks, while others retrieved the remains of those buried at Perth Amboy. Professor Orin G. Libby of the University of Wisconsin, a historian of contemporary Agrarian protest, escorted the trunks from Virginia to North Elba, New York, where Brown was buried. Hinton spoke at the short ceremony of August 30, recalling each of the ten men whose bones were placed in a single coffin alongside their leader. Two years later Hinton himself died on a research trip to England, pursuing Brown's connections to the revolutionary movement in Europe.[22] In the end, the century that inspired and partly realized the hopes of that small circle of determined radicals faded before a future of possibilities immeasurably richer for their having passed this way.

Such efforts had an unexpected ally. Publicly present to constitute the historical memory of the Lost Cause, Jo Shelby remained as individually fearless and thoughtful as he had been as a mounted Confederate raider. Even as he visited Richmond, he described the cause for which they had entered Kansas as "damnable." "I had no business there," he told one interviewer. "I ought to have been shot there and John Brown was the only man who knew it and would have done it. I say John Brown was right." He even suggested that, should Virginia wish to honor its most neglected benefactor, it should raise a statue of John Brown. When Shelby later took up his duties as a U.S. marshal in Kansas City, he hired a black deputy.[23] The history experienced and shaped by individuals often takes unpredictable turns.

Certainly post–World War II realities required better explanations from a historical memory that had accorded only the most marginal role to John Brown and his people, as it had to Tom Paine in the original American Revolution. Still, these radicals' views about standards of institutional legitimacy would remain just as unacceptable. Their aspirations would remain as invisible as the Indian soldiers some of them commanded in the Civil War.

The achievements of the "Second American Revolution" were real enough, but the struggle to maintain the integrity of the republic required the military power and institutional centralization many Unionists feared. The pragmatic course built on the antebellum decades of political domination by the cotton planters. Custom ultimately outweighed "utopian" ideas. The strategy of military conquest triumphed over republican revolution in the South. American "free labor" left a workforce subjugated to a monied aristocracy. In a sense, the rest of American history turned on one question: would ruling circles use the centralized state in their self-interest, as the Founders and their nineteenth-century republican admirers anticipated, or for the promotion of egalitarian social justice? The politics of liberation had only as much room as the Napoleonic conquest might win, and the latter drew strength from the logistics of convenience, the legacy of white supremacy, and the economics of companies, such as McDonald and Fuller, that thrived on both shortages and racism.

In the end, the responses of the little multiracial army that fought on July 17, 1863, reflected a certain wisdom. The veterans of no other battle of similar importance allowed the scene of their combat to remain unmarked. Although Honey Springs Depot remained in use for many years, the exact location of the fighting disappeared into the farmland to its north to await its relocation by metal detectors and archaeologists. As the veterans of Gettysburg or Shiloh or Newtonia or Prairie Grove returned to survey and mark those fields, the men who had battled at Honey Springs knew what they had won there.[24] In this reflexive act of protest, John Brown's body of followers and the veterans they had led declined to collaborate in creating yet another park for officially constructed historical memory. They chose to keep their hopes unconfined by any reservation.

Notes

ABBREVIATIONS

The following abbreviations are used throughout the notes.

BUSAF *Blacks in the United States Armed Forces: Basic Documents*, ed. Morris J. Mac-
Gregor and Bernard C. Nalty, 13 vols. (Wilmington, Del.: Scholarly Resources, 1977).

OR *The War of the Rebellion; A Compendium of the Official Records of the Union
and Confederate Armies, Published under the direction of the . . . Secretary of
War . . .*, 70 vols. in 128 (Washington, D.C.: GPO, 1880–1901).

PCJR *The Papers of Chief John Ross*, ed. Gary E. Moulton, 2 vols. (Norman: University of Oklahoma Press, 1984–85).

SOR *Supplement to the Official Records of the Union and Confederate Armies*, ed.
Janet B. Hewett, Noah Andre Trudeau, and Bryce A. Suderow, 83 vols. in
three parts to date (Wilmington, N.C.: Broadfoot, 1994).

INTRODUCTION

1. Lt. Col. John Bowles to Judson, July 20, James G. Blunt to John M. Schofield, July 26, Blunt to Lt. Col. Wm. T. Campbell, July 19, Henry Hopkins to William A. Phillips, July 21, 1863, in *OR*, 22 (pt. 1): 448, 449, 456, 453; James M. Williams in *BUSAF*, 2:49–50, 58; Bowles's report repr. as doct. 27 in *BUSAF*, vol. 2; Wiley Britton, *The Civil War on the Border*, 2 vols. (New York: G. P. Putnam's Sons, 1899), 2:120; Robert M. Peck, "Wagon-Boss and Mule-Mechanic," *National Tribune*, September 8, 1904, p. 8. ("Our cavalry did not come into the fight, as they were guarding the flanks" ["Later from Fort Gibson," *Leavenworth Daily Conservative*, July 31, 1863, p. 2].) See see also chapter 5.

2. Williams to T. J. Anderson, Jan. 1, 1866, repr. as doct. 28 in *BUSAF*, 2:57, and qtd. from 65; William A. Phillips, "Kansas History," *Collections of the Kansas Historical Society* 4 (1886–90): 359.

3. By the war's close, Kansas had recruited 2,080 blacks; Arkansas, 5,526; and Missouri, 8,344.

4. Early in 1863 the brigade defended the Cherokee National Council, which appointed Lieutenant Colonel Lewis Downing acting principal chief in the absence of Chief Ross and sent Captains James McDaniel and Thomas Pegg to assist Ross in promoting their cause in Washington. Their quest at the U.S. capital proved the longest and most trying campaign of their service; McDaniel died there, his remains to be later joined at Arlington National Cemetery by those of by Captain James S. Vann (Craig W. Gaines, *The Confederate Cherokees: John Drew's Regiment of Mounted

Rifles [Baton Rouge: Louisiana State University Press, 1989], 121, 122; Morris L. Wardell, *A Political History of the Cherokee Nation, 1838–1907* (Norman: University of Oklahoma Press, 1938), 172, 173, 174–75. The modest official figure for the Indian Home Guards is usually given as 3,530, but the peculiar way the regiments recruited makes 4,000 to 5,000 more likely. In addition, several companies and regiments of other Federal units, notably Kansas cavalry, were Indian in composition.

5. Where earlier views correctly identified racism as institutional policies and practices, this new perspective makes racism the mere consensus among individuals of the majority race, to be addressed when whites repudiate their "whiteness." This not only makes the essential discussion of race something about the whites but also embraces the most conservative assumptions about an individual's power to reshape the institutions, market forces, and class relations that frame our social existence. But it never really worked.

CHAPTER 1: THE SHADOW OF JOHN BROWN

1. Phillips interviews originally in the *Atlantic Monthly* 44 (Dec. 1879): 738–44 (repr. in various other sources); Mrs. O. E. Morse, "Sketch of the Life and Works of Augustus Wattles," *Kansas Historical Collection, 1926–1928* 17 (1928): 298–99; David S. Reynolds, *John Brown, Abolitionist: The Man Who Killed Slavery, Sparked the Civil War, and Seeded Civil Rights* (New York: Knopf, 2005), 15, 192, 502–3.

2. Source A-195-209, in U.S. Bureau of the Census, *The Statistical History of the United States: From Colonial Times to the Present* (New York: Basic Books, 1976), 24–37; Russel K. Hickman, "Speculative Activities of the Emigrant Aid Company," *Kansas Historical Quarterly* 4 (Aug. 1935): 235–67; Albert Castel, *A Frontier State at War: Kansas, 1861–1865* (Westport, Conn.: Greenwood, 1979), 10; Morse, "Sketch of Augustus Wattles," 296–97.

3. Castel, *Frontier State*, 14; David Dary, *More True Tales of Old-Time Kansas* (Lawrence: University Press of Kansas, 1987), 274–77; T. F. Robley, *History of Bourbon County, Kansas* (Fort Scott: the author, 1894), 110. See also Richard J. Hinton, "The Suffering in Kansas," *Liberator*, January 4, 1861, p. 3.

4. Castel, *Frontier State*, 13–14.

5. John Bowles, *The Stormy Petrel: An Historical Romance* (New York: A. Lovell; London: Walter Scott, 1892), 83, 80–81, 109. The unpaged preface to this autobiographical novel asserts that the historical content includes material the author "knows personally or has upon reliable testimony," and when Bowles signed a dedication to Mrs. S. J. Walker on Dec. 5, 1893 (the copy used for the microfilm edition), he declared its story "absolutely true."

6. William A. Phillips, *The Conquest of Kansas, by Missouri and Her Allies. A History of the Troubles in Kansas, from the Passage of the Organic Act until the Close of July, 1856* (Boston: Phillips, Sampson, 1856), 42, 71, 233, 234–35, 253, 257–58, 265–66, 318, 359–60, and on the towns, 27, 320. Among the various accounts, see Alice Nichols, *Bleeding Kansas* (New York: Oxford University Press, 1954); Dale E Watts asks a vital question in "How Bloody Was Bleeding Kansas? Political Killings in Kansas Territory, 1854–1861," *Kansas History* 18 (Summer 1995): 116–29.

7. Phillips, *Conquest of Kansas*, on the flag, 45–46, 193. For the rite and Albert Pike's importance to its history, see William L. Fox, *Lodge of the Double-Headed Eagle: Two Centuries of Scottish Rite Freemasonry in America's Southern Jurisdiction* (Fayetteville: University of Arkansas Press, 1997), and C. W. Goodlander, *Memoirs and Recollections of C. W. Goodlander of the Early Days of Fort Scott* (Fort Scott, Kans.: Monitor, 1900), 51–55. See also Duane Schultz, *Quantrill's War: The Life and Times of William Clarke Quantrill* (New York: St. Martin's, 1996); and Edward E. Leslie, *The Devil Knows How to Ride: The True Story of William Clarke Quantrill* (New York: Random House, 1996).

8. Charles Robinson, *The Kansas Conflict* (New York: Harper and Brothers, 1892), 27, 77–78; Gene M. Burnett, "The Uncertain Heroics of Colonel Titus," *Florida's Past: People and Events That Shaped the State*, 3 vols. (Englewood and Sarasota, Fla.: Pineapple, for the author, 1986–91), 3:88–90; Phillips, *Conquest of Kansas*, 324–26; Thomas Schoonover, "Foreign Relations and Kansas in 1858," *Kansas Historical Quarterly* 42 (Winter 1976): 345–52; "Documents: Bleeding Kansas and Spanish Cuba in 1857," trans. and ed. Ebba Schoonover and Thomas Schoonover, *Kansas History* 11 (Winter 1988–89): 240–42.

9. Frank W. Blackmar, *The Life of Charles Robinson: The First State Governor of Kansas* (Topeka: the author, 1902); Don W. Wilson, *Governor Charles Robinson of Kansas* (Lawrence: University Press of Kansas, 1975); Eli Thayer, *A History of the Kansas Crusade: Its Friends and Its Foes*, intro. Rev. Edward Everett Hale (New York: Harper, 1889); Samuel A. Johnson, *The Battle Cry of Freedom: The New England Emigrant Aid Company in the Kansas Crusade* (Lawrence: University Press of Kansas, 1954); *The Monthly Jubilee*, 1852 through 1854, bound and sold as *The Jubilee Harbinger for 1854* (Philadelphia: n.p., n.d.], 134–36.

10. Phillips, *Conquest of Kansas*, 246–47, also 138; Castel, *Frontier State*, 18, 19–21. See William E. Connelley, *James Henry Lane, the "Grim chieftain" of Kansas* (Topeka: Crane, 1899); John Speer, *Life of Gen. James H. Lane, "the Liberator of Kansas"; with corroborative incidents of pioneer history* (Garden City, N.Y.: J. Speer, 1896); Wendell Holmes Stephenson, *The Political Career of General James H. Lane* (Topeka: Kansas State Historical Society, 1930); and Kendall E. Bailes, *Rider on the Wind: Jim Lane and Kansas* (Shawnee Mission, Kans.: Wagon Wheel, 1962).

11. Phillips, *Conquest of Kansas*, 20, 65, 25, 375; "German Emigration to Kansas" (from the *Illinois Staats Zeitung*), *New York Times*, April 4, 1856, p. 1; Russell K. Hickman, "The Vegetarian and Octagon Settlement Companies," *Kansas Historical Quarterly* 2 (Nov. 1933): 377–85; Daniel C. Fitzgerald, *Ghost Towns of Kansas: A Traveler's Guide* (Lawrence: University Press of Kansas, 1988), 130–33; Fitzgerald, *Faded Dreams: More Ghost Towns of Kansas* (Lawrence: University Press of Kansas, 1994), 22 (for "Young America" as a place name); "A Cheap Plan for Getting up Libraries," *Boston Investigator*, August 14, 1861, p. 130.

12. Aileen S. Kraditor, *Means and Ends in American Abolitionism: Garrison and His Critics on Strategy and Tactics, 1834–1850*, 2d ed. (New York: Vintage Books, 1969); Lewis Perry, *Radical Abolitionism: Anarchy and the Government of God in Antislavery Thought* (Ithaca, N.Y.: Cornell University Press, 1973); James Brewer Stewart, *Holy*

Warriors: The Abolitionists and American Slavery (New York: Hill and Wang, 1976); Richard H. Sewell, *Ballots for Freedom: Antislavery Politics in the United States, 1837–1860* (New York: Oxford University Press, 1976); Ronald G. Walters, *The Antislavery Appeal: American Abolitionists after 1830* (Baltimore, Md.: Johns Hopkins University Press, 1976).

13. On the importance of land reform, see Mark A. Lause, *Young America: Land, Labor, and the Republican Community* (Urbana: University of Illinois Press, 2005); "Gerrit Smith's Speech" in "Discussions in the National Abolition Convention, at Syracuse, May 28th and 29th, 1856," *Radical Abolitionist* 1 (July 1856): 104, and in "The Campaign. Gerrit Smith in Brooklyn," *Radical Abolitionist* 4 (Oct. 1858): 22; Richard J. Hinton, "Wendell Phillips: A Reminiscent Study," *The Arena* 13 (July 1895): 240.

14. Phillips, *Conquest of Kansas*, 113–14.

15. William Bishop, "Memorial Discourse," *Transactions of the Kansas State Historical Society* 5 (1896): 102; Clifford C. Baker, "Other Obituary Remarks on Col. Wm. A. Phillips, at the Annual Meeting, January 16, 1894," *Transactions of the Kansas State Historical Society* 5 (1896): 106; Bishop, "Memorial Discourse," 104–5; *Combined History of Randolph, Monroe and Perry Counties, Illinois* (Philadelphia: J. L. McDonough, 1883), 195–96, described local papers favorable to land reform—the *Randolph County Record*, the *Chester Reveille and Homestead Advocate*, the *Kaskaskia Republican*, and the *Chester Herald*. For the favorable citations of these papers by the land-reform movement in the East, see *The Jubilee* (New York: [NRA], 1845), 14, and several articles in *Young America*, including "Hon. Robert Smith," May 24 and Nov. 1 (same title for both), notice of *Young America! Principles and Objects of the National Reform Association, or Agrarian League. By a member* (New York: [NRA], [1846?]), July 5 (quotation), "Progress in Illinois," suggesting its first publisher for the U.S. Senate, December 6, "A Voice from Lower Egypt," Dec. 27, 1845, "Homestead," Jan. 3, and "The Inalienable Homestead," March 7, 1846.

16. Bishop, "Memorial Discourse," 104, 105, 106; *Dictionary of American Biography*, 3d ed. (New York: Scribner's, 1980), 14: 548; newspaper descriptions in *Combined History*, 195–96; Phillips, *Conquest of Kansas*, 189, 321, 365–66, 367, and also 187–202; Bernard A. Weisberger, *Reporters for the Union* (Boston: Little, Brown, 1953), 25–26, 35; Daniel B. Anthony in *Transactions of the Kansas State Historical Society* 5 (1896): 109.

17. Fitzgerald, *Faded Dreams*, 32–33; "Clermont Phalanx," *Harbinger, Devoted to Social and Political Progress*, October 2, 1847, p. 271; William A. Mitchel, *Linn County, Kansas* (Pleasanton Kans.: Linn County Historical Society, 1987 [1928]), 135–36, 136; Morse, "Sketch of Augustus Wattles," 290–93, 294; Isaac M. Martin, *History of the Schools of Cincinnati and Other Educational Institutions, Public and Private* (Cincinnati: the compiler, 1900), 182–83, 185–87; William H. Pease and Jane Pease, *Black Utopia: Negro Communal Experiments in America* (Madison: University of Wisconsin Press, 1963), 38–41; S. S. Prouty, "Kansas as a Factor," *Kansas Historical Society Collections* 1 (1878): 131–42.

18. Hinton, "Wendell Phillips," 226; C. Carroll Hollis, "R. J. Hinton: Lincoln's Reluctant Biographer," *The Centennial Review* 5 (Winter 1961): 66–67; Richard J.

Hinton, *John Brown and His Men* (New York: Funk and Wagnalls, 1894]), 199–200, 201, 203–4n; William E. Connelly, "Col. Richard J. Hinton," *Transactions of the Kansas State Historical Society, 1901–1902* 7 (1902): 490, 493; Thomas Wentworth Higginson, *The Magnificent Activist: The Writings of Thomas Wentworh Higginson,* ed. Howard N. Meyer (New York: Da Capo, 2000), 215, 231–34.

19. "Remarks of Mr. Commerford," *Workingman's Advocate,* April 6, 1844; Phillips, *Conquest of Kansas,* 17, 18. Nicole Etcheson's sesquicentennially published *Bleeding Kansas: Contested Liberty in the Civil War Era* (Lawrence: University Press of Kansas, 2004) seeks to root its importance in slavery by focusing on "the black experience" but ignores both the spectrum of racial views among whites and the very existence of thousands of nonwhite native peoples in Kansas.

20. William A. Phillips, *Labor, Land, and Law: A Search for the Missing Wealth of the Working Poor* (New York: C. Scribner's Sons, 1886), 73–81 and, on Roman law, 409–10, 411.

21. Phillips, *Conquest of Kansas,* 67; *New York Daily Tribune,* Sept. 18, 1856. See also the *Tribune's* "Advice to Filibusterers," Nov. 4, 1852. In general, see David S. and Jeanne T. Heidler, *Old Hickory's War: Andrew Jackson and the Quest for Empire* (Mechanicsburg, Pa.: Stackpole, 1996).

22. *The History of Fond du Lac County, Wisconsin* (Chicago: Western Historical Company, 1880), 314–19, 400–408 (for a portrait and biographical sketch of Bovay, 523, 886). See also David P. Mapes, *History of Ripon, and of Its Founder, David P. Mapes* (Milwaukee: Cramer, Aikens and Cramer, 1873), 67–72, 79–95, 142–43; the Wisconsin Phalanx Reference Materials posted on the Ripon College Web site; and Carl Guarneri, *The Utopian Alternative: Fourierism in Nineteenth-Century America* (Ithaca, N.Y.: Cornell University Press, 1991).

23. John Stauffer, *The Black Hearts of Men: Radical Abolitionists and the Transformation of Race* (Cambridge, Mass.: Harvard University Press, 2001), 8–12, 13–14, 20–24; M. Leon Perkal, "American Abolition Society: A Viable Alternative to the Republican Party?" *Journal of Negro History* 65 (Winter 1980): 58–59; Hinton, *John Brown,* 18–19, 20, 42–43, 57; Phillips, *Conquest of Kansas,* 332.

24. Hinton, *John Brown,* 16, 35, 679; Phillips, *Conquest of Kansas,* 332.

25. Phillips, *Conquest of Kansas,* 208–9; Stauffer, *Black Hearts of Men,* 24–25; Kristen A. Tegtmeier, "The Ladies of Lawrence Are Arming! The Gendered Nature of Sectional Violence in Early Kansas," in *Antislavery Violence: Sectional, Racial, and Cultural Conflict in Antebellum America,* ed. John R. McKivigan and Stanley Harrold, 215–35 (Knoxville: University of Tennessee Press, 1999); "The Forgotten Feminist of Kansas: The Papers of Clarina I. H. Nichols, 1854–1885," ed. Joseph G. Gambone, *Kansas Historical Quarterly* 39 (Spring 1973): 12–57, (Summer 1973): 220–61, and (Autumn 1973): 392–444.

26. Mary Ritchie Jarboe, "John Ritchie, Portrait of an Uncommon Man"; Bill Cecil-Fronsman, "John Ritchie in the Context of History"; and Don Chubb, "Topeka's Oldest House," ed. Daniel Fitzgerald, all in *Shawnee County Historical Society Bulletin,* no. 68 (1991). John Swinton later said, "Well do I remember that winter night," indicating that he may have also been present (Swinton, *Old Ossawattomie Brown: Speech*

on the Twenty-Second Anniversary of John Brown's Death, delivered at the Turn Theatre, *New York, December 2, 1881* [New York: n.p. (for the author?), n.d. (1881?)], 4).

27. Lecompton's Local 36 (which also covered the Lawrence trade until Local 73 was chartered) did not regularly report, but notices from Local 48, at Leavenworth, are in *The Printer* 3 (July 1860): 33, 4 (Apr. 1863): 154, and 5 (Nov. 1863): 22, and a letter of May 28, 1861, reported the members "enlisting in the U.S. service to fight for the glorious old 'Stars and Stripes'" (4 [July 1861]: 8). Richard J. Hinton, "Charley Lenhart" [*sic*], *Leavenworth Daily Conservative,* May 2, 1863, p. 2.

28. Hinton, *John Brown,* 36–37.

29. "John Brown at Dutch Henry's Crossing," *Lippincott's Magazine of Popular Literature and Science* 5 (Jan. 1883): 59–66; Hinton, *John Brown,* 61–63, 87n, also 82–83n, 83–84, 98–99; Phillips, *Conquest of Kansas,* 316–17, 360–61, 403–6, 392–93, 398–99; Swinton, *Old Ossawattomie Brown,* 1; Robert Collins, *General James G. Blunt: Tarnished Glory* (Gretna, La.: Pelican, 2005), 21–23; Reynolds, *John Brown,* 166–67; Harvey R. Hougen, "The Marais des Cygnes Massacre and the Execution of William Griffith," *Kansas History* 8 (1985): 74–94.

30. Statement of W. H. Ambrose, John Brown Papers, Kansas Historical Society, Topeka; Reynolds, *John Brown,* 189–90.

31. Brown tried to get Theodore Parker to write an address to officers and soldiers of the United States Army, but he declined to do so (Jeffery Rossbach, *Ambivalent Conspirators: John Brown, the Secret Six, and a Theory of Slave Violence* [Philadelphia: University of Pennsylvania Press, 1982], 149, 150; "No. 1 Duty of the Soldier [1856–1857]," in Hinton, *John Brown,* 615–16, 616–17).

32. Hinton, *John Brown,* 57. Bowles later noted that the U.S. cavalry responded to the appeals of "unprotected citizens" by taking fifteen hours to cover the twelve miles to Lawrence (*Stormy Petrel,* 140, 142.

33. Hinton, *John Brown,* 48–49, 49–50n; Phillips, *Conquest of Kansas,* 292; Bowles, *Stormy Petrel,* 146; Reynolds, *John Brown,* 203–4. Hinton recalled that the younger men of Lawrence referred to the local Committee of Public Safety as the "Safety Valve" because of its penchant for talk.

34. Hinton, *John Brown,* 107, 52, 88, 105. See also Bowles, *Stormy Petrel,* 10–11, 13, 36–42, 144–46.

35. *Kansas: A Cyclopedia of State History, Embracing Events, Institutions, Industries, Counties, Cities, Towns, Prominent Persons, etc.,* ed. Franck W. Blackmar, 2 vols. (Chicago: Standard, 1912), 2:27 (the text cited in this book comes from a May 2002 transcription by Carolyn Ward and posted on-line at http://skyways.lib.ks.us/genweb/archives/1912 [accessed Nov. 28, 2008]); Goodlander, *Memoirs and Recollections,* 39, 51–55. On Montgomery and Jennison, see Brian Dirck, "By the Hand of God: James Montgomery and Redemptive Violence," *Kansas History* 27 (Spring–Summer 2004): 103–9; William Hutchinson, "Sketches of Kansas Pioneer Experience," *Kansas Historical Collection, 1901–1902* 7 (1902): 395–96; *The United States Biographical Dictionary,* s.v. *Kansas* (Chicago, Ill.: S. Lewis, 1879); and Stephen Z. Starr, *Jennison's Jayhawkers: A Civil War Cavalry Regiment and Its Commander* (Baton Rouge: Louisiana State University Press, 1973).

36. Collins, *General James G. Blunt*, 15–17, 19–20; August Bondi statement on events of 1857 [undated], John Brown Papers. See also Bondi, *Autobiography of August Bondi, 1833–1907* (Galesburg, Ill.: Wagoner, 1910); Reynolds, *John Brown*, 188–89; Robley, *History of Bourbon County*, 100–102 (for Gilpatrick, 83); and Hutchinson, "Sketches of Kansas," 395–96.

37. Robley, *History of Bourbon County*, 129–31, 140; Goodlander, *Memoirs and Recollections*, 11, 33–37, 40–43, 55–56, 63; *Kansas: A Cyclopedia*, 1:196–97; *Biographical Directory of the U.S. Congress*, numerous editions but most accessible on-line at http://bioguide.congress.gov/biosearch.asp (accessed Nov. 28, 2008).

38. William Henry Seward, "On the Irrepressible Conflict," speech delivered at Rochester, N.Y., Oct. 25, 1858.

39. Hinton, *John Brown*, 678–79, 679–80; James Redpath, "Who Were the Friends of Kansas?" *Radical Abolitionist* 4 (Sept. 1858): 12. According to Bowles, Brown did write a letter to Lincoln that remained undelivered (*Stormy Petrel*, 312–14).

40. Bowles reported in Wilbur H. Siebert, *The Underground Railroad from Slavery to Freedom* (New York: Macmillan, 1898), 347, 348–49.

41. "The Prospects of Kansas," *Radical Abolitionist* 3 (Sept. 1857): 12; Bowles, *Stormy Petrel*, 148.

CHAPTER 2: A FREE WEST IN A SLAVE NATION

1. Richard J. Hinton, "John Brown and His Men," *Frank Leslie's Popular Monthly* 27 (June 1889): 695; Hinton, *John Brown and His Men* (New York: Funk and Wagnalls, 1894), 672–73, 674–75, 513n, 514n, 520, 673; Statement of Richard J. Hinton, and Richard Realf to John Brown, Feb. 10, 1858, in John Brown Papers, Kansas Historical Society, Topeka. See also "The Two Systems—the Future," *National Era*, June 17, 1858, p. 94; Ludwell H. Johnson, *Red River Campaign: Politics and Cotton in the Civil War* (Kent, Ohio: Kent State University Press, 1993), 6–7, 7–8, for Edward Atkinson's *Cheap Cotton by Free Labor* (Boston: A. Williams, 1861).

2. "Population of the United States according to the Eighth Census (1860)," *The Merchant's Magazine and Commercial Review* 47 (Oct. 1, 1862): 373.

3. Wiley Britton, *Pioneer Life in Southwest Missouri* (Kansas City, Mo.: Smith-Grieves, 1929), 326–27, 330–31, 332.

4. Laurence M. Hauptman, *The Iroquois in the Civil War: From Battlefield to Reservation* (Syracuse, N.Y.: Syracuse University Press, 1993), 85–86, 90.

5. J. Leitch Wright Jr., *Creeks and Seminoles: The Destruction and Regeneration of the Muscogulge People* (Lincoln: University of Nebraska Press, 1986), 261; "Billy Bowlegs in New Orleans," *Harper's Weekly* 2 (June 12, 1858): 376–78; Jane F. Lancaster, *Removal Aftershock: The Seminole Struggle to Survive in the West, 1836–1866* (Knoxville: University of Tennessee Press, 1994), 144; Carolyn T. Foreman, "Billy Bowlegs," *Chronicles of Oklahoma* 33 (Winter 1855–56): 530–33; Kenneth W. Porter, "Billy Bowlegs (Holata Micco) in the Civil War (Part II)," *Florida Historical Quarterly* 45 (Apr. 1967): 400–401; Annie Heloise Abel, *The American Indian as Slaveholder and Secessionist*, 2d ed. (Lincoln: University of Nebraska Press, 1992 [1915]), 20n.

6. LeRoy H. Fisher, "United States Indian Agents to the Five Civilized Tribes,"

Chronicles of Oklahoma 50 (Winter 1972–73): 410, 411, 412, 413; Cheryl H. Morris, "Choctaw and Chickasaw Indian Agents, 1831–1874," ibid., 415–36; Carol B. Broemeling, "Cherokee Indian Agents, 1830–1874," ibid., 437–57; Caroline T. Foreman, "Dr. William Butler and George Butler, Cherokee Agents," ibid., 30:160–73; David A. Nichols, *Lincoln and the Indian: Civil War Policy and Politics* (Columbia, Mo.: University of Missouri Press, 1978), 8–9, 11; Edmund Danziger, *Indians and Bureaucrats: Administering the Reservation Policy during the Civil War* (Urbana: University of Illinois Press, 1974), 3–4.

7. Nichols, *Lincoln and the Indian*, 14.

8. Angie Debo, *The Rise and Fall of the Choctaw Republic* (Norman: University of Oklahoma Press, 1934), 56, 81–82, 135–36. Patrick N. Minges also points out Pitchlyn's Masonic connection in *Slavery in the Cherokee Nation: The Keetoowah Society and the Defining of a People, 1855–1867* (New York: Routledge, 2003), 165. The book grew from his dissertation, "The Keetoowah Society and the Avocation of Religious Nationalism in the Cherokee Nation, 1855–1867," Ph.D. diss., Union Theological Seminary, New York, 1999, and he has earlier drafts of his research on the Internet at various sites, including http://www.us-data.org/us/minges/.

9. Quoted in Laurence M. Hauptman, *Between Two Fires: American Indians in the Civil War* (New York: Free Press, 1993), 30–31. Panipakuxwe brought to Kansas the gold samples that sparked the Pike's Peak gold rush in 1859 (David Dary, *True Tales of Old-Time Kansas*, rev. ed. [Lawrence: University Press of Kansas, 1984], 274). See also Thurman Wilkins, *Cherokee Tragedy: The Ridge Family and the Decimation of a People*, 2d ed. (Norman: University of Oklahoma Press, 1986); Carolyn Thomas Foreman, *Park Hill* (Muskogee, Okla.: n.p., 1948); and Frank Cunningham, *General Stand Watie's Confederate Indians*, foreword by Brad Agnew, 2d ed. (Norman: University of Oklahoma Press, 1998).

10. Omer Steward, *Peyote Religion: A History* (Norman: University of Oklahoma Press, 1987), 30–34, 37–39, 48–53, 57, 58.

11. For this and the following paragraph, see Abel, *Indian as Slaveholder*, 86 and 86n; Minges, *Slavery in the Cherokee Nation*, 74–84, 96, 85–87; John Ross to George Butler, Sept. 8, 1854, and to G. L. Woodford, Mar. 7, 1858, in *The Papers of Chief John Ross*, ed. Gary E. Moulton, 2 vols. (Norman: University of Oklahoma Press, 1984–85), 2:387, 413; Weer to Moonlight, June 13, 16, 22, July 2, in *OR*, 13:430, 431, 434, 444, 459. See also William G. McLoughlin, *Champions of the Cherokee: Evan and John B. Jones* (Princeton, N.J.: Princeton University Press, 1990).

12. William A. Phillips, *The Conquest of Kansas, by Missouri and Her Allies. A History of the Troubles in Kansas, from the Passage of the Organic Act until the Close of July, 1856* (Boston: Phillips, Sampson, 1856), 22, 378; James A. Clifton, *The Prairie People: Continuity and Change in Potawatomie Indian Culture, 1665–1965* (Lawrence: Regents Press of Kansas, 1977), 380; Hauptman, *Iroquois in the Civil War*, 39, 89; Phillips, *Conquest of Kansas*, 18–19, 21–23; Hinton, *John Brown*, 67–68.

13. Wilbur H. Siebert, *The Underground Railroad from Slavery to Freedom* (New York: Macmillan), 284; Wiley Britton, *The Civil War on the Border*, 2 vols. (New York: G. P. Putnam's Sons, 1899), 2:25; Theda Perdue, *Slavery and the Evolution of Cherokee*

Society, 1540–1866 (Knoxville: University of Tennessee Press, 1979), 129–30; Minges, *Slavery in the Cherokee Nation*, 71–72, 73, 99; "The Two Systems—the Future," *National Era*, June 17, 1858, p. 94.

14. Nichols, *Lincoln and the Indian*, 12; Craig Miner and William E. Unrau, *The End of Indian Kansas: A Study of Cultural Revolution, 1854–1871* (Lawrence: University Press of Kansas, 1978), 51, 61, 63–65, 76–80, 105; Daniel Fitzgerald, *Ghost Towns of Kansas: A Traveler's Guide* (Lawrence: University Press of Kansas, 1988), 61, 63–64, 65; "The New Land-Grab" and "Kansas," by "B." of Iowa Point (the small community where Barr had settled), *New York Daily Tribune*, March 5, 1855, and Feb. 23, 1858.

15. Phillips, *Conquest of Kansas*, 19, 22, 114, 28; Seward's Chicago address "The National Idea: Its Perils," delivered on Oct. 3, 1860, qtd. in Hauptman, *Between Two Fires*, 11; John M. Taylor, *William Henry Seward: Lincoln's Right Hand* (New York: Harper Collins, 1991). Richard Slotkin's generally outstanding work *The Fatal Environment: The Myth of the Frontier in the Age of Industrialization, 1800–1890* (New York: Atheneum, 1965), 267, misreads Phillips, disregarding other statements in his book and ignoring his later marriage to a Cherokee woman.

16. See Mark A. Lause, "Borderland Visions: Maroons and Outlyers in Early American History," *Monthly Review* 54 (Sept. 2002): 38–44; David S. Reynolds, *John Brown, Abolitionist: The Man Who Killed Slavery, Sparked the Civil War, and Seeded Civil Rights* (New York: Knopf, 2005), 107. Martin Delany saw Indian resistance as an inspiration for armed black rebellion; see his *Blake; or, The Huts of America*, intro. Floyd J. Miller (Boston: Beacon, 1970), 85–87.

17. Minges, *Slavery in the Cherokee Nation*, 87–88; Edwin C. McReynolds, *The Seminoles* (Norman: University of Oklahoma Press, 1957), 259; "Billy Bowlegs in New Orleans," *Harper's Weekly* 2 (June 12, 1858): 376–78.

18. Britton, *Civil War*, 2:25. "Lucinda Davis" (p. 59), "John White" (p. 325), "Mary Grayson" (pp. 121, 117), "Nellie Johnson" (p. 157), and "Kiziah Love" (pp. 192, 195), in WPA, Oklahoma Writers Project, "Slave Narratives from the Federal Writers' Project" (typescript, Washington, D.C., 1941). Several of these accounts are reprinted in *Black Indian Slave Narratives*, ed. Patrick Minges (Winston-Salem, N.C.: John F. Blair, 2004), 100–110, 129–34, 175–83.

19. Daniel F. Littlefield, *Africans and Seminoles: From Removal to Emancipation* (Westport, Conn.: Greenwood, 1977), 103–13, 125–28, 132–39, 148–50, 183–84. On the effort, see McReynolds, *The Seminoles*, 257, 261, 263, 266, 268, 279–81. On Chupco, see Kevin Mulroy, *Freedom on the Border: The Seminole Maroons in Florida, the Indian Territory, Coahuila, and Texas* (Lubbock: Texas Tech University Press, 1993), 159. See also *The Jubilee Harbinger for 1854* (Philadelphia: n.p., n.d.), 135.

20. The Kansas Indian named Tooley is quoted by John Speer in *Transactions of the Kansas State Historical Society* 5 (1896): 111. On the Ottawas, see Siebert, *Underground Railroad*, 37, 38, 91–92. Britton, *Civil War*, 1:164; Thomas Wildcat Alford, *Civilization and the Story of the Absentee Shawnees, as Told to Florence Drake* (Norman: University of Oklahoma Press, 1979), 9; Perdue, *Slavery and Cherokee Society*, 130–31, 131–36; David Dary, *More True Tales of Old-Time Kansas* (Lawrence: University Press of Kansas, 1987), 27.

21. John Stauffer, "Advent among the Indians: The Revolutionary Ethics of Gerrit Smith, James McCune Smith, Frederick Douglass, and John Brown," in *Antislavery Violence: Sectional, Racial, and Cultural Conflict in Antebellum America*, ed. John R. McKivigan and Stanley Harrold, 236–73 (Knoxville: University of Tennessee Press, 1999), 236–37, 241, where he concludes that this "reflected their efforts to redefine America as an integrated, egalitarian, and pluralistic society" (242–43). Stauffer's title comes from a chapter of Delany's *Blake; or, The Huts of America*, 85–87.

22. Mark A. Lause, *Young America: Land, Labor, and the Republican Community* (Urbana: University of Illinois Press, 2005), 45, 78–79, 201n17.

23. "Declaration of Independence; and expression of sentiment unanimously adopted by the Working Women and Men, in Mass Meeting at the Jubilee Grove, Fifth day of July, 1852," *Monthly Jubilee* 4 (Mar. 1854): 101–2; "Agrarian League," *Workingman's Advocate*, June 1, 1844; Lewis Masquerier, *Sociology: or, The Reconstruction of Society, Government, and Property* (New York: the author, 1877), 53; "Industrial Congress," *Voice of Industry*, July 2, 1847; West's letter on "Democratic Government," *National Antislavery Standard*, March 1, 1849, p. 159; *Jubilee Harbinger for 1854*, 145; J. E. Thompson, "Black Slavery and White Slavery" and "Rights of Women," *Voice of Industry*, Aug. 27, 1847, p. 2, and April 14, 1848, p. 4.

24. On Bovay, see "Modern Dictionary," *American Freeman*, Nov. 8, 1844 (which mistakenly capitalized "Democrats"); and "Agrarian League" and "Emigration to Oregon," *Workingman's Advocate*, June 1, Dec. 28, 1844. See also "An Indian Letter of Wisdom," *American Freeman*, Nov. 14, 1844; Lause, *Young America*, 78–79, 201n17; and Phillips, *Conquest of Kansas*, 53–54, 55–58, 65, 201, 206–7, 376.

25. The spiritualist *Banner of Light* regularly reported on Beeson's meetings. See issues dated November 20 (p. 5), December 11, 1858 (p. 8), October 29, 1859 (p. 7), March 10 (p. 4), 26 (p. 7), and April 7, 1860 (p. 7), as well as "Are the Indians to be Exterminated?" and James M. Peebles, "From Whence the Indians," Aug. 15, 1863, p. 2, and Oct. 24, 1863, pp. 2–3, respectively. See also Margaret Leech, *Reveille in Washington, 1860–1865* (New York: Harper and Brothers, 1941), 305.

26. John Bowles, *The Stormy Petrel: An Historical Romance* (New York: A. Lovell, 1892), 43, 97, 246, 331, indicating that the relocated black settlement in Kansas became "Claytonville" in the novel. For Wattles, see *Mercer County, Ohio History 1978*, ed. Joyce L. Alig (Celina, Ohio: Mercer County Historical Society, 1980), 740–41, 762.

27. Wattles in Abel, *Indian as Slaveholder*, 226–28n; two pieces entitled "An Indian State" in *The Cincinnati Weekly Herald and Philanthropist*, September 17, 1845, p. 1, and *Young America*, Nov. 15, 1845, p. 1. Trevor Jones's otherwise insightful piece "In Defense of Sovereignty: Cherokee Soldiers, White Officers, and Discipline in the Third Indian Home Guard," *The Chronicles of Oklahoma* 82 (Winter 2004–5): 416–18, accepted the officially imposed view of race among whites as universal.

28. George Henry Evans "Rejoinder to Gerrit Smith," *Young America*, Sept. 27, 1845; Phillips, *Conquest of Kansas*, 67; "The African Race" (from *Voice of Freedom*), *American Freeman*, April 3, 1844; "Freedom of the Public Lands" (from *Seneca Falls Democrat*), *Randolph County Record*, Aug. 12, 1846; "Constitution of the Industrial Congress" and two articles entitled "An Indian State," *Young America*, Sept. 27, Oct.

25, and Nov. 15, 1845; "Our Coloured Population—A Negro State," *The Quarterly Journal and Review* 1 (July, 1846): 193–204; editorial in *Cincinnati Daily Nonpareil*, July 6, 1850, p. 2.

29. Baptiste Peoria negotiated with R. S. Stevens (Miner and Unrau, *End of Indian Kansas*, 76). "Explanation of John Brown Relics and Manuscripts" and John T. Jones to John Brown, Oct. 13, 1857, John Brown Papers. For Brown's friendship with Ottawa Jones, a leader of that tribe married to a Vermont missionary teacher, see Hinton, *John Brown*, 81–82; for the attack on Jones, see Thomas Goodrich, *War to the Knife: Bleeding Kansas, 1854–1861* (Mechanicsburg, Pa.: Stackpole, 158–59; also see Reynolds, *John Brown*, 157–58, 170, 173–74, 203.

30. Reynolds, *John Brown*, 274–75; Jeffery Rossbach, *Ambivalent Conspirators: John Brown, the Secret Six, and a Theory of Slave Violence* (Philadelphia: University of Pennsylvania Press, 1982), 3–4; Thomas Wentworth Higginson, *The Magnificent Activist: The Writings of Thomas Wentworh Higginson*, ed. Howard N. Meyer (New York: Da Capo, 2000), 119–20; Bowles, *Stormy Petrel*, 148; Hinton, *John Brown*, 31; Nat Brandt, *The Town That Started the Civil War* (Syracuse, N.Y.: Syracuse University Press, 1990), 199–200; Mrs. O. E. Morse, "Sketch of the Life and Works of Augustus Wattles," *Kansas Historical Society Collection, 1926–1928* 17 (1928): 298.

31. "An 'Idea of Things in Kansas': John Brown's 1857 New England Speech," ed. Karl Gridley, *Kansas History* 27 (Spring–Summer 2004): 77–85; Franklin B. Sanborn, *Recollections of Seventy Years*, 2 vols. (Boston: R. G. Badger, 1901), 1:134, 135. The literature on John Brown regularly mentions Hugh Forbes but never cites his political associations, though discovering these requires little more than the *National Union Catalogue* and an index to the contemporary New York press. Indeed, a complete run of Forbes's own short-lived *European* has survived.

32. Sanborn, *Recollections*, 1:135; Brandt, *Town That Started the War*, 200.

33. Hinton, *John Brown*, 159.

34. Hinton, "John Brown," 695. For the later New York City connection, see Hinton, *John Brown*, 162–63; Benjamin Quarles, *Allies for Freedom: Blacks and John Brown* (Oxford: Oxford University Press, 1974), 52–53; Daniel C. Littlefield, "Blacks, John Brown, and a Theory of Manhood," in *His Soul Goes Marching On: Responses to John Brown and the Harpers Ferry Raid*, ed. Paul Finkelman, 67–97 (Charlottesville: University Press of Virginia, 1995), 79; Reynolds, *John Brown*, 240–44, 258; Sanborn, *Recollections*, 135; Calvin C. Burt, *Egyption Masonry* (N.p.: n.p., 1879), 203–4, 205, 206, 207, 314–17. "The French Masonic Incident" in the history of Prince Hall masonry is discussed at http://www.freemasonry.org/jawalkes/page_3.htm (accessed Nov. 28, 2008).

35. Osborne P. Anderson, *A Voice from Harper's Ferry: The Unfinished Revolution* (New York: World View, 1974 [1861]), 39–43; Richard Realf to John Brown, Feb. 10, 1858, John Brown Papers; Jean Libby, ed., *John Brown Mysteries: Allies for Freedom* (Missoula, Mont.: Pictorial Histories, 1999), 89–90.

36. Jay Monaghan, *Civil War on the Western Border, 1854–1865* (Boston: Little, Brown, 1955), 91; Morse, "Sketch of Augustus Wattles," 290–99; Siebert, *The Underground Railroad*, 8–9, 65; Quarles, *Allies for Freedom*, 55; Rossbach, *Ambivalent Conspirators*, 188–89, 195; John Brown, "Parallels," *Lawrence Republican*, January

13, 1859; Kagi to W. A. Phillips, from Tabor, Feb. 7, 1859, and Rescue of Missouri Slaves, Dec. 1858, by John Brown, told by James Townley, both in the John Brown Papers.

37. Augustus Wattles to James Smith [John Brown], June 18, 1859, and Theodore Botkin Francis G. Adams, secretary of the Kansas Historical Society, June 16, 1887. In a letter to John Brown dated Aug. 21, 1857, Augustus Wattles discussed the loss of confidence in Robinson and argued against the use of small armed bands for slave liberation: "Whatever might have been intended, much more was threatened & boasted of than could possibly have been performed, unless there was an extensive conspiracy." All these are in the John Brown Papers; the first two also appear in Reynolds, *John Brown*, 280.

38. Phillips to James Smith [John Brown], Kagi to W. A. Phillips (Phillips never received this undated letter sent from Chambersburg), and William A. Phillips, state marshal, to Joel Grover, June 24, 1859, John Brown Papers; William Bishop, "Memorial Discourse," and James F. Legate recollection in *Transactions of the Kansas State Historical Society* 5 (1896): 104–5, 113; "General Summary," *National Era*, June 25, 1857, p. 103.

39. Qtd. in Hinton, *John Brown*, 683, and also see 681–84; Reynolds, *John Brown*, 281–83.

40. Hinton, "John Brown," 695; Richard J. Hinton, "Charley Lenhart" [*sic*], *Leavenworth Daily Conservative*, May 2, 1863, p. 2 (the paper deliberately misreported his birthplace as Iowa, where his mother lived); Hinton, *John Brown*, 253, 253–56; Phillips, *Conquest of Kansas*, 313, 357–58; Thomas Goodrich, *Black Flag: Guerrilla Warfare on the Western Border, 1861–65* (Bloomington: Indiana University Press, 1999), 166–67, 168; Reynolds, *John Brown*, 266.

41. Karen Whitman, "Re-evaluating John Brown's Raid at Harpers Ferry," *West Virginia History* 34 (Oct. 1972): 46–84; Walker to Cooper, May 13, 1861, in *OR*, 3:574.

42. O. E. Morse, "An Attempted Rescue of John Brown from Charleston, Va. Jail," John Brown Papers; Reynolds, *John Brown*, 280. See also John Doy, *The Narrative of John Doy, of Lawrence, Kansas* (New York: T. Holman, for the author, 1860); Dary, *More True Tales*, 90–93.

43. John R. McKivigan, "His Soul Goes Marching On: The Story of John Brown's Followers after the Harpers Ferry Raid," in *Antislavery Violence*, ed. McKivigan and Harrold, 280–81 (Spooner and Hoyt), 283 (LeBarnes); Morse, "Attempted Rescue"; Reynolds, *John Brown*, 379; Hinton, *John Brown*, 335, 370, 396, 397; Hinton, "Charley Lenhart," 2.

44. Editors of the *New York Tribune* knew their regular political writers would not be allowed to cover the trial and execution, so they sent the agricultural editor Henry Steel Olcott and the drama critic Edward H. House, an old bohemian friend of Hinton and John Swinton. See Mark A. Lause, forthcoming book on the antebellum political crisis and the origin of bohemianism.

45. Hinton, "Charley Lenhart," 2; Hinton, "John Brown," 699; Hinton, *John Brown*, 512, 520–25; Reynolds, *John Brown*, 380. Dr. Marximilien Leopold Langenschwarz of

the *Turnerverein* declared "his model Reformer is John Brown" ("Spiritual Lyceum and Conference," *Herald of Progress*, July 7, 1860, pp. 3–4).

46. Reynolds, *John Brown*, 406, 429–30, 430–39; Richard J. Hinton, "Wendell Phillips: A Reminiscent Study," *The Arena* 13 (July 1895): 237, and on the Turners, 236, 238; Bruce Levine, *The Spirit of 1848: German Immigrants, Labor Conflict, and the Coming of the Civil War* (Urbana: University of Illinois Press, 1992), 222–26. See also Henry Metzner, *A Brief History of the American Turnerbund* (Pittsburgh, Penn.: National Executive Committee of the American Turnerbund, 1924).

47. Hinton, "Wendell Phillips," 237; J. K. Hudson, "The John Brown League: An Unwritten Chapter of History," John Brown Papers. See also "Major J. K. Hudson," *Magazine of Western History* 13 (Nov. 1890): 50. There are references to various other societies, the courses of which—if not their existence—remains to be unraveled.

48. Lause, *Young America*, 122–23.

49. "Convention at Boston" and "A Voice from Missouri" (from the *Missouri Democrat*), *Radical Abolitionist* 1 (Dec. 1855): 36 and 3 (Mar. 1858): 57; "Address of the Convention of 'Radical Political Abolitionists,'" *Proceedings of the Convention of Radical Political Abolitionists, held at Syracuse, N.Y., June 26th, 27th, and 28th, 1855 . . .* (New York: Central Abolition Board, 1855), 36, 42.

CHAPTER 3: WAR IN THE FAR WEST

1. Ross to Albert Pike, Feb. 25, 1862, in *SOR*, 1 (ch. 8): 538–39. See also correspondence by and to Chief Ross in *PCJR*, 2:504–9; Morris L. Wardell, *A Political History of the Cherokee Nation, 1838–1907* (Norman: University of Oklahoma Press, 1938), 152; "Phoebe Banks," WPA, Oklahoma Writers Project, "Slave Narratives from the Federal Writers' Project" (typescript, Washington, D.C.), 10, and also in *Black Indian Slave Narratives*, ed. Patrick Minges (Winston-Salem, N.C.: John F. Blair, 2004), 111–15.

2. Benteen qtd. in Charles K. Mils, *Harvest of Barren Regrets: The Army Career of Frederick William Benteen, 1834–1898* (Glendale, Calif.: Arthur H. Clark, 1985), 13, and see also 11, 12–13. Representative governments accord different functions to different bodies.

3. Frank Moore, ed., *The Rebellion Record: A Diary of American Events, with Documents, Narratives, Illustrative Incidents, Poetry, Etc.*, 12 vols., each with independently paged sections (New York: Putnam, 1861–63 [vols. 1–6]; New York: Van Nostrand, 1864–68 [vols. 7–12]), 1 ("Rumors and Incidents"): 27; Carl Moneyhon, "1861: 'The Die Is Cast,'" in *Rugged and Sublime: The Civil War in Arkansas*, ed. Mark K. Christ (Fayetteville: University of Arkansas Press, 1994), 6.

4. Richard J. Hinton, *John Brown and His Men* (New York: Funk and Wagnalls, 1894]), 682; William A. Phillips, *The Conquest of Kansas, by Missouri and Her Allies. A History of the Troubles in Kansas, from the Passage of the Organic Act until the Close of July, 1856* (Boston: Phillips, Sampson, 1856), 193; *The Rebellion Record*, 2 ("Poetry and Incidents"): 31.

5. Mark Grimsley addressed the most obvious manifestation of this disagreement in *The Hard Hand of War: Union Military Policy Towards Southern Civilians, 1861–1865*

(Cambridge: Cambridge University Press, 1995), which traces the ascendancy of this idea of conquest in Federal military thought.

6. John Bowles, *The Stormy Petrel: An Historical Romance* (New York: A. Lovell, 1892), 86, 126, 285, 131 (also describing himself as a freethinker). In addition to including episodic premonitions in this novel, Bowles later wrote *The Masked Prophet, One's Hidden Self: A Romance in Two Lives—Here and Hereafter* (New York: Caxton, 1895).

7. Wiley Britton, *Pioneer Life in Southwest Missouri* (Kansas City, Mo.: Smith-Grieves, 1929), 248–54, 319–24, 345–46, 352, 363–64, 365, 367, 378–93, 393–94.

8. Albert Castel, *A Frontier State at War: Kansas, 1861–1865* (Westport, Conn.: Greenwood, 1979), 15–16, 21, 24–25, 27–28, 30–31, 35; David Dary, *True Tales of Old-Time Kansas*, rev. ed. (Lawrence: University Press of Kansas, 1984), 253–56; Edgar Langsdorf, "Jim Lane and the Frontier Guard," *Kansas Historical Quarterly* 9 (Feb. 1940): 13–25; John G. Clark, "Mark W. Delahay: Peripatetic Politician," ibid., 25 (Autumn 1959): 301–12; Joseph G. Gambone, "Samuel C. Pomeroy and the Senatorial Election of 1861, Reconsidered," ibid., 37 (Spring 1971): 15–32. See also William E. Connelly, "Col. Richard J. Hinton," *Transactions of the Kansas State Historical Society* 7 (1902): 490; Sara T. D. Robinson, "The Wakarusa War," *Collections of the Kansas Historical Society* 10 (1907–8): 463, 465–66.

9. James G. Blunt, "General Blunt's Account of His Civil War Experiences," *Kansas Historical Quarterly* 1 (May 1932): 216, 218. J. K. Hudson, "The John Brown League: An Unwritten Chapter of History," John Brown Papers, Kansas Historical Society, Topeka; "Major J. K. Hudson," *Magazine of Western History* 13 (Nov. 1890): 50; Mary Ritchie Jarboe, "John Ritchie, Portrait of an Uncommon Man," *Shawnee County Historical Society Bulletin*, no. 68 (Topeka, Kans.: Shawnee County Historical Society, 1991).; O. E. Morse, "An Attempted Rescue of John Brown from Charleston, Va. Jail," John Brown Papers; John R. McKivigan, "His Soul Goes Marching On: The Story of John Brown's Followers after the Harpers Ferry Raid," in *Antislavery Violence: Sectional, Racial, and Cultural Conflict in Antebellum America*, ed. John R. McKivigan and Stanley Harrold, 274–97 (Knoxville: University of Tennessee Press, 1999), 281, 288–89. See also "'This Regiment Will Make a Mark': Letters from a Member of Jennison's Jayhawkers, 1861–1862," ed. Jeffrey L. Patrick, *Kansas History* 20 (Spring 1997): 50–58; Bowles, *Stormy Petrel*, 238–45.

10. Bowles, *Stormy Petrel*, 129; Elmo Ingenthron, *Borderland Rebellion: A History of the Civil War on the Missouri-Arkansas Border* (Forsythe, Mo.: Ozark Mountaineer, 1980), 124–25; Bowles, *Stormy Petrel*, 249, also 246–49.

11. Bowles, *Stormy Petrel*, 252–54. On soldierly duties, see Hinton, *John Brown*, 615, 616, 617–618; Hudson, "The John Brown League." When Hinton left for Kansas, Wendell Phillips had asked what he expected to accomplish there, to which Hinton replied that Kansas was "the road to South Carolina!" "Well, Hinton," quipped Phillips after the war's outbreak, "we've reached South Carolina at last!" (Richard J. Hinton, "Wendell Phillips: A Reminiscent Study," *The Arena* 13 [July 1895]: 234–35).

12. Hinton, *John Brown*, 107; Bowles, *Stormy Petrel*, 255–59. Hinton was in the May 1861 occupation of Alexandria in which Elmer Ellsworth was killed. "My place

as a newspaper correspondent was quite near that fatal shot" (Hinton, "Wendell Phillips," 227).

13. For Kapp at a December 1861 mass meeting on behalf of Fremont, see *Rebellion Record*, 4:125. For Kapp's participation in a Jan. 16, 1863, mass meeting on behalf of Franz Sigel, see *Germans for a Free Missouri: Translations from the St. Louis Radical Press, 1857–1862*, selected and trans. Steven Rowan, commentary by James Neal Primm (Columbia: University of Missouri Press, 1983), 295 and 295n.

14. *Rebellion Record*, 1 ("Diary of Events"): 5. Jacob Thompson was the official in question.

15. Philip A. Kalish and Beatrice J. Kalish, "Indian Territory Forts: Charnel Houses of the Frontier, 1839–1865," *Chronicles of Oklahoma* 50 (Spring 1972): 78; Edwin C. McReynolds, *The Seminoles* (Norman: University of Oklahoma Press, 1957), 291. David A. Nichols's *Lincoln and the Indian: Civil War Policy and Politics* (Columbia, Mo.: University of Missouri Press, 1978), 25–26, 33, faults Lincoln for withdrawing the soldiers and pretty much for all else regarding Indian policy during the period.

16. Laurence M. Hauptman, *Between Two Fires: American Indians in the Civil War* (New York: Free Press, 1993), 23, 24, 25–26, 28, 32, 33.

17. Craig W. Gaines, *The Confederate Cherokees: John Drew's Regiment of Mounted Rifles* (Baton Rouge: Louisiana State University Press, 1989), 30; Hinton, *John Brown*, 513n, 514n, 520; Angie Debo, *The Rise and Fall of the Choctaw Republic* (Norman: University of Oklahoma Press, 1934), 80; Walter Lee Brown, *A Life of Albert Pike* (Fayetteville: University of Arkansas Press, 1997).

18. See report of William P. Dole, Oct. 31, 1863, in *The American Indian and the United States: A Documentary History*, 3 vols. (New York: Random House, 1973), 1:114–15; Patrick N. Minges, *Slavery in the Cherokee Nation: The Keetoowah Society and the Defining of a People 1855–1867* (New York: Routledge, 2003), 96, 98 (on the warning out of the Jones family), 102 (on Evan Jones). Perhaps because of the small numbers of the Osage and Quapaw nations, Phillips noted their particular problems as soldiers (John J. Mathews, *The Osages: Children of the Middle Waters* [Norman: University of Oklahoma Press, 1961], 649).

19. Angie Debo, *The Road to Disappearance: A History of the Creek Indians*, 2d ed. (Norman: University of Oklahoma Press, 1979), 143, 145; Thomas Wildcat Alford, *Civilization and the Story of the Absentee Shawnees, as Told to Florence Drake* (Norman: University of Oklahoma Press, 1979), 7–8, 9–10; Minges, *Slavery in the Cherokee Nation*, 99.

20. Debo, *Rise and Fall*, 80–81, 82; Cheryl H. Morris, "Choctaw and Chickasaw Indian Agents, 1831–1874," *Chronicles of Oklahoma* 50 (Winter 1972–73): 415; Minges, *Slavery in the Cherokee Nation*, 105; Nichols, *Lincoln and the Indian*, 30; Arrell M. Gibson, *The Chickasaw* (Norman: University of Oklahoma Press, 1971), 228–30. See also Kenny A. Franks, "An Analysis of the Confederate Treaties with the Five Civilized Tribes," *Chronicles of Oklahoma* 50 (Winter 1972–73): 459.

21. Debo, *Road to Disappearance*, 145, 147. Daniel F. Littlefield Jr., *Africans and Creeks: From the Colonial Period to the Civil War* (Westport, Conn.: Greenwood, 1979), 182, 183; McReynolds, *The Seminoles*, 292. In April 1862 Charles DeMorse described

Jumper as "a full blood Seminole" who "speaks no English" (DeMorse, "Indians for the Confederacy," *Chronicles of Oklahoma* 50 [Winter 1972–73]: 475). Christine Schultz White and Benton R. White, in *Now the Wolf Has Come: The Creek Nation in the Civil War* (College Station: Texas A&M Press, 1996), exmine the disintegration of the nation and the outbreak of hostilities but do not question the commonplace apologetics for "the Lost Cause."

22. Ross, "Proclamation to the Cherokee People, May 17, Rector to Ross, Jan. 29, Ross to Rector, Feb. 22, 1861, in *OR*, 13:489–90, 490–91, 491–92; Minges, *Slavery in the Cherokee Nation*, 99–100. See also the February–March correspondence in *PCJR*, 2:458–67.

23. Citizens of Boonsborough to Ross, May 9, 1861, in *OR*, 13:493–94; Lt. Col. J. R. Kannasy to Ross, May 15, 1861, ibid., 13:492; McCulloch to Ross, June 12, 1861, ibid., 13:495; David Hubbard to Ross, June 12, 1861, ibid., 13:497–98; Ross' responses of May 10, 17, June 12, and June 17, 1861, ibid., 13:494–95, 493, 495–96, 498–99; Gaines, *Confederate Cherokees*, 16–17. Also May-July correspondence in *PCJR*, 2:468–78.

24. Procedings and address in *OR*, 13:499–505. See also Minutes of the National Executive Council, Aug. 11, "Address to the Cherokee Nation," Aug. 21, Ross to George W. Clark and to Benjamin McCullough, both Aug. 24, 1861, and Ross, L. Downing, McDaniel, and Evan Jones to U.S. Senate and House of Representatives, June 14, 1864, *PCJR*, 2:479, 482–83, 491: Gaines, *Confederate Cherokees*, 11–13, 16–17, 21–2, 46–48, 93–94, 105–6, 121–23; "Lucinda Davis," WPA, Oklahoma Writers Project, "Slave Narratives," 59.

25. Ross letters and annual message, Sept. 19, Oct. 8, Oct. 4, 8, 9, 1861, *PCJR*, 2:485–88, 487–88, 490–91, 491–92, 492–95; Littlefield, *Africans and Creeks*, 135–36, 138; W. David Baird, *The Quapaw Indians: A History of the Downstream People* (Norman: University of Oklahoma Press, 1980), 97; Laurence M. Hauptman, *The Iroquois in the Civil War: From Battlefield to Reservation* (Syracuse, N.Y.: Syracuse University Press, 1993), 89, 91–93; Gary L. Cheatham, "Confederate Government Interests in the Quapaw, Osage, and Cherokee Tribal Lands of Kansas," *Kansas History* 27 (Autumn 2003): 172–85.

26. Kip Lindberg and Matt Matthews euphemistically called this "aggressive recruiting" ("'To Play a Bold Game': The Battle of Honey Springs," *North and South* 6 [Dec. 2002]: 58).

27. Kenneth W. Porter, "Billy Bowlegs (Holata Micco) in the Civil War (Part II)," *Florida Historical Quarterly* 45 (Apr. 1967): 394; McReynolds, *The Seminoles*, 293; Gaines, *Confederate Cherokees*, 29. See also Littlefield, *Africans and Creeks*, 135–36, 138; Debo, *Road to Disappearance*, 147–48; Britton, *Civil War*, 1:164–66. A Shawnee paraphrased Lincoln: "This is no fight of yours, it is between the white people. You keep out of it. If you cannot remain in your country in peace, come out of it, and if you loose property the government will pay you for it" (qtd. in Alford, *Civilization and Absentee Shawnees*, 6). See, too, Robert W. DeMoss' fictional *Exodus to Glory* (Tulsa, Okla.: the author, 1991).

28. Porter, "Billy Bowlegs," 394; McReynolds, *The Seminoles*, 293–94. The U.S.

Indian agent E. H. Carruth implied that military support might be forthcoming (Minges, *Slavery in the Cherokee Nation*, 112, 124).

29. Minges, *Slavery in the Cherokee Nation*, 111–12; "Sarah Wilson" (pp. 344, 346–47, 350–51), "Lucinda Davis" (p. 53), and "Morris Sheppard" (pp. 290–91), WPA, Oklahoma Writers Project, "Slave Narratives."

30. "Phoebe Banks" (pp. 8–9) and "Mary Grayson" (pp. 117–19, 123), WPA, Oklahoma Writers Project, "Slave Narratives."

31. Gaines, *Confederate Cherokees*, 27; Ross and Joseph Vann to Motley Kennard and Echo Harjot, Oct. 10, *PCJR*, 2:498; Ross to William P. Ross, Nov. 16, 1861, ibid., 2:503.

32. Ross to Opothleyahola, Sept. 19, Oct. 8, 11, 1861, *PCJR*, 2:487–88, 491–92, 495–96. See also Ross to Motley Kennard, Oct. 4, 8, 1861, Motley Kennard and Echo Harjo to Ross, Oct. 18, 1861, and Ross to Motley Kennard and Echo Harjo, Oct. 20, 1861, ibid., 2:490, 490–91, 496–97, 497–99.

33. Britton, *Civil War*, 1:165–67; McReynolds, *The Seminoles*, 295 and n, 298; Minges, *Slavery in the Cherokee Nation*, 115–17. The location of the site remains controversial, some favoring the remains of a camp on the Red Fork of the Arkansas River, while others favor Twin Mounds, near the present Yale, Oklahoma.

34. Baird, *The Quapaw Indians*, 98, 99; Mathews, *The Osages*, 628, 630–36, 637; Weer in *OR*, 13:431, 444; Hauptman, *Between Two Fires*, 31 (for Panipakuxwe ["Fall Leaf"]). See also Gary L. Cheatham, "Divided Loyalties in Civil War Kansas," *Kansas History* 11 (Summer 1988): 97–99.

35. Annie Heloise Abel, *The American Indian as Slaveholder and Secessionist*, 2d ed. (Lincoln: University of Nebraska Press, 1992 [1915]), 46–47n, 53–54n, 57, 229, 231; Dean Trickett, "The Civil War in the Indian Territory 1862," *Chronicles of Oklahoma* 19 (Mar. 1941): 56–57; Hauptman, *Iroquois in the Civil War*, 94.

36. Porter, "Billy Bowlegs," 395; Gaines, *Confederate Cherokees*, 30–31, 45, 46; Britton, *Civil War*, 1:167–68, 168–69.

37. Minges, *Slavery in the Cherokee Nation*, 117–22; Gaines, *Confederate Cherokees*, 46–47; Britton, *Civil War*, 1:170–71.

38. Porter, "Billy Bowlegs," 395–96; Minges, *Slavery in the Cherokee Nation*, 122–23; James M. McIntosh congratulatory order and report of Dec. 26, 1861, the latter from the *Washington [Arkansas] Telegraph*, Jan. 15, 1862, in *SOR*, 1 (ch. 8): 537, 538; Gaines, *Confederate Cherokees*, 55; Britton, *Civil War*, 1:172–73; McReynolds, *The Seminoles*, 266–67, 300, 301–2.

39. Porter, "Billy Bowlegs," 396; on Feb. 28, 1862, Coffin wrote Dole that Billy was among the "good commanders" and had arrived "recently" (qtd. in Abel, *Indian as Slaveholder*, 277n); Gaines, *Confederate Cherokees*, 59.

40. McReynolds, *The Seminoles*, 303, 304; Alford, *Civilization and the Absentee Shawnees*, 10–12; Debo, *Road to Disappearance*, 150–52; Hauptman, *Iroquois in the Civil War*, 96; Daniel C. Fitzgerald, *Ghost Towns of Kansas: A Traveler's Guide* (Lawrence: University Press of Kansas, 1988), 140–41, 144–45; Larry Lapssley, "The Story of a Kansas Freedman," ed. Alberta Pantle, *Kansas Historical Quarterly* 11 (Nov. 1942): 341–69; William A. Dobak, ed., "Civil War on the Kansas-Missouri Border: The

Narrative of Former Slave Andrew Williams," *Kansas History* 6 (Winter 1983–84): 237–39; Richard Sheridan, "From Slavery in Missouri to Freedom in Kansas: The Influx of Black Fugitives and Contrabands into Kansas, 1854–1865," *Kansas History* 12 (Spring 1989): 41–43.

    41. Porter, "Billy Bowlegs," 396–97; Col. William Weer to Moonlight, July 12, 1862, in *OR*, 13:487.

    42. William L. Shea, "1862: 'A Continual Thunder,'" in *Rugged and Sublime*, ed. Christ, 27, 29; Hauptman, *Iroquois in the Civil War*, 93. In general, see William L. Shea and Earl J. Hess, *Pea Ridge: Civil War Campaign in the West* (Chapel Hill: University of North Carolina Press, 1992), 274–75; Gaines, *Confederate Cherokees*, 80–89; Minges, *Slavery in the Cherokee Nation*, 135.

    43. Ross to Pike, Mar. 22 and Apr. 10, to Jefferson Davis, May 10, to Thomas C. Hindman, June 25, 1862, *PCJR*, 2:510, 511, 512–13, 513–15, 515; Minges, *Slavery in the Cherokee Nation*, 131–32, 147.

    44. Blunt to Caleb Smith, Nov. 21, 1862, the Abraham Lincoln Papers, Library of Congress, posted on-line as part of the American Memory Project at http://memory.loc.gov/ammem/alhtml/malhome/html (accessed Nov. 28, 2008). For a more critical view of the expedition, see Nichols, *Lincoln and the Indian*, 40–47, 48–50.

    45. In late October 1861 proponents of the expedition appealed to Lincoln to authorize raising "a Company of Mounted Sappers, Miners, & Engineers" for the expedition (*The Collected Works of Abraham Lincoln*, ed. Roy P. Basler, 9 vols. [New Brunswick, N.J.: Rutgers University Press, 1953–55], 5:9); Abel, *Indian as Slaveholder*, 235 and 235n; Hauptman, *Iroquois in the Civil War*, 94; Minges, *Slavery in the Cherokee Nation*, 124–25, 127–28.

    46. "The Indian Expedition," *Leavenworth Daily Conservative*, July 8, 1862, p. 2; Minges, *Slavery in the Cherokee Nation*, 137–39; Porter, "Billy Bowlegs," 397; Blunt to Caleb Smith, Nov. 21, 1862, the Abraham Lincoln Papers; Baird, *The Quapaw Indians*, 98, 99; Hauptman, *Between Two Fires*, 32, 33; Annie Heloise Abel, *The American Indian in the Civil War, 1862–1865* (Lincoln: University of Nebraska Press, 1992), 77 and 77n.

    47. "Mary Grayson," WPA, Oklahoma Writers Project, "Slave Narratives," 123; Littlefield, *Africans and Creeks*, 239; Hauptman, *Between Two Fires*, 32, 33. About half the unit essentially deserted after this campaign, and the ranks filled again with Cherokee warriors, many of them Confederate deserters, including James McDaniel, Moses Price, Archibald Scraper, Bud Gritts, Dirtthrower, Springfrog. Minges mistakenly moves Cherokee composition to earlier (*Slavery in the Cherokee Nation*, 137–38).

    48. Wiley Britton, *Memoirs of the Rebellion on the Border 1863* (Chicago: Cushing, Thomas and Col, 1882), 200. Later, the Indian regiments began receiving the new rifled muskets. Wiley Britton, *The Union Indian Brigade in the Civil War* (Kansas City, Mo.: F. Hudson, 1922), 58–79; Britton, *Civil War*, 1:297, 298–99; and, on Elder's involvement in the town council at Fort Scott, T. F. Robley, *History of Bourbon County, Kansas* (Fort Scott: the author, 1894), 177.

    49. Debo, *Road to Disappearance*, 159, 160; and, on the Creeks in Washington, White

and White, in *Now the Wolf Has Come*, 142, 174n; Tom Holman, "William G. Coffin, Lincoln's Superintendent of Indian Affairs for the Southern Superintendency," *Kansas Historical Quarterly* 39 (Winter 1973): 491–514.

CHAPTER 4: WHITENESS CHALLENGED

1. Wiley Britton, *The Civil War on the Border*, 2 vols. (New York: G. P. Putnam's Sons, 1899), 1:299; Robert M. Peck, "Wagon-Boss and Mule-Mechanic," *National Tribune*, July 28, 1904, p. 2; Patrick N. Minges, *Slavery in the Cherokee Nation: The Keetoowah Society and the Defining of a People 1855–1867* (New York: Routledge, 2003),139.

2. Craig W. Gaines, *The Confederate Cherokees: John Drew's Regiment of Mounted Rifles* (Baton Rouge: Louisiana State University Press, 1989), 95–96; Laurence M. Hauptman, *The Iroquois in the Civil War: From Battlefield to Reservation* (Syracuse, N.Y.: Syracuse University Press, 1993), 86, 94; Britton, *Civil War*, 1:296–97; Weer to Moonlight (Blunt), June 13, 16, 21, 22, 1862, in *OR*, 13:430, 434, 441, 444. As a reminder of Northern support for national expansion, even in the interest of the slaveholding South, Charles W. Doubleday, commander of the Second Ohio Cavalry, left his memoir *Reminiscences of the Filibuster War in Nicaragua* (New York: the author, 1886).

3. Weer to Moonlight (Blunt), June 13, 16, 21, 22, 23, July 2, Blunt to Weer, July 3, 1862, in *OR*, 13:430–431, 434, 441, 444–45, 460–61; "The Indian Expedition" and "The Fight at Cabin Creek," *Leavenworth Daily Conservative*, July 8, 19, 1863, both p. 2; Peck, "Wagon-Boss and Mule-Mechanic," *National Tribune*, July 28, August 4, 11, 18, 1904, all p. 2; "A Trip to Fort Blunt" (from the *Republican*), *Denver Weekly Commonwealth*, September 3, 1863, p. 3; Samuel R. Curtis to Abraham Lincoln, Feb. 28, 1864, the Abraham Lincoln Papers, Library of Congress, posted on-line as part of the American Memory Project at http://memory.loc.gov/ammem/alhtml/malhome/html (accessed Nov. 28, 2008).

4. Weer to Moonlight (Blunt), June 13, 16, 22, July 2, 1862; James A. Phillips to Ross, June 26, 1862, James A. Phillips to W. R. Judson, June 28, Salomon to Weer, June 30, Weer to Moonlight, July 2, 1862, in *OR*, 13:430, 431, 434, 444, 459, 450, 456, 458, 460; *History of Newton, Lawrence, Barry and McDonald Counties, Missouri* (Chicago: Goodspeed, 1888), 313; "The Indian Expedition," *Leavenworth Daily Conservative*, July 10, 1862, p. 2; Gaines, *Confederate Cherokees*, 98–100, 114; Peck, "Wagon-Boss and Mule-Mechanic," *National Tribune*, July 28, 1904, p. 2.

5. Weer to Moonlight, July 4, 5, 6, 1862, in *OR*, 13:137, 137–38, 138; Watie's Report, July 6, 1862, and Clarkson to Cooper, Feb. 29, 1864, *SOR*, 3 (ch. 13): 19–22, 35–36; Gaines, *Confederate Cherokees*, 100–103; *History of Newton*, 313, 473–74; Henry A. Franks, *Stand Watie and the Agony of the Cherokee Nation* (Memphis, Tenn.: Memphis State University Press, 1979), 128–29; Maumee (pseud.), "From the Cherokee Nation" and "Affairs in the Indian Country," *Leavenworth Daily Conservative*, July 15, 20, 1862, both p. 2; J. Leitch Wright Jr., *Creeks and Seminoles: The Destruction and Regeneration of the Muscogulge People* (Lincoln: University of Nebraska Press, 1986), 307.

6. Ritchie to Blunt, July 5, 1862, Weer to Moonlight, July 6, 1862, Ross to Weer, July 8, 1862, Capt. H. S. Greeno to Weer, July 15, 1862, in *OR*, 13:138, 463–64, 473, 516–18; Watie's report, July 6, 1862, *SOR*, 3 (ch. 13): 22; Britton, *Civil War*, 1:303–4, 304, 305–6; "Notes from the Diary of Susan E. Foreman," ed. Linda Finley, *Chronicles of Oklahoma* 47 (Winter 1969): 395, 396; Gaines, *Confederate Cherokees*, 103–4, 105, 107–8, 110–11; Minges, *Slavery in the Cherokee Nation*, 132–33, 142, 143, 146–47; James G. Blunt, "General Blunt's Account of His Civil War Experiences," *Kansas Historical Quarterly* 1 (May 1932): 224; Trevor Jones, "In Defense of Sovereignty: Cherokee Soldiers, White Officers, and Discipline in the Third Indian Home Guard," *The Chronicles of Oklahoma* 82 (Winter 2004–5): 413; Maumee (pseud.), "From the Cherokee Nation" and "The Indian Expedition," *Leavenworth Daily Conservative*, July 15, July 31, 1862, both p. 2.

7. Weer to Moonlight, July 2, 4, 6, 1862, in *OR*, 13:460–61, 137, 137–38. For information on other individuals, see also Gaines, *Confederate Cherokees*, 17, 46–48, 57, 93, 121, 109, 121–22 (Pegg), 123 (Scraper), 123 (McDaniel), 28, 40–41, 121–22 (W. P. Ross), 18, 121, 122 (Downing), 18, 123 (Vann), 124 (members of Ross family); Kenneth W. Porter, "Billy Bowlegs (Holata Micco) in the Civil War (Part II)," *Florida Historical Quarterly* 45 (Apr. 1967): 397. See report of William P. Dole, Oct. 31, 1863, in *The American Indian and the United States: A Documentary History*, 3 vols. (New York: Random House, 1973), 1:114–15; "The Indian Expedition" and "Wm. A. Phillips" (quoting T. Dwight Thatcher in the *Lawrence Republican*), *Leavenworth Daily Conservative*, July 31 and August 2, 1862, both p. 2.

8. Weer to Moonlight, June 13, 1862, James A. Phillips to Salomon, June 27, 1862, Weer to Moonlight, July 2, 12, 1862, in *OR*, 13:431, 452, 461, 487–88 (all these letters complained about the lack of arms, clothing, or rations for 1,500 Cherokee recruits); Maumee (pseud.), "From the Cherokee Nation," *Leavenworth Daily Conservative*, July 15, 1862, p. 2; Peck, "Wagon-Boss and Mule-Mechanic," *National Tribune*, July 28, August 11, 1904, both on p. 2. They initially sent "about 250 negroes" north by wagons.

9. Blunt to Stanton, July 20, 1862, to Weer, July 19, 1862, ibid., in *OR*, 13:483, 489; Glenn L. Carle, "The First Kansas Colored," *American Heritage* 43 (Mar. 1992): 82; Richard Sheridan, "From Slavery in Missouri to Freedom in Kansas: The Influx of Black Fugitives and Contrabands into Kansas, 1854–1865," *Kansas History* 12 (Spring 1989): 44; Williams in *BUSAF*, 2:51–52; Lane to Matthews, Aug. 18, 1862, in *Freedom: A Documentary History of Emancipation 1861–1867: Selected from the Holdings of the National Archives of the United States, Series II: The Black Military Experience*, ed. Ira Berlin (Cambridge: Cambridge University Press, 1982), 69; "Lucinda Davis," WPA, Oklahoma Writers Project, "Slave Narratives from the Federal Writers' Project 1936–38" (typescript, Washington, D.C., 1941), 59; "The Colored Regiment," *Leavenworth Daily Conservative*, August 6, 1862, p. 2.

10. Williams in *BUSAF*, 2:52–53; Carle, "The First Kansas Colored," 82; *Collected Works of Abraham Lincoln*, ed. Roy P. Basler, 9 vols. (New Brunswick, N.J.: Rutgers University Press, 1953–55), 6:188, 395–96; "The Colored Regiment," with ongoing coverage under "Arming the Negroes" and "A colored Brigade from Kansas,"

Leavenworth Daily Conservative, March 5, 1863, April 10, 12, 13, 25, 1863, all on p. 2; Lary C. Rampp; "Negro Troop Activity in Indian Territory, 1863–1865," in *The Price of Freedom: Slavery and the Civil War*, ed. Martin H. Greenberg and Charles G. Waugh (Nashville, Tenn.: Cumberland House, 2000), 173–75.

11. Salomon to all commanders, July 18, 1862, in *OR*, 13:476; Salomon to Blunt, July 20, 29, 1862, ibid., 485 and 521; Blunt to Salomon, Aug. 3, 1862, ibid., 532; Britton, *Civil War*, 1:249, 306; Gaines, *Confederate Cherokees*, 112–13; Minges, *Slavery in the Cherokee Nation*, 143–44. See also David A. Nichols, *Lincoln and the Indian: Civil War Policy and Politics* (Columbia, Mo.: University of Missouri Press, 1978), 52–53; Blunt, "General Blunt's Account," 223–24; Blunt to Caleb Smith, Nov. 21, 1862, the Abraham Lincoln Papers.

12. Britton, *Civil War*, 1:310; E. H. Carruth and H. W. Martin to Blunt, July 19, 1862, Lt. A. C. Ellithorpe, General Order No. 1, July 19, 1862, R. W. Furnas to Blunt, July 25, 1862, Salomon to Blunt, July 29, 1862, in *OR*, 13:478, 481; 512, 521; Gaines, *Confederate Cherokees*, 114, 115–16; John J. Mathews, *The Osages: Children of the Middle Waters* (Norman: University of Oklahoma Press, 1961), 649; W. David Baird, *The Quapaw Indians: A History of the Downstream People* (Norman: University of Okalahoma Press, 1980), 99. See also Thomas Weston Tipton, *Forty Years of Nebraska at Home and in Congress* (Lincoln, Neb.: n.p., 1902), 120, 122.

13. Phillips to Furnas, July 27, Aug. 6, 1862, Blunt to Stanton, July 21, 1862, in *OR*, 13:181–82, 183, 184, 486; Gaines, *Confederate Cherokees*, 116–17; Britton, *Civil War*, 1:310–11; Minges, *Slavery in the Cherokee Nation*, 145. Panipakuxwe ("Fall Leaf") to the commissioner of Indian affairs, Dec. 4, 1863, qtd. in Laurence M. Hauptman, *Between Two Fires: American Indians in the Civil War* (New York: Free Press, 1993), 34.

14. Britton, *Civil War*, 1:308, 309–10, 311–12, 337–38; "The Indian Expedition," *Leavenworth Daily Conservative*, July 31, 1862, p. 2; Blunt to Caleb Smith, Nov. 21, 1862, the Abraham Lincoln Papers.

15. "Diary of Susan E. Foreman," 397; Britton, *Civil War*, 1:306, 312; Wiley Britton, *The Aftermath of the Civil War Based on Investigation of War Claims* (Kansas City, Mo.: printed by Smith-Grieves, 1925), 212; B. S. Henning to Blunt, Oct. 11, 1862, in *OR*, 13:726; Blunt to Caleb Smith, Nov. 21, 1862, the Abraham Lincoln Papers.

16. Blunt to Stanton, July 21, Phillips to Furnas, Aug. 6, Blunt to Lincoln, Aug. 13, General Order No. 4, Aug. 24, 1862, in *OR*, 13:183, 485–505, 565–66, 595; Britton, *Civil War*, 1:306–7, 308. Blunt later ordered the white troops to Fort Scott.

17. Alvin M. Josephy Jr., *The Civil War in the American West* (New York: Knopf, 1991), 99–100, 106; Tipton, *Forty Years of Nebraska*, 120, 122. For Whipple and other critics of Indian policy, see Robert W. Mardock, *The Reformers and the American Indian* (Columbia, Mo.: University of Missouri Press, 1971), and Francis Paul Prucha, *American Indian Policy in Crisis: Christian Reformers and the Indian, 1865–1900* (Norman: University of Oklahoma Press, 1976).

18. Salomon to Blunt, Aug. 2, 9, E. B. Brown to Schofield, Aug. 5, B. S. Henning to John Richie, Aug. 5, to Lt. Blocki, Aug. 6, 1862, Salomon to Schofield, Blunt to Curtis, and Col. George H. Hall to Gen. E. B. Brown, all Oct. 1, 1862, Blunt to Lane,

Sept. 16, 1862, in *OR*, 13:287, 289, 529, 552, 540, 543, 576–79, 641, 697; Richard S. Brownlee, *Gray Ghosts of the Confederacy* (Baton Rouge: Louisiana State University Press, 1958), 93–95, 98–99; *History of Newton*, 474, 640, 315; Edwin C. Bearss and Arrell M. Gibson, *Fort Smith: Little Gibraltar on the Arkansas*, 2d ed. (Norman: University of Oklahoma Press, 1979), 259; "General Blunt's Late Expedition," *Leavenworth Daily Conservative*, Oct. 9, 1862, p. 2.

19. Blunt's Special Order No. 28, Sept. 13, 1862, in *OR*, 13:630; Cheryl H. Morris, "Choctaw and Chickasaw Indian Agents, 1831–1874," *Chronicles of Oklahoma* 50 (Winter 1972–73): 415; Hauptman, *Iroquois in the Civil War*, 86–87, 95; R. Halliburton Jr., *Red over Black: Black Slavery among the Cherokee Indians* (Westport, Conn.: Greenwood, 1971), 129; Morris L. Wardell, *A Political History of the Cherokee Nation, 1838–1907* (Norman: University of Oklahoma Press, 1938), 158–59; Carol B. Broemeling, "Cherokee Indian Agents, 1830–1874," *Chronicles of Oklahoma* 50 (Winter 1972–73): 452; LeRoy H. Fisher, "United States Indian Agents to the Five Civilized Tribes," *Chronicles of Oklahoma* 50 (Winter 1972–73): 412, 413.

20. Ward L. Schrantz, *Jasper County, Missouri, in the Civil War*, 2d ed. (Carthage, Mo.: Carthage Kiwanis Club, 1988 [1923]), 75–77, 80–86; Phillips to Blunt, Sept. 5, Weer to Moonlight, Sept. 12, Ritchie to Blunt, Sept. 21, Sept. 23, Ritchie to Wattles, Sept. 23, Salomon to E. B. Brown, Sept. 23, Weer to Blunt, Sept. 24, 1862, in *OR*, 13:277, 615, 627, 659, 661, 662, 666; Samuel Crawford, *Kansas in the Sixties* (Chicago: A. C. McClurg, 1911), 52, 53; Blunt to Caleb Smith, Nov. 21, 1862, the Abraham Lincoln Papers; Peck, "Wagon-Boss and Mule-Mechanic," *National Tribune*, July 28, 1904, p. 2; Glenn Shirley, *Belle Starr and Her times: The Literature, the Facts, and the Legend* (Norman: University of Oklahoma Press, 1982). White criminals sometimes disguised themselves as Indians, according the December 29, 1862, complaint against John Willis from Newton County; see Missouri's Union Provost Marshal Papers: 1861–1866, F 1489, available at http://www.sos.mo.gov/archives/provost/ (accessed Nov. 28, 2008).

21. Phillips to Blunt, Sept. 5, Weer to Moonlight, Sept. 10, Blunt to Weer, Sept. 12, Blunt's Special Order No. 28, Sept. 13, Blunt to Lane, Sept. 16, Salomon to Blunt, Blunt to Weer and to Salomon, all Sept. 22, 1862, Weer to Blunt, Sept. 24, Blunt to Salomon and Weer to Salomon, Sept. 26, 1862, in *OR*, 13:615, 622, 626, 630, 641, 657, 666, 294; *History of Newton*, 315, 474–75; Blunt, "General Blunt's Account," 224–27; Britton, *Aftermath of the Civil War*, 212.

22. For the order, see Blunt to Salomon, Sept. 30, 1862, in *OR*, 13:692. Blunt to Salomon, Sept. 30, Lynde to Salomon, Salomon to Schofield, Weer to Blunt, and Hall to Brown, all Oct. 1, Lt. Col. Arthur Jacobi to Salomon, Oct. 3, 1862, William R. Judson's undated report, in *OR*, 13:287, 288, 289, 291–92, 293–94, 295–96, 672, 692; Cooper to Rains, Oct. 2, 1862, in *OR*, 13:287, 288, 290, 293, 296, 301; James S. Rains, Oct. 4, 1862, *SOR*, 3 (ch. 13): 58; *PCJR*, 2:521; Britton, *Civil War*, 1:353; Britton, *Aftermath of the Civil War*, 201–2, 205–7; Edwin C. Bearss, "The Army of the Frontier's First Campaign: The Confederates Win at Newtonia," *Missouri Historical Review* 60 (Apr. 1966): 283–319; Bruce Nichols, *Guerrilla Warfare in Civil War Missouri* (Jefferson, N.C.: McFarland, 2004), 176–77; Crawford, *Kansas in the Sixties*,

54; James Lemuel Clark, *Civil War Recollections of James Lemuel Clark and the Great Hanging of Gainesville, Texas, in October 1862*, ed. L. D. Clark (Plano: Republic of Texas Press, 1997), 70, 16–18, 56–64, 68, 69; *History of Newton*, 317–18. The *Leavenworth Daily Conservative* hardly gives more than a mere notice in "The Last Great Battle," October 9, 1862, p. 2. On Cooper's drunkenness, see Robert Collins, *General James G. Blunt: Tarnished Glory* (Gretna, Miss.: Pelican, 2005), 78.

23. "The Battle of Helena, Arkansas," *Leavenworth Daily Conservative*, July 28, 1863, p. 2.

24. "Spiritualist Conference at Clinton Hall, New York. Tuesday Evening, April 30, 1861," "Father Beeson and the Indians," "The Indians," and "Spiritualism and the Indians," *Banner of Light*, May 18 (p. 8), October 5 (p. 5), December 14 (p. 6), 1861, August 23 (p. 4), October 18 (p. 3), 1862, August 15 (p. 2), 1863; Ross to Lincoln, Sept. 16, 17, Ross to Lewis Downing, Sept. 19, 1862, two letters of Ross to Dole, Oct. 13, 1862, Ross to Edwin M. Stanton, Nov. 8, Ross to Phillips, Jan. 4, 1863, *PCJR*, 2:516–18, 518, 518–19, 519–20, 521, 520–22, 525; Lincoln to Curtis, Oct. 10, Curtis to Lincoln, Oct. 16, 1862, in *OR*, 13:723; Curtis qtd. in *History of Newton*, 642; "The Refugee Indians," *Leavenworth Daily Conservative*, December 18, 1862, p. 2; Nichols, *Lincoln and the Indian*, 33–36, 56–57; Lincoln to Whipple and Beeson qtd. in Mardock, *Reformers and the Indian*, 12–13, 14–15. Dole asked to take Phillips's letter to the president; Ross gave it to him, but the correspondence subsequently disappeared.

25. Schofield to Curtis, Oct. 11, General Order No. 6, Oct. 20, Lt. Col. Owen A. Bassett, Oct. 24, 1862, Cooper's report Oct. 25, Blunt to Schofield, Oct. 28, Cooper's report Dec. 15, 1862, in *OR*, 13:324, 325, 326, 328, 330, 331, 335, 725, 754; Hindman to T. Holmes, Oct. 20, Oct. 25, Michael W. Busten to Cooper, Nov. 4, Major R. C. Newton, Oct. 24, Nov. 3, 1862, *SOR*, 3 (ch. 13): 59–62, 62–64, 64–67, 68–69, 69–70; Crawford, *Kansas in the Sixties*, 54–55, 55–56, 56–57, 58–59, 59–61, 61–62; Britton, *Civil War*, 1:364–64, 366–67, 368–74; *History of Newton*, 643–44; *History of Benton, Washington, Carroll, Madison, Crawford, Franklin, and Sebastian Counties, Arkansas* (Chicago: Goodspeed, 1889; repr., *Benton County* section, Siloam Springs, Ark.: Benton Historical Society, [1978]), 111–12; Philip A. Kalish and Beatrice J. Kalish, "Indian Territory Forts: Charnel Houses of the Frontier, 1839–1865," *Chronicles of Oklahoma* 50 (Spring 1972): 66, 67–68; Blunt, "General Blunt's Account," 227–28; Collins, *General James G. Blunt*, 81–82 (Cooper rumor); "Letter from the Kansas Army in Arkansas," by Pen (pseud.), and "From the Eleventh Kansas," *Leavenworth Daily Conservative*, October 29, November 13, 1862, both p. 2; Blunt to Caleb Smith, Nov. 21, 1862, the Abraham Lincoln Papers.

26. "Loyal Indians Victorious," *Leavenworth Daily Conservative*, November 29, 1862, p. 2; Hauptman, *Between Two Fires*, 28–29, 29–30, 35–36; F. Johnson to Dole, Jan. 20, 1863, qtd. in Annie Heloise Abel, *The American Indian in the Civil War, 1862–1865* (Lincoln: University of Nebraska Press, 1992), 183, 329–30n, and also 184, though this account does not note the crucial presence of the Kickapoo.

27. Blunt to Curtis, Nov. 29, Dec. 2, and 3, 1862, in *OR*, 22 (pt. 1): 41–42, 42–43, 43–46 (also other reports from both Federal [46–52] and Confederate [53–59]

sources), along with Harrison to Herron, Dec. 11, 1862, *SOR*, 4 (ch. 22): 29–33; Britton, *Civil War*, 1:377, 379, 380, 381, 382–83, 384, 385–86, 388, 390, 391, 392–93, 395; Jay Monaghan, *Civil War on the Western Border, 1854–1865* (Boston, Little, Brown, 1955), 258; Blunt, "General Blunt's Account," 228–29, 229–30. For accounts depicting Federal (and even Confederate) Indians as uncivilized savages slaughterable in vast numbers by a few virtuous whites, see John N. Edwards, *Shelby and His Men*, (Cincinnati: Miami, 1867), 85, 91–92, 99–103, 99–103; Edwards, *Noted Guerrillas* (St. Louis: Bryan, Brand; Chicago: Thompson and Wakefield, 1877), 320, 330, 331.

28. "The Civil War Diary of John Howard Kitts," *Kansas State Historical Society Collections* 14 (1915–18): 321, 322, 323; Kim Allen Scott, "The Fighting Printers of Company E, Eleventh Kansas Volunteer Infantry," *Arkansas Historical Quarterly* 46 (Autumn 1987): 271–73, 273–74; Theda Perdue, *Slavery and the Evolution of Cherokee Society, 1540–1866* (Knoxville: University of Tennessee Press, 1979), 136; William G. McLoughlin, *Champions of the Cherokee: Evan and John B. Jones* (Princeton, N.J.: Princeton University Press, 1990), 227–29, 364, 378.

29. Federal reports in *OR*, 22 (pt. 1): 68–138, with Confederate reports on 138–58 and in *SOR*, 4 (ch. 22): 33–92; Crawford, *Kansas in the Sixties*, 76–78; Collins, *General James. G. Blunt*, 116–20; Monaghan, *Civil War on the Western Border*, 260, 263, 264–69, 269–70; Britton, *Civil War*, 1:398–99, 401–32; Wiley Britton, *The Union Indian Brigade in the Civil War* (Kansas City, Mo.: F. Hudson, 1922), 131–41; Wattles, Dec. 12, 1862, in *OR*, 22 (pt. 1): 93, 94; Porter, "Billy Bowlegs," 397; *OAR*, VII, 274; Blunt, "General Blunt's Account," 232–33, 233–34.

30. For the movement on Van Buren, see *OR*, 22 (pt. 1): 167–71, and Hindman's Feb. 5, 1863, report on his abandonment of the town, ibid., 171–73; Scott, "Fighting Printers of Company E," 279; Britton, *Civil War*, 1:431, 433, 434–36, 436–38, 438, 439–40, 441; William L. Shea, "1862: 'A Continual Thunder,'" in *Rugged and Sublime: The Civil War in Arkansas*, ed. Mark K. Christ (Fayetteville: University of Arkansas Press, 1994), 56; Blunt, "General Blunt's Account," 234–38. "H.J. Sr." reported that Arkansans, including wounded rebels, cheered the Federals' march (Frank Moore, ed., *The Rebellion Record: A Diary of American Events, with Documents, Narratives, Illustrative Incidents, Poetry, Etc.*, 12 vols. [New York: Putnam, 1861–63 (vols. 1–6); New York: Van Nostrand, 1864–68 (vols. 7–12)], 6:307–10, also in *SOR*, 4 [ch. 22]: 97–105).

31. Britton, *Civil War*, 1:441, 443, 2:3; Brownlee, *Gray Ghosts*, 145, 146, 149–50, 151–54.

32. Battery (pseud.), "The 1st Kansas Colored Regiment," dated July 13, in *New York Daily Tribune*, July 22, 1863, p. 3; Joseph T. Glatthaar, *Forged in Battle: The Civil War Alliance of Black Soldiers and White Officers* (New York: Free Press; London: Collier-Macmillan, 1990), 187; Noah Andre Trudeau, *Like Men of War: Black Troops in the Civil War, 1862–1865* (Boston: Little, Brown, 1998), 3–7. See sources cited in Dudley T. Cornish, "Kansas Negro Regiments in the Civil War," *Kansas Historical Quarterly* 20 (May 1953): 419n, 420n (these include the *New York Times*, Oct. 12, 1862).

33. Brownlee, *Gray Ghosts*, 103, 104; Carle, "The First Kansas Colored," 84, 86; Williams in *BUSAF*, 2:53; "The Engagement at Island Mound," *Leavenworth Daily Conservative*, November 13, 1862, p. 2; Cornish, "Kansas Negro Regiments," 421,

42 1n; *Lawrence Republican,* Nov. 6, 1862, qtd. from Sheridan, "From Slavery to Freedom," 44; Trudeau, *Like Men of War,* 3–7; Richard J. Hinton, "The Kansas Negro Regiment," *Liberator,* November 21, 1862, p. 186; "The 1st Kansas Colored Regiment," *New York Daily Tribune,* July 22, 1863, p. 3.

34. Blunt to Curtis, Apr. 29, May 30, 1863, in *OR,* 22 (pt. 2): 260, 261.

35. Carle, "The First Kansas Colored," 82, 84; *Anti-Slavery Standard,* Jan. 24, 1863, qtd. in Benjamin Quarles, *Allies for Freedom: Blacks and John Brown* (New York: Oxford University Press, 1974), 161, 222n54; Richard J. Hinton, "Muster of the Colored Regiment," *Leavenworth Daily Conservative,* January 17, 1863, p. 2.

36. Williams et al. to Lane, Jan. 9, 1863, in *Freedom,* 334–35, 335n; Williams in *BUSAF,* 2:54. Among its officers signing the protest was Captain William Smallwood, a future Greenback leader. See also Matthews to Lane and Hinton to Lane, *Freedom,* 69–70, 70n, 335–36.

37. "The Colored Regiment," *Leavenworth Daily Conservative,* May 8, 1863, p. 2; Williams in *BUSAF,* 2:54; Cornish, "Kansas Negro Regiments," 422–23; Williams to Capt. H. G. Loring, Apr. 21, 1863, in *Freedom,* 72–73.

38. Huckleberry Downing et al. to Ross, Jan. 8, 1863, *PCJR,* 2:527; Phillips to Blunt, Dec. 25, 1862, in *OR,* 22 (pt. 1): 873; Phillips to Curtis, Jan. 29, Feb. 4, 1863, ibid., 22 (pt. 2): 85, 96–97; Britton, *Civil War,* 1:432, 440.

39. White Catcher et al. to Ross and Daniel H. Ross to Ross, both Dec. 2, 1862, *PCJR,* 2:522–23, 523; Britton, *Civil War,* 2:36.

40. Scott, "Fighting Printers of Company E," 279–80. The *Van Buren Press* had ceased publication in January 1862.

41. Richard J. Hinton, *Rebel Invasion of Missouri and Kansas, and the Campaign of the Army of the Border, against Sterling Price, in October and November, 1864* (Chicago: Church and Goodman; Leavenworth, Kan.: F. W. Marshall, 1865), 331; Blunt to Lynde, Apr. 16, 1863, in *OR,* 22 (pt. 2): 222; Blunt, "General Blunt's Account," 239; Collins, *General James G. Blunt,* 120–23, 124; Peck, "Wagon-Boss and Mule-Mechanic," *National Tribune,* July 28, 1904, p. 2. On Daniels, see Michael Fellman, *Inside War: The Guerilla Conflict in Missouri during the American Civil War* (New York: Oxford University Press, 1989), 161.

42. For Federal reports, in *OR,* 22 (pt. 1): 178–94; for Confederate reports, ibid., 194–211, along with *SOR,* 4 (ch. 22): 105–10; Frederick W. Goman, *Up from Arkansas* (Springfield, Mo.: Wilson's Creek National Battlefield Foundation, 1999); Frank W. Klingberg, *The Southern Claim Commission* (Berkeley: University of California Press, 1955), 101; Wiley Britton, *Pioneer Life in Southwest Missouri* (Kansas City, Mo.: Smith-Grieves, 1929), 347–48, 352–53; David Pickering and Judy Falls, *Brush Men and Vigilantes: Civil War Dissent in Texas* (College Station: Texas A&M University Press, 2009), 69, 71–72, 75; A. W. Bishop, *Loyalty on the Frontier* (St. Louis: R. P. Studley, 1863), 78; Richard Current, *Lincoln's Loyalists: Union Soldiers from the Confederacy* (New York: Oxford University Press, 1994), 4–10, 168, 210; *History of Benton,* 544–45.

43. *Rebellion Record,* 6 ("Documents"): 60–70 (for reports), 70–79 (for newspaper accounts); Monaghan, *Civil War on the Western Border,* 267, 269, 262, 270–71, 432; Collins, *General James G. Blunt,* 101–2.

44. Britton, *Civil War*, 2:23, 32–33; [James W. Demby], *Mysteries and Miseries of Arkansas* (St. Louis: the author, 1863).

45. Craig Miner and William E. Unrau, *The End of Indian Kansas: A Study of Cultural Revolution, 1854–1871* (Lawrence: University Press of Kansas, 1978), 40, 31, 65; Collins, *General James G. Blunt*, 111; Albert E. Castle, *Civil War Kansas: Reaping the Whirlwind*, 2d ed. (Lawrence: University Press of Kansas, 1997), 94–95; Charles Robinson, *The Kansas Conflict* (New York: Harper and Brothers, 1892), 419–20; "Removal of the Indians" and "Organization of the Indian Territory," *Leavenworth Daily Conservative*, Dec. 21, 27, 1862, both p. 2; "The Indians" and "Meeting for the Indians" (from the *Washington Sunday Times*), *Banner of Light*, February 7 (p. 3), 21 (p. 3, with editorial on p. 5), May 2 (p. 3), 1863; discussions of Indian rights in *Banner of Light*, August 23, 1862, p. 4, August 15, 1863, p. 2.

CHAPTER 5: THE UNION AS IT NEVER WAS

1. Hinton to Lane, Jan. 12, 1863, in *Freedom: A Documentary History of Emancipation 1861–1867: Selected from the Holdings of the National Archives of the United States, Series II: the Black Military Experience*, ed. Ira Berlin (Cambridge: Cambridge University Press, 1982), 335, 336. Hinton likely wrote the *Missouri Democrat* account of an expedition "composed of Nebraska and Kansas volunteers, one regiment from Colorado and 5000 Indians": "Every effort is being made to start the expedition by the 10th of May. A negro regiment has nearly completed the fortification of Fort Scott" ("Gen. Blunt's Texas Expedition" *Boston Herald*, May 5, 1863, p. 2).

2. Blunt to Caleb Smith, Nov. 21, 1862, the Abraham Lincoln Papers, Library of Congress, posted on-line as part of the American Memory Project at http://memory.loc.gov/ammem/alhtml/malhome/html (accessed Nov. 28, 2008); Curtis to Lincoln, Oct. 16, 1862, and the brigade returns of June 30, 1863, in *OR*, 13:723, 22 (pt. 2): 342; James G. Blunt, "General Blunt's Account of His Civil War Experiences," *Kansas Historical Quarterly* 1 (May 1932): 238–39; Ross to Phillips, Jan. 4, 1863, statement by Nat Fish, et al., Jan. 23, 1863, and Daniel H. Ross to John Ross, Jan. 23, 1863, *PCJR*, 2:525, 526, 533; Wiley Britton, *The Civil War on the Border*, 2 vols. (New York: G. P. Putnam's Sons, 1899), 2:22.

3. Britton, *Civil War*, 2:7–8; Laurence M. Hauptman, *The Iroquois in the Civil War: From Battlefield to Reservation* (Syracuse, N.Y.: Syracuse University Press, 1993), 94, 94–95; Huckleberry Downing et al. to Ross, Jan. 8, 1863, Ross to Evan Jones (ca. Feb. 15, 1864) and to the U.S. Senate and House of Representatives, Feb. 18, 1865, *PCJR*, 2:528, 561, 625; Angie Debo, *The Road to Disappearance: A History of the Creek Indians*, 2d ed. (Norman: University of Oklahoma Press, 1979), 154; "The Refugee Indians," *Leavenworth Daily Conservative*, December 18, 1862, p. 2; Dole's report, Oct. 31, 1863, in *The American Indian and the United States: A Documentary History*, 3 vols. (New York: Random House, 1973), 1:116–17, 118; Edwin C. McReynolds, *The Seminoles* (Norman: University of Oklahoma Press, 1957), 305–6. By 1864 officials counted some 14,790 refugees of the territory in Kansas (Jane F. Lancaster, *Removal Aftershock: The Seminole Struggle to Survive in the West, 1836–1866* [Knoxville: University of Tennessee Press, 1994], 147).

4. Correspondence in *PCJR*, 2:528, 529, 530, 533, and correspondence in *OR*, 22 (pt. 2): 152, 163, 165, 181, 168, 181, 190; Blunt to Caleb Smith, Nov. 21, 1862, the Abraham Lincoln Papers; "The Refugee Indians," "The Indian Brigade" (from the *New York Times*), "From Arkansas," "Slavery Abolished in the Cherokee Nation," and "Action of the Cherokee Legislature," *Leavenworth Daily Conservative*, December 18, 31, 1862, February 22, 1863, March 19, 29, 1863, all p. 2; *History of Newton, Lawrence, Barry and McDonald Counties, Missouri* (Chicago: Goodspeed, 1888), 319–20, 330–31, 328, 759; Kenneth W. Porter, "Billy Bowlegs (Holata Micco) in the Civil War (Part II)," *Florida Historical Quarterly* 45 (Apr. 1967): 398.

5. Morris L. Wardell, *A Political History of the Cherokee Nation, 1838–1907* (Norman: University of Oklahoma Press, 1938), 172, 174–75; Patrick N. Minges, *Slavery in the Cherokee Nation: The Keetoowah Society and the Defining of a People 1855–1867* (New York: Routledge, 2003), 152–53; Huckleberry Downing et al. to Ross, Jan. 8, Ross to Henry C. Meigs, Mar. 11, 1863, *PCJR*, 2:528, 534; Britton, *Civil War*, 2:23–26, 27; R. Halliburton Jr., *Red over Black: Black Slavery among the Cherokee Indians* (Westport, Conn.: Greenwood, 1971), 132; Theda Perdue, *Slavery and the Evolution of Cherokee Society, 1540–1866* (Knoxville: University of Tennessee Press, 1979), 137–38; "The Cherokees," "Slavery Abolished in the Cherokee Nation," and "Action of the Cherokee Legislature," *Leavenworth Daily Conservative*, February 22, March 12, 19, 1863, all p. 2; Phillips to Blunt, Mar. 19, Apr. 2, 27, May 1, 1863, in *OR*, 22 (pt. 2): 162, 190, 256, 266.

6. Britton, *Civil War*, 2:26. Richard J. Hinton, "Charley Lenhart" [*sic*], *Leavenworth Daily Conservative*, May 2, 1863, p. 2.

7. Britton, *Civil War*, 2:28–29, 33, 34–35, 37; Wiley Britton, *The Aftermath of the Civil War Based on Investigation of War Claims* (Kansas City, Mo.: printed by Smith-Grieves, 1925), 213, 214; Annie Heloise Abel, *The American Indian in the Civil War, 1862–1865* (Lincoln: University of Nebraska Press, 1992), 206, 207–8, 209; Phillips to Blunt, Apr. 2, 8, 12, 24 (referring to orders), Blunt to Phillips, Apr. 11, 1863, in *OR*, 22 (pt. 2): 190, 205, 212, 247; Carolyn Thomas Foreman, *Park Hill* (Muskogee, Okla.: n.p., 1948), 123; Robert M. Peck, "Wagon-Boss and Mule-Mechanic," *National Tribune*, August 11, 1904, p. 2.

8. Philip A. Kalish and Beatrice J. Kalish, "Indian Territory Forts: Charnel Houses of the Frontier, 1839–1865," *Chronicles of Oklahoma* 50 (Spring 1972): 66, 67, 68, 73–74, 75 (quotation on 69); Britton, *Civil War*, 2:37–38, 39; Chief John Ross' annual messages, Oct. 3, 1859, and Oct. 4, 1860, *PCJR*, 2:426, 451. For a survey of what remains, see Q. B. Boydstun, "Fort Gibson Barracks, Powder Magazine, and Bake Oven," *Chronicles of Oklahoma* 50 (Fall 1972): 289–96; Phillips to Blunt, published as "From Arkansas," *Leavenworth Daily Conservative*, May 15, 1863, p. 2.

9. "The Cherokees," "Roster of the Fourth and Fifth Indian Regiments," Phillips to Blunt, "From Arkansas," and "A Card," *Leavenworth Daily Conservative*, February 22, March 6, May 15, August 16, 1863, all p. 2; Britton, *Civil War*, 2:40, 48; Minges, *Slavery in the Cherokee Nation*, 151–52; Phillips to Blunt, Dec. 28, 1862, Phillips to Blunt, Apr. 2, 1863, in *OR*, 22 (pt. 1): 881, 22 (pt. 2): 190, 256; Huckleberry Downing et al. to Ross, Jan. 8, 1863, *PCJR*, 2:527; Debo, *The Road to Disappearance*, 154.

10. Britton, *Civil War*, 2:25; Angie Debo, *The Rise and Fall of the Choctaw Republic* (Norman: University of Oklahoma Press, 1934), 133, 196; Billy Bowlegs to Commissioner Dole, May 2, 13, 1863, qtd. in Porter, "Billy Bowlegs," 398; Lancaster, *Removal Aftershock*, 143–44, 151 (citing Pascofar to Lincoln, May 10, 1864); Abel, *American Indian in the Civil War*, 206, 207–8.

11. Phillips to Curtis, in *OR*, 22 (pt. 2): 149; Indian (pseud.), March 21, "From the Indian Brigade," *Leavenworth Daily Conservative*, March 31, 1863, p. 2; Wiley Britton, *Memoirs of the Rebellion on the Border 1863* (Chicago: Cushing, Thomas and Col, 1882), 154, 161–63; Britton, *Civil War*, 2:41, 47–48, 48–49, 49–50, 54–56, 338–39; Russell L. Mahon, *Fayetteville, Arkansas, in the Civil War* (Fayetteville: Washington County Historical Society, 2003), 70–86. On Hart, see Edwin C. Bearss and Arrell M. Gibson, *Fort Smith: Little Gibraltar on the Arkansas*, 2d ed. (Norman: University of Oklahoma Press, 1979), 263; David Pickering and Judy Falls, *Brush Men and Vigilantes: Civil War Dissent in Texas* (College Station: Texas A&M University Press, 2000), 78–79. See also David Dary's chapter "Hugh Cameron, the Kansas Hermit," in his *More True Tales of Old-Time Kansas* (Lawrence: University Press of Kansas, 1987), 133–41.

12. Blunt to Phillips, Feb. 23, Phillips to Curtis, Mar. 20, and to Blunt, Apr. 2 (on salt lick), 9, 12, May 15, 1863, in *OR*, 22 (pt. 2): 121–23, 165, 166, 190, 208, 212, 284; Britton, *Civil War*, 2:34, 36, 39, 40–44; Peck, "Wagon-Boss and Mule-Mechanic," *National Tribune*, August 11, 18 (both p. 2), and 25 (p. 8), 1904; Minges, *Slavery in the Cherokee Nation*, 154–55; "From Fort Gibson and the Indian Country. Success of Colonel Phillips. Death of Dr. Gilpatrick" and "From Arkansas," *Leavenworth Daily Conservative*, May 7, 15, 1863, both p. 2; Robert Collins, *General James G. Blunt: Tarnished Glory* (Gretna: Pelican, 2005), 137–38.

13. Mahon, *Fayetteville*, 86, 89 (for the September return of the Union troops); Britton, *Civil War*, 2:42–43, 59–60, 61, 74; "From Fort Gibson and the Indian Country. Success of Colonel Phillips. Death of Dr. Gilpatrick" and "From Arkansas" (two separate items), *Leavenworth Daily Conservative*, May 7, 10, 15, 1863, all p. 2; Phillips to Curtis, Mar. 2, to La Rue Harrison, Mar. 21, Apr. 2, 12, 18, Harrison to Curtis, Apr. 2, 1863, in *OR*, 22 (pt. 2): 137–38, 191, 212, 224–25, 212; Wiley Britton, *The Union Indian Brigade in the Civil War* (Kansas City, Mo.: F. Hudson, 1922), 223, 224; Ross to Evan Jones (ca. Feb. 14, 1864), *PCJR*, 2:562.

14. Phillips to Blunt (two items), Apr. 24, to Curtis, Apr. 27, Blunt to Phillips, Apr. 30, Phillips to Blunt, May 1, Curtis to Halleck, May 6, Lincoln to Stanton, May 11, Phillips to Blunt, May 15, Halleck and Lincoln to Schofield, both May 27, Schofield to Blunt, May 30, June 10, Schofield to E. D. Townsend, Oct. 3, 1863, in *OR*, 22 (pt. 2): 247, 256, 258, 262, 266, 270, 277, 284, 290, 293, 296, 315, 596; Britton, *Civil War*, 2:28, 37, 64; Phillips to Blunt, "From Arkansas," and J.B.M., "From Fort Gibson," *Leavenworth Daily Conservative*, May 15, June 7, 1863, both p. 2; entries for Dec. 29, 1862, and Jan. 14, 1863, in *Lincoln, Day by Day: A Chronology, 1809–1865*, ed. Earl Schenk Miers (Dayton, Ohio: Morningside, 1991 [1960]), 152–53, 154; *The Collected Works of Abraham Lincoln*, ed. Roy P. Basler, 9 vols. (New Brunswick, N.J.: Rutgers University Press, 1953–55), 6:234.

15. Blunt to Col. N. P. Chipman, May 14, 1863, in *OR*, 22 (pt. 2): 280, 284. Phillips to Curtis, Mar. 9, 11, 20, 27, and to Blunt, Mar. 19, Apr. 8, 27, May 1, 9, 15, Blunt to Schofield, June 26, 1863, in *OR*, 22 (pt. 2): 150, 162, 166, 189, 205, 256, 266, 276, 282, 283, 284, 337. (These obstructionist officers were likely Captain George Lewis Gaylor, in charge of the commissary with "his excellent clerk, Walker." The quartermaster was Aaron M. Thomas, son of Capt. Chester Thomas; the paymaster, Major Daniel Marsh Adams of New Hampshire.) See also "The Fight at Cabin Creek," *Leavenworth Daily Conservative*, July 19, 1863, p. 2; Blunt to Caleb Smith, Nov. 21, 1862, the Abraham Lincoln Papers.

16. Ewing qtd. in "The Colored Regiment," *Leavenworth Daily Conservative*, May 8, 1863, p. 2; Captain David Mefford to Col. W. R. Judson, Mar. 14, Major Charles W. Blair to Gen. Blunt, May 9, Livingston to Sterling Price, May 28, E. A. Smith to Maj. H. Z. Curtis, June 30, 1863, in *OR*, 22 (pt. 1): 238–39, 320–21, 321–22, 322, and Blunt to Curtis, Apr. 6, Schofield to Halleck, June 13, Schofield to E. D. Townsend, assistant adjutant general in Washington, July 15, and to Ewing, June 16, 17, Blunt to Schofield, June 26, in *OR*, 22 (pt. 2): 200, 318, 319, 320–22, 337–38; "Movements Below," "The First Kansas Colored," Letter of "Cherokee," and "From Ft. Gibson & Ft. Smith: Arrival of Gen. Blunt," *Leavenworth Daily Conservative*, April 26, May 31, July 22, 1863, all p. 2.

17. Hindman to Totten, Sept. 10, Totten's response, Sept. 17 (with the predictable recollection of Pea Ridge), Holmes to Curtis, Oct. 11, Curtis to E. A. Carr, Oct. 21, 1862, in *OR*, 13:623, 648, 727; John Bowles, *The Stormy Petrel: An Historical Romance* (New York: A. Lovell; London: Walter Scott, 1892), 287; Michael Fellman, *Inside War: The Guerilla Conflict in Missouri during the American Civil War* (New York: Oxford University Press, 1989), 165; Britton, *Civil War*, 2:64–66, 66–68, 69–73, 76, 77, 101–2; Britton, *Aftermath of the War*, 213; Ward L. Schrantz, *Jasper County, Missouri, in the Civil War*, 2d ed. (Carthage, Mo.: Carthage Kiwanis Club, 1988 [1923]), 124–27; Larry Lapssley, "The Story of a Kansas Freedman," ed. Albverta Pantle, *Kansas Historical Quarterly* 11 (May 1942): 346 and 346n; Britton, *Civil War*, 2:65, 77, 78; "From Baxter's Springs" and two articles entitled "The First Kansas Colored," *Leavenworth Daily Conservative*, May 23, 31, June 23, 1863, all p. 2; Bruce Nichols, *Guerrilla Warfare in Civil War Missouri* (Jefferson, N.C.: McFarland, 2004), 178–79; T. R. Livingston to Williams, May 20, and Williams to T. R. Livingston, May 21, 1863, *Freedom*, 575; Williams in *BUSAF*, 2:54–55. For Bowles's fictionalized version of the fight, see *Stormy Petrel*, 290, in which "Tom Livingstone" is a recurring figure from the Border War.

18. "The First Kansas Colored," *Leavenworth Daily Conservative*, May 31, 1863, p. 2; T. R. Livingston to Williams, May 20, 23, 27, June 8, 23, 1863, *Freedom*, 575; Williams to T. R. Livingston, May 21, 26, June 8, 1863, *Freedom*, 575; Williams in *BUSAF*, 2:54–55; Williams to Major C. W. Blair, June 9, 1863, in *OR*, 22 (pt. 2): 314; Britton, *Civil War*, 2:77–78; Joseph T. Glatthaar, *Forged in Battle: The Civil War Alliance of Black Soldiers and White Officers* (New York: Free Press; London: Collier-Macmillan, 1990), 203. See, too, "Important from the Frontier," *New York Times*, May 31, 1863, p. 1.

19. Britton, *Union Indian Brigade*, 226–27, 228–29, 230–31.

20. Peck, "Wagon-Boss and Mule-Mechanic," *National Tribune*, August 18, 1904, p. 2; Phillips to Blunt, May 22, 1863, in *OR*, 22 (pt. 1): 336–37, 337–38; Phillips to Blunt, "Good News from Col. Phillips," *Leavenworth Daily Conservative*, May 30, 1863, p. 2; Minges, *Slavery in the Cherokee Nation*, 155; Britton, *Civil War*, 2:74–76, 80–81, 81–82, 82–83. Toward the end of 1863, a John Thornton later enlisted in the First Missouri Colored, the Sixty-second USCT.

21. Phillips to Blunt, May 22, 1863, in *OR*, 22 (pt. 1): 338; "Good News from Col. Phillips," and J.B.M., "From Fort Gibson," *Leavenworth Daily Conservative*, May 30, June 7, 1863, both p. 2; Peck, "Wagon-Boss and Mule-Mechanic," *National Tribune*, August 25, 1904, p. 8; J.B.M.; Britton, *Civil War*, 2:84–85, 85–86 and also 2:83–84; McReynolds, *The Seminoles*, 307. Also at this time, the Confederates sent a delegation to the Osages in May 1863 (John J. Mathews, *The Osages: Children of the Middle Waters* [Norman: University of Oklahoma Press, 1961], 639–40).

22. Britton, *Civil War*, 2:86–91, 93; "From Fort Blunt, Cherokee Nation," *Leavenworth Daily Conservative*, July 4, 1863, p. 2; Porter, "Billy Bowlegs," 399; Peck, "Wagon-Boss and Mule-Mechanic," *National Tribune*, August 11, 1904, p. 2; "Report of Col. William A. Phillips," June 20, and "Report of Col. Stephen H. Wattles," June, 1863, in *OR*, 22 (pt. 1): 348–50, 350–52; DeMorse to Cooper, June 21, 23, Major Joseph A. Carroll to DeMorse, June 20, 1863, in *SOR*, 4 (ch. 22): 133–40, 140–44. DeMorse claimed to have killed twenty-eight Federals, wounded twenty-nine, and taken six prisoners, and Carroll noted the presence of several blacks among the Federals' dead (142).

23. Phillips to Blunt, Apr. 2, June 6, 20, 1863, in *OR*, 22 (pt. 2): 190, 311, 331; Britton, *Civil War*, 2:94; "The Fight at Cabin Creek," *Leavenworth Daily Conservative*, July 19, 1863, p. 2.

24. Phillips to Blunt, May 30, 31, June 6, Williams to Maj. C. W. Bliss, June 9, Blunt to Schofield, June 8, 1863, in *OR*, 22 (pt. 2): 297–98, 298, 311, 314, 341–42; Britton, *Civil War*, 2:78–80, 91; Peck, "Wagon-Boss and Mule-Mechanic," *National Tribune*, August 25, 1904, p. 8, recalling an exchange in which one rebel asked, "Say, Yanks, what's we'uns done to you'ens that you-ens is all time shootin' at we-uns," to which the Federals laughed and asked if he was one of those "Arkansas 'haw-eaters.'"

25. Reports of Phillips, July 7, Williams, July (no date), and Foreman, July 5, 1863, in *OR*, 22 (pt. 1): 378, 379, 392; Britton, *Civil War*, 2:94, 95; Bearss and Gibson, *Fort Smith*, 263–66; Collins, *General James G. Blunt*, 139–41; Williams in *BUSAF*, 2:56; "The First Kansas Colored," including the June 12 letter from Col. Williams, *Leavenworth Daily Conservative*, June 23, 1863, p. 2, which publication included the following relevant pieces: "The Second Colorado," June 26, p. 3, with "Meeting of Colored Citizens" and "Colored War Meeting," July 2, 10, both p. 2. For the assignment of the Second Colorado, see *Denver Weekly Commonwealth*, June 25, 1863, p. 4.

26. See, in addition to the sources cited above, Palmer Boeger, "Flowing with Blood and Whiskey: Stand Watie and the Battles of First and Second Cabin Creek," *Journal of the Indian Wars* 1 (2000): 45–68; Lary Rampp, "Negro Troop Activity in Indian Territotry, 1863–1865," *Chronicles of Oklahoma* 47 (Spring 1969): 531–55.

27. Britton, *Civil War*, 2:112.

28. "Gen. Blunt Departs," "Gen. Blunt Moving to the Arkansas," and "From Gen. Blunt's Command," *Leavenworth Daily Conservative*, June 20, July 9, 17, 1863, all on p. 2; Britton, *Civil War*, 2:113; Peck, "Wagon-Boss and Mule-Mechanic," *National Tribune*, September 8, 1904, p. 8; James G. Blunt to Abraham Lincoln, July 31, 1863, the Abraham Lincoln Papers.

29. "Cherokee" (pseud.), "From Ft. Gibson & Ft. Smith: Arrival of Gen. Blunt," *Leavenworth Daily Conservative*, July 22, 1863, p. 2; Collins, *General James G. Blunt*, 142; Blunt, "General Blunt's Account," 243–44; Kip Lindberg and Matt Matthews, "'To Play a Bold Game': The Battle of Honey Springs," *North and South* 6 (Dec. 2002): 60; Phillips to Blunt, July 7, 1863, in *OR*, 22 (pt. 2): 355, 356; on the arrival of the supply train, Williams's report, July (no date), in *OR*, 22 (pt. 1): 381; Britton, *Civil War*, 2:112–13; Lindberg and Matthews, "'To Play a Bold Game,'" 61; Williams in *BUSAF*, 2:58.

30. Blunt letter, July 25, published as "Battle of Honey Springs! Private Letter from Maj. Gen. Blunt," *Leavenworth Daily Conservative*, August 6, 1863, p. 2; Blunt to Schofield, July 26, in *OR*, 22 (pt. 1): 447; Blunt to H. Z. Curtis, July 13, 26, Curtis to Lt. Col. C. W. Marsh, A.A.G., St. Louis, July 16, 1863, *OR*, 22 (pt. 2): 367, 379; Britton, *Civil War*, 2:116; Blunt, "General Blunt's Account," 244; Peck, "Wagon-Boss and Mule-Mechanic," *National Tribune*, September 8, 1904, p. 8; Britton, *Civil War*, 2:117, 118; Lindberg and Matthews, "'To Play a Bold Game,'" 61. Dodd described the Union numbers as only 2,200 men ("From the Second Colorado," *Denver Weekly Commonwealth*, August 20, 1863, p. 1).

31. "Lucinda Davis," WPA, Oklahoma Writers Project, "Slave Narratives from the Federal Writers' Project" (typescript, Washington, D.C.), 53, 59–60, 60–61; Britton, *Civil War*, 2:118.

32. See, in addition to the other citations on Honey Springs, Britton, *Civil War*, 2:112–25; Peck, "Wagon-Boss and Mule-Mechanic," *National Tribune*, September 8, 15, 1904, both p. 8; Federal reports by Blunt, Bowles, Schuarte, Capt. Edward R. Stevens, Lt. Col. Wm. T. Campbell, Capt. Edward A. Smith, Wattles, Maj. J. Nelson Smith, Capt. Henry Hopkins, in *OR*, 22 (pt. 1): 447–51, 453–56; Confederate reports and orders by Cooper, *OR*, 22 (pt. 1): 458–60, 461–62; reports from Cooper, De-Morse, and Welch, in *SOR*, 4 (ch. 22): 145–46, 146–47, 148–49; Williams in *BUSAF*, 2:49–58; Evan Jones to Ross, July 21, 1863, *PCJR*, 2:538; "Another Victory," "The Battle at Elk Creek," and "Later from Fort Gibson," *Leavenworth Daily Conservative*, July 25, 26, 31, 1863, all p. 2.

33. "Lucinda Davis," 61.

34. Entries for Jan. 14, June 20, July 13, 23, 1863, in *Lincoln, Day by Day*, 154, 191–92; *Collected Works of Abraham Lincoln*, 6:289, 291, 326, 344–45; Britton, *Civil War*, 2:125–26; Blunt to Abraham Lincoln, July 31, Sept. 24, 1863, Abraham Lincoln Papers. On Lawrence, see Thomas Goodrich, *Bloody Dawn: The Story of the Lawrence Massacre* (Kent, Ohio: Kent State University Press, 1991); Burton J. Williams, "Quantrill's Raid on Lawrence: A Question of Complicity," *Kansas Historical Quarterly* 34 (Summer 1968): 143–49; Burton J. Williams, "Erastus D. Ladd's Description of

the Lawrence Massacre," *Kansas Historical Quarterly* 29 (Summer 1963): 116, 115, 120; Britton, *Civil War*, 2:147–48. The son of Evan Jones was killed in Lawrence, one daughter died within a month, and two other daughters died the following winter (Minges, *Slavery in the Cherokee Nation*, 160–61). Capt. Fall Leaf's Delawares requested "about 200 guns with powder and lead" to defend themselves and their lands from the rebels (Laurence M. Hauptman, *Between Two Fires: American Indians in the Civil War* [New York: Free Press, 1993], 36).

35. Blunt to Schofield, Sept. 3, Cloud to Blunt, Sept. 20, Cabell to Capt. B. G. Duball, Dec. 7, Schofield's report, Dec. 10, 1863, in *OR*, 22 (pt. 1): 601–2, 602–4, 604–8, 14; Britton, *Civil War*, 2:149, 152–53, 153–54, 154–55, 159–60, 209, 519–20; Samuel Crawford, *Kansas in the Sixties* (Chicago: A. C. McClurg, 1911), 96, 97, 98–99, 99–100, 101–2; Collins, *General James G. Blunt*, 147; Bearss and Gibson, *Fort Smith*, 267–68; Collins, *General James G. Blunt*, 147–49; Britton, *Civil War*, 2:149, 152–53, 153–54, 154–55, 155–56, 156–57, 157–58, 160–61. See also Edwin C. Bearss, "The Federals Capture Fort Smith, 1863," *Arkansas Historical Quarterly* 28 (Summer 1969): 156–90; Bearss and Gibson, *Fort Smith*, 268–69; Holmes qtd. in Shelby Foote, *The Civil War: A Narrative*, 3 vols. (New York: Random House, 1963), 707; Thomas A. DeBlack, "1863: 'We Must Stand or Fall Alone,'" in *Rugged and Sublime: The Civil War in Arkansas*, ed. Mark K. Christ, 59–103 (Fayetteville: University of Arkansas Press, 1994), 88. See also Blunt, "General Blunt's Account," 246–47.

36. Bearss and Gibson, *Fort Smith*, 274–79; On Baxter Springs, see reports in *OR*, 22 (pt. 1): 688–701; Blunt, "General Blunt's Account," 247–48; Collins, *General James G. Blunt*, 149, 150–51, 153–62; Britton, *Civil War*, 2:159–60, 166–69, 172–74, 213, 216–21, 224–25, and, on guerrilla activity, 162–65. See also Richard S. Brownlee, *Gray Ghosts of the Confederacy* (Baton Rouge: Louisiana State University Press, 1958), 128–29, 135–36, 136–37; Britton, *Memoirs*, 451; Lary C. Rampp, "Incident at Baxter Springs," *Kansas Historical Quarterly* 36 (Summer 1970): 183–97; *Rebellion Record*, 7 ("Documents"): 552–54. For Pond, see Walter F. Beyer and Oscar F. Keydel, eds., *Deeds of Valor: From Records in the Archives of the United States Government; How American Heroes Won the Medal of Honor*, 2 vols. (Detroit, Mich.: Perrien-Keydel, 1906–7). See also Mark E. Scott, *The Fifth Season: General "Jo" Shelby's the Great Raid of 1863* (Independence, Mo.: Two Trails, 2001), 69–121.

37. Blunt to Lincoln, July 31, Sept. 24, 1863, the Abraham Lincoln Papers; Samuel R. Curtis to Abraham Lincoln, Feb. 28, 1864, the Abraham Lincoln Papers; Collins, *General James G. Blunt*, 126, 131, 133–34, 180–82 (though Collins seems not to have understood the significance of these conflicts); "The Carney Swindle and Ten Cents for the Missionary Fund," "Carney's Last Rhetorical Flourish," and "Soldiers on the Fraud," *Leavenworth Daily Conservative*, March 6, April 14, 17, 1864, all on p. 2; entries for Dec. 29, 1862, Jan. 14, Oct. 2, 28, Nov. 20, and Dec. 11, 13, 18, 21, 1863, in *Lincoln, Day by Day*, 211, 216, 219, 226, 228, 229; *Collected Works of Lincoln*, 6:234, 495, 543–45, 7:8, 61, 78–79, 84–85; Brownlee, *Gray Ghosts*, 169–70, 181; Blunt, "General Blunt's Account," 248–50; Collins, *General James G. Blunt*, 164–65, 167, 170–71; Frank A. Burr and Richard J. Hinton, *The Life of General Philip H. Sheridan*,

Its Romance and Reality: How One Humble Lad Reached the Head of an Army (Providence, R.I.: Reid, 1888), 153, 322. See also Fellman, *Inside War,* 47–48, 173.

38. Phillips to Blunt, Mar. 2, 19, to Curtis, Mar. 3, 20, 1863, in *OR,* 22 (pt. 2): 140, 141–42, 162, 166; Britton, *Civil War,* 2:39, 36–37; Samuel R. Curtis to Abraham Lincoln, Feb. 28, 1864, Abraham Lincoln Papers; Lapssley, "Story of a Kansas Freedman," 362, 365–66 (for Lapssley's later settlement in Saline County, 341). Unknown to them, the news that the Federals were feeding civilians forced the more sorely pressed Confederate authorities in Texas to do the same.

39. Minges, *Slavery in the Cherokee Nation,* 155, noting that William G. McLoughlin called the move "an effort to redistribute the wealth by the Keetoowah" and the Home Guards (McLoughlin, *After the Trail of Tears: The Cherokees' Struggle for Sovereignty, 1839–1880* [Chapel Hill: University of North Carolina Press, 1993], 211).

40. Lancaster, *Removal Aftershock,* 144, 149, 150–51, 151, citing Long John to Lincoln, Mar. 10, 1864, and Pascofar to Lincoln, May 10, 1864; Britton, *Civil War,* 2:161, 236; Porter, "Billy Bowlegs," 399 and 399n. Consumption claimed the life of the Seminole hero Halpatter Mico (or Halputta Micco); So mik-mix-ko or Su-nuk-mik-ko died of the disease Oct. 29, 1863. Britton, *Civil War,* 2:197, 234–35, 235–36, 239–40, 242–43, 345–46; Halliburton, *Red over Black,* 129; Jay Monaghan, *Civil War on the Western Border, 1854–1865* (Boston: Little, Brown, 1955), 296; Williams in *BUSAF,* 2:62; Samuel R. Curtis to Abraham Lincoln, Feb. 28, 1864, Abraham Lincoln Papers.

41. Phillips to Curtis, Feb. 16, 24, and undated itinerary, Phillips to Gov. Colbert of Chickasaw Nation, to Choctaw General Council, to Jumper of the Seminole, Feb. 15, Thayer to Steele, Feb. 22, Major Moses B. C. Wright to Lt. William Gallaher, Feb. 27, 1864, in *OR,* 34 (pt. 1): 106–8, 108–9, 109–10, 111–12, 112–13, with Phillips to McIntosh of the Creeks, also Feb. 15, appended to Confederate Gen. Maxey's report, in *OR,* 34 (pt. 2): 997; John C. Waugh, *Sam Bell Maxey and the Confederate Indians* (Fort Worth, Tex.: McWhiney Foundation Press, 1995), 34, 35–36; Debo, *Rise and Fall,* 82 and 83, quoting McCurtain to McNeil, Dec. 16, 1863; Britton, *Civil War,* 2:237, 238; Abel, *American Indian in the Civil War,* 312n; Lancaster, *Removal Aftershock,* 149; "Lucinda Davis," 62–63.

42. "Kiziah Love," WPA, Oklahoma Writers Project, "Slave Narratives from the Federal Writers' Project" (typescript, Washington, D.C.), 195–96; Britton, *Civil War,* 2:238–39; Debo, *Rise and Fall,* 83; Ariel Gibson, *The Chickasaws* (Norman: University of Oklahoma Press, 1971), 236–37; Phillips to Thayer, Feb. 8, 1864, in *OR,* 34 (pt. 2): 272; Frank Cunningham, *General Stand Watie's Confederate Indians,* foreword by Brad Agnew, 2d ed. (Norman: University of Oklahoma Press, 1998) 134.

43. Britton, *Civil War,* 2:239; "Proclamation of Amnesty and Reconstruction," Dec. 8, 1863, *Collected Works of Abraham Lincoln,* 7:53–56. Choctaw Confederates who reenlisted for the war supposedly voted an ultimatum to their General Council mandating universal conscription (Debo, *Rise and Fall,* 83–84). Phillips to Jumper, Feb. 15, 1864, in *OR,* 34 (pt. 2): 111; Cunningham, *Stand Watie's Confederate Indians,*

134–35 (which romantically asserts Jumper's "determination to stay true to Dixie"); James Lemuel Clark, *Civil War Recollections of James Lemuel Clark and the Great Hanging of Gainesville, Texas, in October 1862*, ed. L. D. Clark (Plano: Republic of Texas Press, 1997), 86, 89, 91. See also Bearss and Gibson, *Fort Smith*, 266–67.

CHAPTER 6: BEYOND THE MAP

1. F. J. Herron to Lt. Col. C. T. Christensen, Nov. 18, 1864, in *OR*, 41 (pt. 2): 605–6. Not surprisingly, Cunningham understates the fact that Phillips was "briefly replaced" (Frank Cunningham, *General Stand Watie's Confederate Indians*, foreword by Brad Agnew, 2d ed. [Norman: University of Oklahoma Press, 1998], 182).

2. On Brainerd, see Ross to Sara F. Stapler, Feb. 12, Ross to Mary Ross, Feb. 13, Ross and Evan Jones to Brainerd, Feb. 15, Ross to Nanson et al., Mar. 2, 1864, in *PCJR*, 2:558, 559, 563–64, 568. "Meeting in Behalf of the Indians," *Banner of Light*, March 26, 1864, p. 5, and April 2, 1864, pp. 2–3; see also, for the later meeting in California, "The Indians," *Banner of Light*, July 30, 1864, p. 4.

3. John Besson, letter to "The National Convention," and Cora Wilburn, "The Convention—Spiritual Séance—A Plea for the Indians," *Banner of Light*, July 30, 1864, p. 8, and September 3, 1864, p. 3. See also "Spiritualist National Convention. Byran Hall, Chicago, Illinois, August 9th, 10th, 11th, 12th, 13th, and 14th, 1864," and "Official Report of the National Convention of Spiritualists, Held in Chicago, Ill., August 9th to 14th, 1864," *Banner of Light*, August 20 (p. 4), 27 (p. 8), September 3 (p. 8), 10 (p. 8), 17 (p. 8), 24 (p. 8), October 1, 1864 (pp. 5, 8); *Journal of the Senate of the United States of America, 1789–1873*, posted at http://memory.loc.gov/ (accessed Apr. 16, 2008).

4. Thomas Weston Tipton, *Forty Years of Nebraska at Home and in Congress* (Lincoln, Neb.: n.p., 1902), 122, 123; Alvin M. Josephy Jr., *The Civil War in the American West* (New York: Knopf, 1991), 145–46.

5. Edwin L. Sabin, *Kit Carson Days, 1809–1868*, rev. ed., 2 vols. (Lincoln: University of Nebraska, 1995 [1935]), 2:725–48; Eugene Ware, *The Indian War of 1864, Being a Fragment of the Early History of Kansas, Nebraska, Colorado and Wyoming* (Topeka, Kans.: Crane, 1911); "The Santa Fe Mail," "The Kansas Valley Route to Santa Fe," "American Indian War Threatened," and "Pawnee Need Chastisement," *Leavenworth Daily Conservative*, November 2, December 17, 1862, July 11, 12, 1863, all on p. 2; Stan Hoig, *The Sand Creek Massacre* (Norman: University of Oklahoma Press, 1961).

6. "The Loyal Creeks in Council; an Official Conference," *Leavenworth Daily Conservative*, May 6, 1864, p. 2 (the article mistakenly identifies the loyal Creeks as being in the Third Indian Home Guard rather than the First).

7. Williams in *BUSAF*, 2:57; "From Gen. Blunt's Command—Near Fort Gibson—A Rapid March—Skirmish with Gen. Cooper—Situation and Prospects," *Leavenworth Daily Conservative*, July 17, 1863, p. 2, repr. as "Gen. Blunt's Expedition—The Approach to Port Gibson" *New York Tribune*, July 24, 1863, p. 5. This postwar assessment ignored both the Indian presence and the participation of black members of the Indian Home Guard at Locust Grove thirteen months earlier.

8. Robert M. Peck, "Wagon-Boss and Mule-Mechanic," *National Tribune*, July 28, 1904, p. 2, and September 8, 15, 1904, both p. 8.

9. Edwin C. Bearss and Arrell M. Gibson, *Fort Smith: Little Gibraltar on the Arkansas*, 2d ed. (Norman: University of Oklahoma Press, 1979), 273.

10. Frank A. Burr and Richard J. Hinton, *The Life of General Philip H. Sheridan, Its Romance and Reality: How One Humble Lad Reached the Head of an Army* (Providence, R.I.: Reid, 1888), 153; Ludwell H. Johnson, *Red River Campaign: Politics and Cotton in the Civil War* (Kent, Ohio: Kent State University Press, 1993), 40, 42, 47–48, 49–78, 170–72, 184–87 (quoting Sherman, 88); Samuel Crawford, *Kansas in the Sixties* (Chicago: A. C. McClurg, 1911), 102; Williams in *BUSAF,* 2:62; Mike Fisher, "The First Kansas Colored—Massacre at Poison Springs," *Kansas History* 2 (Summer 1979): 121–28; Mark K. Christ, ed., *"All Cut to Pieces and Gone to Hell": The Civil War, Race Relations, and the Battle of Poison Spring* (Little Rock, Ark.: August House, 2003); Noah Andre Trudeau, *Like Men of War: Black Troops in the Civil War, 1862–1865* (Boston: Little, Brown, 1998), 182–200; Wiley Britton, *The Civil War on the Border,* 2 vols. (New York: G. P. Putnam's Sons, 1899), 2:253–311.

11. Richard S. Brownlee, *Gray Ghosts of the Confederacy* (Baton Rouge: Louisiana State University Press, 1958), 186–87; Britton, *Civil War,* 2:240–43, 341–42, 346, 347, 354–60; Ross, Lewis Ross, Downing, and McDaniel to Stanton, May 25, Phillips to Ross, June 26, 1864, *PCJR,* 2:579, 595–96. In this rather rare case, John N. Edwards agrees with other sources on Quantrill's passage in his *Noted Guerrillas* (St. Louis: Bryan, Brand; Chicago, Thompson and Wakefield, 1877), 226–27.

12. Thomas A. DeBlack, "1863: 'We Must Stand or Fall Alone,'" in *Rugged and Sublime: The Civil War in Arkansas,* ed. Mark K. Christ (Fayetteville: University of Arkansas Press, 1994), 88, 105; Daniel E. Sutherland, "1864: 'A Strange, Wild Time,'" in ibid., 107, 109, 110, 124, 131, 134, 139, 238. See also James Lemuel Clark, *Civil War Recollections of James Lemuel Clark and the Great Hanging of Gainesville, Texas, in October 1862,* ed. L. D. Clark (Plano: Republic of Texas Press, 1997), 88–89, 90–91; and "Indian," (pseud.), "From the Indian Brigade" (Mar. 21), *Leavenworth Daily Conservative,* March 31, 1863, p. 2. See also Michael A. Hughes, "Wartime Gristmill Destruction in Northwest Arkansas and Military Farm Colonies," *Arkansas Historical Quarterly* 46 (Summer 1987): 175, repr. in Anne J. Bailey and Daniel E. Sutherland, *Arkansas: Beyond Battles and Leaders* (Fayetteville: University of Arkansa Press, 2000), 31–46.

13. Sutherland, "1864," 128, 138. The discussion, unbelievably, lingered into the closing months of the war (Carl Moneyhon, "1865: 'A State of Perfect Anarchy,'" in *Rugged and Sublime,* ed. Christ, 148).

14. Blunt to Abraham Lincoln, July 31, 1863, the Abraham Lincoln Papers, Library of Congress, posted on-line as part of the American Memory Project at http://memory.loc.gov/ammem/alhtml/malhome/html (accessed Nov. 28, 2008).; Robert Collins, *General James G. Blunt: Tarnished Glory* (Gretna: Pelican, 2005), 128, 131–32, 167–68; T. F. Robley, *History of Bourbon County, Kansas* (Fort Scott: the author, 1894), 129–31; C. W. Goodlander, *Memoirs and Recollections of C. W. Goodlander of the Early Days of Fort Scott* (Fort Scott, Kans.: Monitor, 1900), 65, 66–67, 68, 69, 72, 78, also

74, 75, 80, 85, 95–96, 101; untitled items on the year's sales and article reprinted from the *Fort Scott Bulletin*, *Leavenworth Daily Conservative*, January 22, 1863, p. 2, and June 26, 1863, p. 3.

15. Wiley Britton, *The Union Indian Brigade in the Civil War* (Kansas City, Mo.: F. Hudson, 1922), 379–80; Jay Monaghan, *Civil War on the Western Border, 1854–1865* (Boston: Little, Brown, 1955), 305; J. B. McAfee in *Transactions of the Kansas State Historical Society* 5 (1896): 109–10; McDonald's wartime association is noted also in Richard J. Hinton, *Rebel Invasion of Missouri and Kansas, and the Campaign of the Army of the Border, against Sterling Price, in October and November, 1864* (Chicago: Church and Goodman; Leavenworth, Kan.: F. W. Marshall, 1865), 40. About June 15, 1863, "the large store room owned and occupied by D. H. Ross & Co, with its contents—about ten thousand dollars—was burned up" ("The Fight at Cabin Creek," *Leavenworth Daily Conservative*, July 19, 1863, p. 2).

16. Ross to Nanson et al., Mar. 2, Ross, Lewis Ross, Downing, and McDaniel to Stanton, May 25, Daniel H. Ross to Ross, July 7, Ross to McDonald and Co., Aug. 4, Smith Christie to Ross, Aug. 19, 1864, in *PCJR*, 2:568, 579, 597, 601, 602, 604; Phillips to Herron, Jan. 16, 1865, in *OR*, 48 (pt. 1): 543; Cunningham, *Watie's Confederate Indians*, 183.

17. Morris L. Wardell, *A Political History of the Cherokee Nation, 1838–1907* (Norman: University of Oklahoma Press, 1938), 195–96; Angie Debo, *The Road to Disappearance: A History of the Creek Indians*, 2d ed. (Norman: University of Oklahoma Press, 1979), 160. On the unaided government stonewalling on the Neutral Tract, see McDaniel, Downing, and E. Jones to Dole, Nov. 21, 1863, Downing to Ross and E. Jones, Oct. 18, 1864, *PCJR*, 2:544–45, 612–14.

18. David E. Long, *The Jewel of Liberty: Abraham Lincoln's Re-election and the End of Slavery* (Mechanicsburg, Penn.: Stackpole, 1994), 36–37, 171; John Niven, *Salmon P. Chase: A Biography* (New York: Oxford University Press, 1995), 357, 359–60, 361, 363–64.

19. Daniel H. Ross to Ross, July 7, 1864, *PCJR*, 2:597; James A. Clifton, *The Prairie People: Continuity and Change in Potawatomie Indian Culture, 1665–1965* (Lawrence: Regents Press of Kansas, 1977), 374; Carol B. Broemeling, "Cherokee Indian Agents, 1830–1874," *Chronicles of Oklahoma* 50 (Winter 1972–73): 452; *The Collected Works of Abraham Lincoln*, ed. Roy P. Basler, 9 vols. (New Brunswick, N.J.: Rutgers University Press, 1953–55), 8:34n; Britton, *Civil War*, 2:345; James G. Blunt, "General Blunt's Account of His Civil War Experiences," *Kansas Historical Quarterly* 1 (May 1932): 239.

20. Collins, *General James G. Blunt*, 131, 167–69, 177–79; Thomas Ewing to Schofield, Nov. 2, 1863, William R. Judson to Halleck, Apr. 7, 1864, in *OR*, 22 (pt. 2): 692, 34 (pt. 3): 79. Blunt was attending a mock circus at Fort Scott that introduced a mock elephant as "General Blunt" because, like his namesake, he was said to be "a good drinker" (Goodlander, *Memoirs and Recollections*, 85).

21. Annie H. Abel, *American Indians under Reconstruction* (Cleveland, Ohio: Arthur H. Clark, 1925), 85–86; Ross to Sarah F. Stapler, Apr. 30, Ross, Lewis Ross, Downing, and McDaniel to Stanton, May 25, Daniel H. Ross to Ross, July 7, Smith Christie

to Ross, Aug. 19, 1864, *PCJR*, 2:575, 579, 595–96, 597, 603, 604; Bearss and Gibson, *Fort Smith*, 279.

22. McAfee in *Transactions of the Kansas State Historical Society* 5 (1896): 109; Harlan to Ross, Dec. 7, 1863, Smith Christie to Ross, Aug. 19, 1864, *PCJR*, 2:563, 579, 603–4, 605. See also Capt. W. Doudna (Co. G, Ninth Kansas Cavalry), Apr. 16, Elder to Blunt, May 17, 1863, in *OR*, 22 (pt. 2): 221, 286. Rather defensive about the military, Kansas cavalryman Wiley Britton blamed "white men who did not belong to the army" (Britton, *Civil War*, 2:34).

23. William Bishop, "Memorial Discourse," *Transactions of the Kansas State Historical Society* 5 (1896): 104, 105; John Speer in *Transactions of the Kansas State Historical Society* 5 (1896): 111; Nat Fish et al, Jan. 23, 1863, Ross to Sarah F. Stapler, Apr. 30, Daniel H. Ross to Ross, July 7, Smith Christie to Ross, Aug. 19, 1864, *PCJR*, 2:533, 575, 597, 603; Phillips to Blunt, Dec. 25, 1862, Apr. 24, May 15, 1863, in *OR*, 22 (pt. 1): 874, 22 (pt. 2): 190, 256, 284; Britton, *Civil War*, 2:19; J.B.M., "From Fort Gibson," *Leavenworth Daily Conservative*, June 7, 1863, p. 2. Those so charged made counteraccusations against Phillips but never tried to prove them, despite every opportunity to do so.

24. *Proceedings of the National Union convention held in Baltimore, Md., June 7th and 8th, 1864. Reported by D. F. Murphy* (New York: Baker and Godwin, 1864), 3; "Topeka Convention! The End of Fraud-Carney!" *Leavenworth Daily Conservative*, April 23, 1864, p. 2.

25. Phillips to Ross, June 26, Daniel H. Ross, on behalf of the Keetowah society, to Chief Ross, July 7, 1864, *PCJR*, 2:596, 597.

26. Phillips to Frederick Steele, July 11, with endorsements from Thayer, July 17, and final disposition by Steele on July 25, 1864, in *OR*, 41 (pt. 2): 123–24.

27. Britton, *Civil War*, 2:346, 347–48, 348–50, 351; Lary C. Rampp, "Negro Troop Activity in Indian Territory, 1863–1865," in *The Price of Freedom: Slavery and the Civil War*, volume 1: *The Demise of Slavery*, ed. Martin H. Greenberg and Charles G. Waugh (Nashville, Tenn.: Cumberland House, 2000), 185–86; untitled item, *Fort Smith New Era*, May 28, 1864, p. 2.

28. Phillips to Thayer, July 10, 1864, in *OR*, 41 (pt. 2): 108; Britton, *Union Indian Brigade*, 431–32.

29. See note 26.

30. Anderson to Phillips, July 19, 1864, in *OR*, 41 (pt. 2): 265; Britton, *Union Indian Brigade*, 432, 430; Daniel H. Ross to Ross, July 7, 1864, *PCJR*, 2:597. See also Phillips to Herron, Jan. 16, 1865, in *OR*, 48 (pt. 1): 542–43; Cunningham, *Watie's Confederate Indians*, 183.

31. Daniel H. Ross to Ross, July 7, John Ross and Evan Jones to Stanton, July 25, Ross to John P. Usher, July 27, 29, 1864, *PCJR*, 2:594, 597, 597–98, 599–600.

32. Special Order No. 117, July 30, 1864, in *OR*, 41 (pt. 2): 476. The index to *OR* indicates references to Phillips on pp. 927 and 935 and on 41 (pt. 3): 984, but these could not be found. Nor were any records of the court-martial or his reinstatement among the service records of the National Archives.

33. Britton, *Union Indian Brigade*, 460–62; Ross and Evan Jones to Stanton, Aug. 24, Ross to Lincoln, Nov. 7, 1864, *PCJR*, 2:606, 614–15.

34. Sykes to Curtis, Sept. 28, Herron to Lt. Col. C. T. Christensen, Nov. 18, 1864, in *OR*, 41 (pt. 2): 605–6, 41 (pt. 3): 461, 462.

35. Britton, *Civil War*, 2:148, 433–50, 462–74, 475–76, 338–39; Hinton, *Rebel Invasion*, 37–38, 39–40, 46, 49, 66, 69–70, 79; Paul B. Jenkins, *The Battle of Westport* (Kansas City, Mo.: Franklin Hudson, for the author, 1906), 143, 166. Robinson, Weer, Montgomery, and others led the Kansas State Militia, while others meeting the invasion included Ritchie, Cloud, and Crawford (then a candidate for governor), as well as John M. Mentzer, the union printer; Hugh Cameron, the Kansan second-in-command of the Second Arkansas Cavalry; Lieutenant S. S. Prouty of the Third Indian Home Guard; and Major H. S. Greeno, then in the Fourth Arkansas Cavalry. Hinton took "general charge of the movements and organization of the colored men" under Blunt and the former chief recruiter for Hinton's old regiment, the now-commissioned Lieutenant William D. Matthews, had both a section of guns and some three hundred black volunteer civilians at Fort Scott.

36. Herron to Lt. Col. C. T. Christensen, Nov. 18, 1864, in *OR*, 41 (pt. 3): 605, and also correspondence of Oct. 16, Nov. 10, 28, 1864, *OR*, 41 (pt. 5): 504–5, 708; see also the discussion among Grant, Halleck, and others of the Union high command over the situation in Arkansas in *OR*, 41 (pt. 3): 157, 373, 434, 569–70, and 41 (pt. 4): 575, 630, 879, 882, as well as Thayer's note of Oct. 4, 1864, trying to make Wattles answerable to the needs of McKee, McDonald, and others, 41 (pt.3): 610; Hinton, *Rebel Invasion*, 307–8; Wiley Britton, *Memoirs of the Rebellion on the Border 1863* (Chicago: Cushing, Thomas and Col, 1882), 154; Josephy, *Civil War in the West*, 302, 304.

37. F. J. Herron to Lt. Col. C. T. Christensen, Nov. 18, 1864, in *OR*, 41 (pt. 2): 605–6; Smith Christie to Ross, Aug. 19, 1864, *PCJR*, 2:605.

38. Herron to Lt. Col. C. T. Christensen, Nov. 18, 1864, in *OR*, 41 (pt. 2): 605–6; *Collected Works of Lincoln*, 8:564; Greeley to John G. Nicolay, Sept. 11, 1864, Abraham Lincoln Papers; Cunningham, *Watie's Confederate Indians*, 182. Regrettably, all such documents were excluded from the U.S. Army War College's later publication of *Official Records*, and no record was found of any court-martial.

39. Organization of the district as of the end of Dec. 1864, Phillips to Herron, Jan. 16, 1865, in *OR*, 41 (pt. 4): 985, 48 (pt. 1): 542; Eliza Jan Ross to Ross, Dec. 31, 1864, Ross to Dole, Jan. 30, 1865, *PCJR*, 2:616; 619–20.

40. *Official Army Register of the Volunteer Force of the United States Army for the Years 1861, '62, '63, '64, '65*, 8 vols. (Washington, D.C.: GPO, 1865–67), 3: 365, 368. Anderson would be absent at the time the regiment was mustered out.

41. Cunningham, *Watie's Confederate Indians*, 184–85; Phillips to Herron, Jan. 16, to Canby, Feb. 16, to John Pope, Feb. 16, 1865, in *OR*, 48 (pt. 1): 870–74; See also P. P. Elder to Lt. John Chess, Jan. 12, 1865, Coffin to Alexander Hamilton, Sept. 22, 1864, and Joel Moody to Phillips, Aug. 22, 1864 (documenting a contradictory policy of saying that taking Indian cattle required sale and authorization and permitting it without such authorization), in *OR*, 48 (pt. 1): 872–73.

42. Britton, *Union Indian Brigade*, 453–54, 455–56; Phillips to Herron, Jan. 16, 1865, in *OR*, 48 (pt. 1): 542–43; Cunningham, *Watie's Confederate Indians*, 183.

43. Debo, *Road to Disappearance*, 162–63, 163–64; Ross to Dole, Jan. 30, to Lincoln, Feb. 15, 1865, *PCJR*, 2:619–20, 621–22 (in support of the petition of Micco Hutke).

44. Clark, *Recollections of James Clark*, 90, 91 (transferred to the Second Kansas, presumably the Second Kansas Cavalry).

45. Ross to Mary B. Ross, Mar. 22, 1865 in *PCJR*, 2:638, this volume also includes his petition to the Senate and House, Feb. 18, his letters to Mary B. Ross, Feb. 28, Mar. 5, to Dole, Mar. 20, 1865, 624–27, 627, 631–32, 633–34, and the communications of Ross with other representatives to Stanton, Mar. 23, Grant, Mar. 23, Stanton, Mar. 27, the Senate, Mar. 27, 1865, 635, 635–36, 638–39, 641.

46. Britton, *Union Indian Brigade*, 430–31; Monaghan, *Civil War on the Western Border*, 305; *The American Indian and the United States: A Documentary History*, 3 vols. (New York: Random House, 1973), 2:1327, 1358, 1359; quotation in Laurence M. Hauptman, *The Iroquois in the Civil War: From Battlefield to Reservation* (Syracuse, N.Y.: Syracuse University Press, 1993), 89. As early as 1848 the Potawatomie had begun to drift south into the territory, a group even joining the Kickapoo and Seminole effort to plant a colony in Mexico (Clifton, *The Prairie People*, 380). By September 1863 Dole had proposed formal government action to clear Kansas of Indians, beginning with the Sac and Fox (William T. Hagan, *The Sac and Fox Indians* [Norman: University of Oklahoma Press, 1958], 241).

47. Ross to Dole, Jan. 30, 1865 in *PCJR*, 2:619–20; Hauptman, *Iroquois in the Civil War*, 89; Debo, *Road to Disappearance*, 165.

48. William H. Armstrong's *Warrior in Two Camps: Ely S. Parker, Union General and Seneca Chief* (Syracuse, N.Y: Syracuse University Press, 1978), 29, 90, understates the importance of Parker's presence; Anthony C. Parker, in *The Life of Gen. Ely S. Parker: Last Grand Sachem of the Iroquois and General Grant's Military Secretary* (Buffalo: Buffalo Historical Society, 1919), chose not even to mention his presence; Robert M. Utley, *The Indian Frontier of the American West, 1846–1890* (Albuquerque: University of New Mexico Press, 1984), 117; Jane F. Lancaster, *Removal Aftershock: The Seminole Struggle to Survive in the West, 1836–1866* (Knoxville: University of Tennessee Press, 1994), 156–57, 185, 234; Bearss and Gibson, *Fort Smith*, 305–8; Christine Schultz White and Benton R. White, *Now the Wolf Has Come: The Creek Nation in the Civil War* (College Station: Texas A&M Press, 1996), 174n16. As was usual, black Indians such as Caesar Bruner, a Seminole, attended as interpreters (Helen Jackson, *A Century of Dishonor: A Sketch of the United States Government's Dealings with Some of the Indian Tribes* [New York: Harper and brothers, 1881], 287–91).

CONCLUSION

1. "Tom W. Woods," WPA, Oklahoma Writers Project, "Slave Narratives from the Federal Writers' Project" (typescript, Washington, D.C.), 354.

2. Daniel O'Flaherty, *General Jo Shelby, Undefeated Rebel* (Chapel Hill: University of North Carolina Press, 1954), 393.

3. Patrick N. Minges, *Slavery in the Cherokee Nation: The Keetoowah Society and the Defining of a People 1855–1867* (New York: Routledge, 2003), 160. Already, by 1863, a third of the adult women were widows and a quarter of the children had been orphaned.

4. Robert W. Mardock, *The Reformers and the American Indian* (Columbia, Mo.: University of Missouri Press, 1971), 16–17, 21, 33–34, 39–42, 47. See also Francis Paul Prucha, *American Indian Policy in Crisis: Christian Reformers and the Indian, 1865–1900* (Norman: University of Oklahoma Press, 1976), 3, 28–29. William P. Tomlinson published Lydia M. Childs's *An Appeal for the Indian* (New York, 1868). These works mention the involvement of Samuel F. Tappan, Cora Daniels, Aaron M. Powell, Gerrit Smith, and Henry T. Childs, all more or less associated with the spiritualist movement, as was Alfred H. Love, whose Universal Peace association took up the issue.

5. Thomas Weston Tipton, *Forty Years of Nebraska at Home and in Congress* (Lincoln, Neb.: n.p., 1902), 121, 122, 123, 125–26; Alvin M. Josephy Jr., *The Civil War in the American West* (New York: Knopf, 1991), 145–46; Everett Dick, *Conquering the Great American Desert: Nebraska* (Lincoln: Nebraska State Historical Society, 1975), 61, 122, 188–89, 195, 327.

6. "Major J. K. Hudson," *Magazine of Western History* 13 (Nov. 1890): 50.

7. Minges, *Slavery in the Cherokee Nation*, 128; Christine Schultz White and Benton R. White, *Now the Wolf Has Come: The Creek Nation in the Civil War* (College Station: Texas A&M Press, 1996), 150, 151. Minges added that there was no evidence of hostility to blacks before contact with "civilization" (84). Nor is there any evidence of contact with blacks before "civilization" (for the assumption that Drew's regiment had black members, see 118–19).

8. "Labor in the Interior," *Leavenworth Daily Conservative*, May 6, 1864, p. 2.

9. "Mary Grayson," WPA, Oklahoma Writers Project, "Slave Narratives," 122.

10. "Property," *Leavenworth Daily Conservative*, February 12, 1863, p. 2; "High Prices and 'Strikes,'" *Leavenworth Daily Conservative*, April 22, 1864, p. 2. The paper was also subtly skeptical about immigrants and their drinking habits; see "To the Friends of Temperance in Kansas," *Leavenworth Daily Conservative*, May 5, 1864, p. 2.

11. Robert Collins, *General James G. Blunt: Tarnished Glory* (Gretna: Pelican, 2005), 211, 219, 220–22; Craig Miner and William E. Unrau, *The End of Indian Kansas: A Study of Cultural Revolution, 1854–1871* (Lawrence: University Press of Kansas, 1978), 117–18.

12. Miner and Unrau, *End of Indian Kansas*, 35.

13. *Biographical Directory of the U.S. Congress*, numerous editions but most accessible on-line at http://bioguide.congress.gov/biosearch.asp (accessed Nov. 28, 2008); Miner and Unrau, *End of Indian Kansas*, 64, 76, 129, 65.

14. Phillips to Ross, June 26, 1864, Ross to John B. Jones, Dec. 16, 1865, Ross to Johnson, June 28, 1866, in *PCJR*, 2:596, 659, 679; William A. Phillips, "Kansas History," *Collections of the Kansas Historical Society* 4 (1886–90): 358. "Trusts, encroaching corporations, the gambling spirit," insisted Phillips toward the close of his life, "must be placed under the iron hand of law."

15. Theodore Botkin to Francis G. Adams, secretary of the Kansas Historical Society, June 16, 1887, John Brown Papers, Kansas Historical Society, Topeka.

16. "The Forgotten Feminist (Part Four. 1867–1868)," *Kansas Historical Quarterly* 39 (Winter 1973): 528 and 528n; Mary Ritchie Jarboe, "John Ritchie: Portrait of an Uncommon Man," ed. Daniel C. Fitzgerald, *Shawnee County Historical Society Bulletin*, no. 68 (Topeka, Kans.: Shawnee County Historical Society, 1991).

17. See also Harold Piehler, "Henry Vincent: Kansas Populist and Radical Reform Journalist," *Kansas History* 2 (Spring 1979): 14–25. After an 1861 marriage in Pennsylvania, Tibbles may have served in an Ohio regiment, but he and his wife had brought the gospel into northwestern Missouri and joined the new settlers in western Nebraska just in time (Thomas Henry Tibbles, *Buckskin and Blanket Days: Memoirs of a Friend of the Indian* [Chicago: Donnelly, 1985 (1905)], 180, 207–12, 215, and, for the printers, 224).

18. David Dary, "Hugh Cameron, the Kansas Hermit," *More True Tales of Old-Time Kansas* (Lawrence: University Press of Kansas, 1987), 137–41; David Montgomery, *Beyond Equality: Labor and the Radical Republicans, 1862–1872*, 2d ed. (Urbana: University of Illinois Press, 1981),

19. James M. McPherson, *The Struggle for Equality: Abolitionists and the Negro in the Civil War and Reconstruction* (Princeton, N.J.: Princeton University Press, 1964), 382, 384, 424; Richard J. Hinton, "The New Politics," *The Arena* 2 (Jan. 1895): 219.

20. William A. Phillips, *Labor, Land and Law: A Search for the Missing Wealth of the Working Poor* (New York: C. Scribner's Sons, 1886), 81, 73, 77, 79–81; *PCJR*, 2:736 (discussing Ann Stapler), 745–56. Enemies of the Ross family and former secessionists resented Phillips's role in Cherokee affairs (Morris L. Wardell, *A Political History of the Cherokee Nation, 1838–1907* [Norman: University of Oklahoma Press, 1938], 341, 343).

21. Phillips, "Kansas History," 359; Richard J. Hinton, "Making Kansas a Free State," *The Chautauquan: A Weekly Newsmagazine* 31 (July 1900): 351.

22. Benjamin Quarles, *Allies for Freedom: Blacks and John Brown* (Oxford: Oxford University Press, 1974), 173–74.

23. Andrew Rolle, *The Lost Cause: The Confederate Exodus to Mexico* (Norman: University of Oklahoma Press, 1965), 204–5; O'Flaherty, *General Jo Shelby*, 44.

24. House Committee on Natural Resources, Subcommittee on National Parks, Forests, and Public Lands, *Honey Springs and Stones River National Battlefields: Hearing on H.R. 4821*, 103d Cong., 2d sess., 1994 (Washington, D.C.: GPO, 1994).

Index

MARK A. LAUSE is a professor of American history at the University of Cincinnati and the author of *Young America: Land, Labor, and the Republican Community* and other books.

The University of Illinois Press
is a founding member of the
Association of American University Presses.

Composed in 10/13.5 Janson Text
with Electra display
by Jim Proefrock
at the University of Illinois Press
Manufactured by Thomson-Shore, Inc.

University of Illinois Press
1325 South Oak Street
Champaign, IL 61820-6903
www.press.uillinois.edu